PETER MOSSMAN 89©

10

Colour profiles of KB726 in wartime battle colours of No.419 Squadron VR.A and FM213
post-war No.405 Squadron with original H2S...

- Peter Mossman

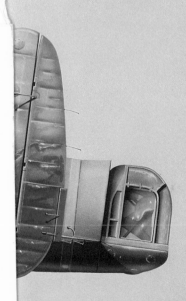

PETER MOSSMAN 89©

MYNARSKI'S
LANC

A painting of KB726 VR.A being shot down by a piece Ju-88 at 00:13 hrs on June 13, 1944 near Amiens, France. - *Don Connolly*

Ant de Breyne
Pilot

Roy Vigars
Engineer

Jack Friday
Bomb Aimer

Bob Bodie
Navigator

Jim Kelly
Wireless Operator

Pat Brophy
Rear Gunner

Ken Branston
M./U. Gunner *Prior to Mynarski U.C.*

MYNARSKI'S
LANC

*The story of two famous Canadian
Lancaster Bombers KB726 & FM213*

Compiled and Edited by
BETTE PAGE
Canadian Warplane Heritage Museum

THE BOSTON MILLS PRESS

Canadian Cataloguing in Publication Data

Main entry under title:

Mynarski's Lanc

Bibliography: p.
Includes index.
ISBN 1-55046-006-4

1. Lancaster (Bombers). 2. Canada. Royal
Canadian Air Force. Squadron, 419 - History.
3. Mynarski, Andrew, 1916-1944. I. Page, Bette.

UG1242.B6M85 1989 623.74′63 C89-093548-3

Published in Canada by:

THE BOSTON MILLS PRESS
132 Main Street
Erin, Ontario N0B 1T0
(519) 833-2407
Fax: (519) 833-2195

American Association
for State and Local History
Award of Merit

Winners of the
Heritage Canada
Communications Award

Designed by John Denison, Erin
Cover Design by Gill Stead, Guelph
Typography by Lexigraf, Tottenham
Printed by Ampersand, Guelph

Drawings and colour profiles by Bill Bishop and
Peter Mossman.

The Publisher gratefully acknowledges the assistance of
the Canada Council and the Ontario Arts Council.

TABLE OF CONTENTS

ACKNOWLEDGEMENTS

This book was put together with much research, and the knowledge and combined effort of many people, but without the continued help, persistence and persuasion of my husband Ron, it would never have reached completion.

I would like to thank the many, many people who came to me with information and who answered a myriad of questions, and especially those whose names I have failed to record. Your help was appreciated.

Without Norm Etheridge's excellent records the remarkable story of the restoration would be very limited.

Art de Breyne was a tower of strength in helping with the crew stories and gave much time and patience to the foreword. The crew, too, did an admirable job in recollecting their exploits of so many years ago, and patiently answered Ron's penetrating questions.

My sincere gratitude to the many contributors of material and encouragement in writing the book: Norm Etheridge, Bill Gregg, Bill Clancy, Murray Smith, Vince Elmer, Art de Breyne, Bob Bodie, Pat Brophy, Jim Kelly, Roy Vigars, Jack Friday, Ken Branston, Gregg Hannah, Bill Randall, Al Topham, Karl Coolen, Cy Dunbar, Chuck Sloat, Gil Hunt, Roy Freckleton, Larry Melling, Jim Buckel, C.W.H.M. Archives, Glenn Wright (National Archives of Canada), and the Lanc Support Club.

PHOTOGRAPHY CREDITS

The many photographs which add so much to the book were loaned to me very generously from many sources, and many have great sentimental value to their owners. Your generosity is very much valued. Thank you to Vince Elmer for significant historic pictures, and to Jim Challoner, Murray Smith, Chuck Sloat, Gregg Hannah, Jim Hoover, Roy Freckleton, Larry Melling, George and Irene Sobering, Murray Smith, Bill Gregg, Art de Breyne, Jim Kelly, Al Topham, Karl Coolen, Pat Brophy, Bill Randall,the National Aviation Museum, the Armed Forces Negative Library, Aidan Finn, Nick Fragis and the Royal Canadian Air Force Association 447 Wing.

Special mention should be made of the artists and draftsman who provided the paintings and drawings of the Lancaster. They are Don Connolly, Peter Mossman and Bill Bishop.

FOREWORD

I am honoured to be asked to write a foreword to this book.

Restoration of a Canadian Avro Lancaster bomber in poor condition, to the state of airworthiness, would be an ambitious project under the most favourable conditions. It was accomplished however by a group of very determined men and women, without significant resources, to perpetuate its existence and thereby honour a brave man.

Preservation in flying condition of one single Lancaster, should have been a national duty. To have rebuilt it almost from the ashes with volunteer help adds infinitely to its value and is an indication of the esteem in which it is held.

This book is a necessary and integral part of the overall project. Only after reading it can one begin to understand the innumerable problems that had to be solved along the way and appreciate the perseverance of the restoration crew in seeing the job through to completion. A multitude of Lanc Support Club members across the country and around the world undoubtedly played a part in sustaining the morale of this work force over a nine-year period.

The end product of this labour of love, the reborn version of VR.A KB726, is to me an exciting vision to behold. From all angles it is a thing of beauty, but never more so than when viewed from beneath. Her place is in the sky, where she triumphs as a living memorial to one special man and to all bomber crews who gave their lives for the cause of freedom. The story of our crew survival is in tribute to the untold stories of many other crews who did not survive the long and bloody conflict.

As a Lanc supporter from early days of the project it is a source of pride and joy to be able to say that in a small way I was part of this magnificent aircraft. And I would like to express my gratitude on behalf of the thousands who contributed to the project, to the hundreds of workers who gave so much, and in particular to the restoration crew and Norm Etheridge.

Long may she ride the skies.

Art de Breyne
original pilot of the
Mynarski Lanc

LIST OF THE RESTORATION CREW VOLUNTEERS

ALWOOD, BARRY
ARGUE, ROBERT
ARTES, FRANK
ATKINSON, DOUG
BALFOUR, MRS.& MR.
BANNERMAN, TERRY
BARTON, SHANE
BARTON, EAN
BARTON, HENRY
BEACAGE, PHIL
BICKHAM, ART
BRADFORD, ANNA
BRADLEY, DENNIS
BUCKEL, JIM
CAMPBELL, BILL
CARSON, NORM
CHALK, DOUG
CHAPMAN, BOB
CHARTERS, MICHAEL
CHISLETT, LES
CLANCY, BILL
CLIFFORD, JOHN
COOLEN, KARL
CRABTREE, GRAHAM
CUMMINS, JOHN
DEHAAN, JOHN
DELUCE, BILL
DICKIE, GORD
DORS, JAMIE
DUKE, MARION
DUNPHY, AL
EDWARDS, ERIC
ELLIOT, KEN
ELLIOT, SCOTT
ELNISKY, BILL
ESSERY, ROB
ETHERIDGE, NORM
FEDUCK, DON
FISHER, TOM
FRECKLETON, ROY
GAGNON, RENE
GIBSON, JIM
GILMOUR, JOHN
GRAHAM, ROD
GREEN, ERIC
GREGG, BILL
GROVE, ERIC
GRUBER, ART
HALES, ERIC
HALTROP, SYDNEY
HANNAH, GREG
HARROD, CAM

HAYCOCK, CARL
HILL, BOB
HINDMARSH, JOHN
HOFFMAN, HARRY
HOOKER, JACK
HOOVER, BARB
HOOVER, JIM
HORMANN, HEINZ
HUNT, DAVE
HYDE, PETER
INGRASSIA, JOANNE
JACQUES, CLAVETTE
JOHNSTON, DWAYNE
JOHNSTON, KENNETH
JONASSON, PETER
JONES, JACK
KAYE, RON
KERR, WAYNE
KUIACK, TED
LAVALLEE, GUY
LIDDLE, JOHN
LOOP, BILL
LOWE, FRED
MADERICH, SALLY
MARTIN, STEVE
MASSARO, ART
MATHERS, MARG
MAY, ROGER
MCCALL, DONALD
MCCOY, BRIAN
MCDONALD, PAUL
MCGEE, MILT
MERRICAN, BILL
MESSMER, BOB
MEHTAH, MONTH
MELLING, LARRY
MILLER, JIM
MOLS,TIM
MOON, STEVE
NELSON, PHIL
NESS, ALAN
NORTON, BOB
ONKEN, TREVOR
OSBORNE, MURRAY
PACEY, RAY
PAGE, RON
PAGE, BETTE
PARK, STEVE
PASTRAK, NICK
PATTERSON, J.S.
PERRY, JAMES
POLLARD, JIM

PORTER, JIM
PORTINGA, ED
PRENDERGAST, DON
REGINSKI, WES
RANDALL, BILL
READING, W/O
REES, BOB
REGIS, REG
REGINISKY, WES
RIDDLE, WILF
ROBERGE, ROLEY
RODRIGUES,
ROOT, NEVILLE
ROSSADITA, MIKE
ROTHDEUTCH, BILL
ROUTSKY, PAUL
SANFORD, W/O
SAVERS, LARRY
SAWYER, CAROLYN
SCHADE, NEIL
SCHAFER, DAVE
SCHOFIELD, DON
SCRUTIN, ED
SLADE, PAT
SLADE, BILL
SLOAN, ART
SLOAT, CHUCK
SMITH, HARRY
SMITH, JOHN
SMITH, MURRAY
SMITH, WAYNE
SOBERING, IRENE
SOBERING, GEORGE
STEVENS, TOM
STRIOWSKI, BILL
SULLY, BRUCE
SWARTZ, BETH LYNN
SWIFT, BILL
TOPHAM, AL
VANCE, W/O
VANDEN, HEUVAL CASE
VARDY, JANET
WALTERS, COLIN
WARDEN, BILL
WARREN, SPENCER
WEATHERSTON, DOUG
WHITE, BILL
WLODARCZYKI, ADAM
WYLIE, RON
YORK, HERB

INTRODUCTION

The story of the famous WWII Avro Lancaster bomber has been told many times and many books have been written about the plane and its exploits and achievements. This book is unique in that it presents an account of the Canadian Lancasters built at Malton by Victory Aircraft and stories about two of these aircraft in particular. The first story is that of the aircraft and crew of the Mynarski V.C. Lancaster, in which Andrew Mynarski earned his Victoria Cross (posthumously), and the second one is the history of Lancaster Mark X FM213. The latter has been restored to flying condition by the Canadian Warplane Heritage Museum (CWHM), with the enthusiastic help and dedication of the Lanc Support Club, which is made up of a great many capable and willing volunteers. The aircraft has been dedicated in honour of P/O Andrew Mynarski, V.C., his crew, and the many other Canadians who sacrificed so much in the conflict more than 40 years ago.

The book is presented in three major parts: the Lancaster and Canadian Mark X bombers in general; the Canadian No.6 Bomber Group and its squadrons, with special emphasis on the crew of KB726 VR.A of No.419 "Moose" Squadron on that fateful night of 12/13 June 1944; and finally, the life history of Lancaster FM213 and restoration to its first flight after 24 years in retirement. This Lancaster is now the only flying example in North America, and one of only two flying in the world.

The story must begin with the formation and history of Canadian Warplane Heritage Museum, "Canada's Flying Museum of WWII Aircraft."

The nucleus of CWHM was formed by a number of pilots, two of whom were the late Alan Ness, and Dennis Bradley, who met regularly at Toronto Island Airport and dreamed of flying something bigger and more powerful than Cessnas. In 1970 they decided to do something about this and started to search for a suitable World War II fighter aircraft to restore and fly. After much exploring and research they finally found a Fairey Firefly in Georgia, which they then had ferried to Canada. This Firefly, after many hundreds of hours of painstaking restoration and many dollars, did become airborne and was to be the flagship of the organization as the collection grew. In 1972 the founders incorporated the group into a non-profit company and later into a non-profit charitable foundation, and CWHM came of age. In the succeeding 16 years the aircraft collection has grown to more than 40 aircraft and the membership to over 600 worldwide. The organization now has permanent headquarters and facilities, consisting of two WWII hangars at Hamilton Airport, Mount Hope, Ontario. The largest of their acquired aircraft was the North American B-25 Mitchell two-engined bomber, until CWHM acquired the massive four-engined Avro Lancaster bomber in 1978.

This book includes the story of that aircraft and how it was restored and supported. It lay around dejectedly for more than five years without much progress on its restoration, until 1983, when three things happened:

a) a federal employment grant was obtained to fund engineers to work on the aircraft
b) Norm Etheridge took on the job as chief engineer of the project
c) and later the Lanc Support Club was formed to raise funds and provide assistance to meet the needs of this costly and ever-hungry project. It was the Lanc Support Club that initiated the decision to write this book, and therefore it is pertinent to record a brief history of this unique club in the introduction.

LANCASTER SUPPORT CLUB OF CANADIAN WARPLANE HERITAGE MUSEUM

The idea of a support club grew out of the concerns of the original members who were part of the Lancaster restoration crew, some of whom worked on the aircraft when it was still at Goderich. When the aircraft was brought to Mount Hope, this crew grew as the serious restoration started under the guiding hand of Norm Etheridge, and an official club was finally organized in support of the Lancaster restoration and as part of the Canadian Warplane Heritage Museum. The first meeting took place in October 1984. Its mandate was to:

a) promote interest in the restoration of the Lancaster FM213
b) to enrol club members on a worldwide basis
c) to raise funds for the purpose of supplementing the cost of restoration.

Restoration members took on a network of responsibilities: financial memberships, public relations, exhibits and memorabilia/souvenirs.

They met regularly to discuss and make the decisions necessary to maintain the club. Newsletters were prepared and sent bi-annually to members, advising them of restoration progress.

Exhibits and sales of souvenirs were presented by the club administrators at reunions, banquets, fall fairs, expositions, shopping malls, etc. Display boards were fabricated depicting restoration processes, Lancaster bomber crews, missions accomplished, and also the Mynarski story. These display boards were improved upon over the period and served as the backbone and major attraction to the presentations.

Examples of the display boards that the Lanc Support Club used.   - K. Coolen

Club chapters were established by supporting people in communities other than Hamilton: one in Listowel, one in Niagara and one was even developed in the U.K., at Buxton.

The club gained credibility at its first Hamilton Airshow exhibit in the summer of 1985. From that time on there seemed to be no end to the membership enrolment. Members came from all age groups and all walks of life, veterans, relatives and service personnel in particular. The club now enjoys membership from the U.K., New Zealand, Australia, France, Belgium, the Netherlands, U.S.A. and Zimbabwe. The majority of members are, of course, from the provinces and territories of Canada.

Not enough praise can be given for the enthusiasm of the people who administer the club. Their dedication and vitality have been responsible through successful P.R., for worldwide attention to the project. Their ability to cope with the growing pains of such a large membership is complementary to the services of the gallant men and women who built, serviced and manned the 7,377 Lancaster bombers of WWII. It is to be especially noted that the thousands of people who supported the restoration of this bomber were the real reason for the success of the program which brought to airworthy condition Lancaster FM213, painted to represent KB726 VR.A of No.419 "Moose" Squadron, dedicated in memory of P/O Andrew Mynarski, V.C.

The CWHM Support Club was honoured in having Mrs. Margaret Dove, the daughter of the late Sir Roy Chadwick, C.B.E., M.Sc., F.R.S.A., F.R.Ae.S., the designer of the Lancaster bomber, become its Honourary President. In June 1987 she was presented with a scroll prepared by the CWHM proclaiming her Honourary President of the CWHM Lanc Support Club.

The club has been very successful in raising money in the last four years from membership enrolment and renewal, garage sales, dances, mall exhibits and raffles. The final total may reach over $400,000, when all the receipts are in, by the time this book goes to the publisher at the end of 1988. This is a terrific achievement for this type of organization, where all the manpower was voluntary.

Special mention must be made of one stalwart of this club, Irene Sobering, for her undying enthusiasm and hard work in all areas of fund-raising, and in particular for the way she manages to organize the catering for any visiting group, no matter how large or on how short notice.

The club's support, together with the assistance of the many contributing companies, carried the project, which is a unique piece of restoration history, to completion.

This book attempts to give this multitude of people, who gave so much over such a long term, some of the recognition they so richly deserve.

The volunteers who worked on the aircraft are listed here. If anybody has been left out it is deeply regretted, but over the nine years there have been many changes, and even though faces are remembered, names seem to have faded.

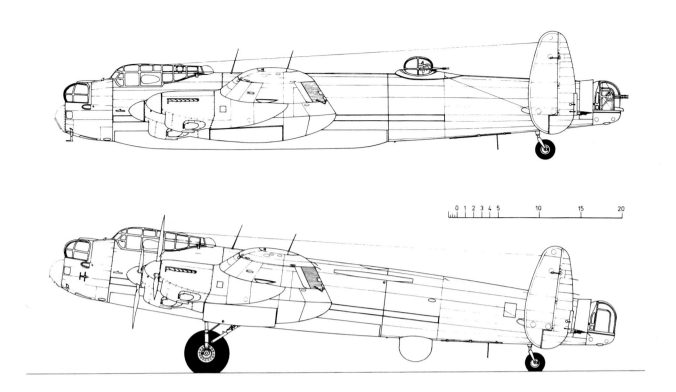

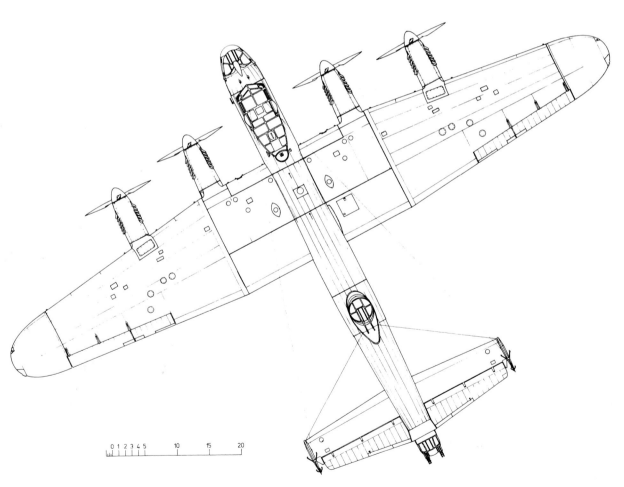

Two-view drawings of KB726 & FM213.   - *Bill Bishop.*

I

AVRO LANCASTER MARK X

DESIGN ORIGIN OF THE AVRO LANCASTER BOMBER - MANCHESTER

The Avro Lancaster bomber of WWII fame was originated in 1936, when the British Air Ministry issued two specifications. The first of these, B12/36 for four-engine bombers, would be Britain's answer to the development of a new class of bomber, slightly superior to the new four-engine Boeing 299, which later became the B-17 Flying Fortress. A range of at least 2,000 miles was required, with the ability to defend themselves in daylight. The power-operated turrets had fortunately been developed by two ex-Royal Flying Corps pilots, "Tommy" Thompson and "Archie" Frazer-Nash, in the early 30s. These gun turret designs were put into production in 1935 and reached high gear by 1939.

The aircraft designs that evolved from these enquiries were the four-engine Short Stirling and the Vickers-Supermarine 318, which became stillborn when the prototype was lost due to the bombing of the Supermarine plant in 1940, and Spitfire production had maximum priority. The second specification was the P13/36 "Prototypes." This called for a heavy-medium bomber to be faster than the B12/36, with a cruising speed of 275 mph, a range of 3,000 miles and with a bomb load of 4,000 lbs. This resulted in proposals from Handley Page and A.V. Roe, which were accepted and construction was authorized. A new specification, B19/37, was then issued and resulted in the Avro 679 Manchester. At that time the biggest aircraft that A.V. Roe had under construction was the A.V. Roe Anson, a twin-engine bomber and reconnaissance aircraft, so the step to the Manchester proposal was a large one. A wooden mock-up was built in 1938 and the first prototype flew on July 25 1939, with Capt. H.A. Brown at the controls. In this flight,and after further testing, the poor flight characteristics of the Manchester were observed, failings which were to plague the aircraft for the rest of its life. Most of the poor behaviour was due to the inability of the Rolls Royce Vulture engines to deliver their designed power of 2,000 hp each.

The design concept of the aircraft by Roy Chadwick (later Sir Roy) was sound, but the choice of the two untried Rolls Royce Vulture X-type 24-cylinder engines was not. These engines were actually a combination of four Rolls Royce Peregrine's blocks joined to a common crankshaft, not Kestrels as some references say.

(Note - The Merlin was developed from the Kestrel as P.V.12. The Griffon which was developed using many features of the famous R engines of Schneider Trophy fame filled the void left by the termination of the Vulture, until the limited appearance of the Eagle at 3,500 hp).

The engine was afflicted with many problems, which in turn reflected on the aircraft as a whole. This choice of an untried engine with a new aircraft design, broke one of Roy Dobson's cardinal rules "never put an untried engine in a brand new aircraft design." The biggest of these problems was lack of power due to distortion of the cylinder blocks and the crankcase, which caused excessive friction to be generated, preventing delivery of power to the propeller. This lack of power made the Manchester difficult, if not impossible, to keep airborne on one engine if the other failed or caught fire due to overheating, which could result from this excessive friction.

According to John Martin ex-Orenda Engines and of Pratt & Whitney Canada fame, who was working at Rolls Royce at that time, said "the real problem was the method of supporting the engine on the aircraft", as he used many Vulture engines on a test bed to drive the Whittle centrifugal test compressors and had no trouble with the solid mounting in the test cell. The engine operated well at over 2,000 hp and achieved in excess of 3,000 hp on a few occasions. The gear boxes to the test compressors were the limiting hardware. He believed that A.V. Roe would not change their engine mount design and blamed their aircraft's poor performance problems on the engine manufacturer.

The problems with the Vulture development and its planned production also affected Handley Page Aircraft in the decision to switch their proposal HP.57 from the Vultures to four Rolls Royce Merlins early in the prototype construction. The result was the Handley Page Halifax.

Even though the Manchester entered service on November 1 1940, and took part in many operations, the aircraft required many modifications to improve its performance. These included an extra 10 feet added to the wingspan (90 ft. 1 in.) and a third dorsal fin to the fuselage (length 70 ft.) to correct the lateral instability problem. This fin was later replaced by the two large fins and a 50% increase in the tailplane span, from 22 ft. to 36 ft. This modification was later to be used on the Lancaster. In parallel with the Manchester I and IA development, design work was done on a Manchester II using either the Bristol Centaurus or Napier Sabre engines in an attempt to overcome the Manchester's engine problem.

The Manchester bomber never made the grade. Out of 741 aircraft dispatched on raids, 73 aircraft were lost from all causes (10%) and they were only able to drop 794 tons of bombs in 1941 and 1,032 in 1942. The Manchester was withdrawn from service in June 1942.

LANCASTER MK B.1

The controversy over the Vulture engine was to sway back and forth between Rolls Royce Derby and the Air Ministry. Rolls Royce feared the development of both the Napier Sabre and the Bristol Centaurus engines, which were capable of beating them in the 2,000 hp class. The Air Ministry wanted to limit the number of different types of large-horsepower engines in production to five, in order to maximize production volume. They were the two air-cooled radials (Hercules and Centaurus) and three liquid-cooled units (Merlin, Griffon and Sabre). Therefore, the Peregrine, or half-size Vulture and the Vulture were terminated.

Rolls Royce was reluctant to admit defeat with the Vulture, which had now achieved 1,845 hp but was still unreliable. The agreement by Rolls Royce and the American Packard Engine and Car Company to mass-produce Merlins under licence resulted in the easing of pressure on the Merlin supply and allowed for the consideration of more four-engine bombers.

Chadwick's solution to the poor performance of the Manchester was to redesign the wing and centre section to take four Rolls Royce Merlins, and this was designated the Manchester III. This was a private venture and did not receive much enthusiasm from either the Ministry of Defence or the Ministry of Aircraft Production, who were more concerned with actual production of aircraft, rather than improvements. The combination of the new wing and centre section, capable of taking four Rolls Royce Merlins and mated to the Manchester body, turned into a winner as the Manchester III or Avro Type 683. Before production started on the Manchester III, it was thought advisable to change the name to Lancaster, to reflect the major modification of the aircraft and to disassociate it from the miserable performance of the Manchester I and IA in service. Thus was the Lancaster B.1 born.

The prototype (BT308) first flew on January 11, 1941, fitted with Merlin Xs

14

producing 1,280 hp at take-off. The first production Lancaster B.1 aircraft (L7527), fitted with Merlin X engines rated at 1,390 hp on take-off, entered service with No.44 (Rhodesian) Squadron on Christmas Eve 1941. It first saw operations on March 3, 1942, on a "gardening" operation, laying mines. The Lancaster first dropped bombs on Germany on March 10 during a raid on Essen. A total of 7,377 Lancasters were built in many variations, including the Lancaster B.II powered by Bristol Hercules sleeve-valve radial engines, and parts for a further 622 were manufactured to maintain the Lancasters in service. The Mark III Lancaster was fitted with either the Packard Merlin engines Mark 28 of 1,300 hp, Mark 38 of 1,390 hp, or 224 of 1,620 hp. When the Mark III was built in Canada with the Packard Merlin 224s, it was designated Mark X.

During their WWII service Lancasters made 156,192 sorties and dropped 608,612 tons of bombs, including 51,513,106 incendiary bombs, and they consumed 228,000,000 gallons of fuel to do the job. The Lancaster was modified for many roles, such as the famous "Dambuster," the 12,000 lb. "Tallboy" bombs which sank the *Tirpitz*, a German pocket battleship and the 22,000 lb. "Earthquake or Grand-slam" bomb which was used to destroy the concrete submarine pens in France, as well as viaducts and collapse tunnels. Of the 7,377 built, a total of 3,349 Lancasters were lost in action and 487 were damaged. This large number of sorties and tonnage of bombs dropped had the tragic price of 55,573 aircrew killed or missing in action in all Bomber Command during the war years, which included 9,919 personnel from the R.C.A.F., though not all these aircrew were lost in Lancasters.

Air Chief Marshal Sir Arthur Harris, Commander in Chief, Bomber Command, suggested that the Lancaster was the greatest single factor in winning the Second World War and considered its efficiency incredible, both in performance and in the way in which it could be saddled with ever-increasing loads without breaking the camel's back. It is amazing that an aircraft as small as the Lancaster could so easily take the weight (22,000 lbs) of the grand-slam, bomb which no other aircraft could carry, nor can any aircraft do so today.

According to one pilot, the Lanc was fantastically strong, and he considered that if there was one quarter of one left by the enemy defence, that quarter would fly home.

Another story is told about two members of a squadron discussing the source of a Lancaster's strength. One, from the automotive industry, talked of the integral body-cum-chassis construction. The other member was a chaplain and felt that the strength lay in the nave and transept, adding with tongue in cheek that pilots sat in the choir.

Both were right. The central portion was extremely strong. It was reinforced in the fore and aft directions by a flat floor which also formed the roof of the bomb bay, to which bombs weighing up to ten tons were slung. It was crossed by two waist-high main spars extending sideways from the fuselage and carrying a Merlin on its triangular steel tube mounting at each end. Especially strong wing ribs absorbed the loadings behind each engine and into this key structure formed by front spar and engine mountings were fed loads from the Dowty oleo-pneumatic undercarriage. When retracted, the undercarriage legs were housed in rearward extensions of the inboard engine nacelles. To this immensely sturdy cruciform structure were bolted the mainplanes and rear section of the fuselage.

It is interesting to note that the Chadwick design team also saw the need for a transport aircraft using the same wing, power plants, tail assembly and undercarriage, but with a rectangular fuselage, at the same time as they designed the Lancaster. This was designated as Avro Type 685 and was to become the Avro York two years later, due to pressure on Lancaster production, rather than new types of transport. One of these Yorks was produced in Canada in November 1944 as a Canadian York FM 400.

LANCASTER B.X

As the war situation worsened in England in 1940, the British were looking for ways to improve aircraft production, out of the range of the German bombers. As the United States was not yet in the war, Canada became the Dominion to which Britain turned in her time of need.

The place chosen to build the Lancaster in Canada was Malton, in the National Steel Car Corporation's new building for their Aircraft Division. The National Steel Car Corporation, which made railway rolling stock in Hamilton, decided to build a plant at Malton for its new Aircraft Division when an order was received for Westland Lysanders in March 1938. The company also made Handley Page Hampden wings for the Ontario group of companies, as part of the Canadian Associated Aircraft Ltd., and became involved with the assembly of British Anson Is and North American Harvards, as well as the conversion of the French Yales in 1940. They were also assembling Hurricane wings and received an order in early 1941 for 300 Martin B-26 Marauder bombers.

At a meeting in Washington on Thursday, September 18, 1941 at the offices of the British Supply Council in Washington, this was all changed. As this was such a significant meeting with respect to production of the Lancaster bombers in Canada, it is worth recording the details of how and what was decided.

The meeting was attended by the following major players in Canada's wartime history:

Mr. E.P. Taylor (Chairman)	Mr. C.R. Fairey
Sir Henry Self	Mr. Ralph P. Bell
Hon. Mr. C.D. Howe	Mr. J.B. Carswell
Air Marshal Harris	Mr. F. Smye
Air Vice-Marshal Stedman	Mr. Leslie Chance (Secretary)

The minutes of the meeting record the following discussion:

Mr. Taylor said that on his recent visit to England, the Minister of Aircraft Production had stressed to him the importance which the Home Government attached to production in Canada of heavy bombers of the British type (Lancaster).

Mr. Howe said that the Canadians would be glad to undertake the production of heavy bombers provided that the requirements of the Royal Canadian Air Force for 218 medium bombers (Marauder) could be protected. He pointed out that Canadians had undertaken production in Canada of these machines and hoped for deliveries beginning in August 1942 which would give a total of 75 machines in that year and thereafter 25 a month.

After discussion it was finally agreed that Canadians would undertake production of the Lancaster-type heavy bomber in Canada, subject to the following conditions:

a) that provisions be made for the requirements of the R.C.A.F. for 218 medium bombers from the U.S. production at approximately the same rate as set out above for the proposed Canadian production. The type of machine which would be acceptable to the R.C.A.F. would be agreed between Air Vice-Marshal Stedman and the British Air Commission. The dollar value of deliveries to Canada of medium bombers from U.S. production would be offset against the dollar value of Canadian production of Lancasters.

b) that the necessary negotiations with the U.S. for the transfer to Canada under the terms of the Lend-Lease Act of the 218 medium bombers referred to above would be undertaken by the U.K.

c) that the initial order placed with Canada for Lancaster aircraft should be for not less than 250 machines.

d) that the U.K. would undertake the necessary negotiations for the supply of suitable engines for installation in the Lancaster airframes agreed to be produced in Canada as above.

e) that the U.K. agree to supply to Canada 240 Merlins from the Packard production for installation in the Hurricane aircraft being produced in Canada and intended for delivery to the Chinese Republic. (An interesting record of history in the making.)

So from this meeting the Marauder bomber contract was cancelled, after a little tooling had been made, at the end of October. The Lancaster order was announced in December 1941 and work started immediately, with the first drawings arriving in January 1942. A Lancaster Mk I (R5727) was flown over from England by Clyde Pangborn on August 25, 1942, to act as a master tool and pattern standard, thus making the first east to west crossing of the Atlantic Ocean by a Lancaster. After it was demonstrated to the high command and government officials in Ottawa, Mr. C.D. Howe and Ralph Bell flew in it back to Malton on August 31, 1942. This aircraft was later acquired by Trans-Canada Airways (T.C.A.) and modified with the nose and tail turrets positions faired over and windows fitted in the fuselage. It entered service with the airline, ferrying freight and mail across the Atlantic, and was later modified by Avro U.K. with 10 seats and extra fuel tanks. It inaugurated a transatlantic service on 22 July 1943.

The design and manufacture of the Mark X Lancasters in Canada were to be the same as the Mark III in England, but with Packard Merlin 224 engines, though the first 75 aircraft were fitted with Rolls Royce Merlin 38s. The following changes were made to the Canadian aircraft to fit the parts supply problem. All instruments, radios and ball bearings would come from Canadian or American sources. A completely new and novel wiring system would be installed, which by simply unclamping four ground connections from the fuselage could be changed from a one-wire to a two-wire circuit. In case of local battle damage to the wiring, parts of the system could be isolated by pulling out a plug and converting that section to a two-wire circuit. One of the major targets of production was to ensure interchangeability between English and Canadian sub-assemblies — allowing modification, repair and replacement of battle-damage — for all major parts of the aircraft, without costly spares having to be shipped from Canada. The design of the Lancaster lent itself to this objective, as it was made up of 31 major sub-assemblies. One of the reasons given for the dimension of the largest sub-assemblies was the length of a British railway freight car, which was 29 feet. This was necessary for the dispersal method of production by many companies to prevent any serious interference from bombing. These sub-assemblies were as follows:

1 Nose section of fuselage
2 Front fuselage, including cockpit
3 Rear centre fuselage
4 Rear fuselage, including rear turret mount
5 Port outboard nacelle
6 Port inboard nacelle
7 Starboard inboard nacelle
8 Starboard outboard nacelle
9 Centre section, including inner wings, landing gear, and inboard engine mounts
10 Port outer wing
11 Port leading edge
12 Starboard outer wing
13 Starboard leading edge
14 Port wing-tip

R5727 first Lancaster in Canada to act as a master tooling model. Note - Lysander and Anson in background.

- CWHM

First fuselage being assembled at Victory Aircraft KB700. Note the original windows in the fuselage which were deleted on future aircraft. *- N.A.M.*

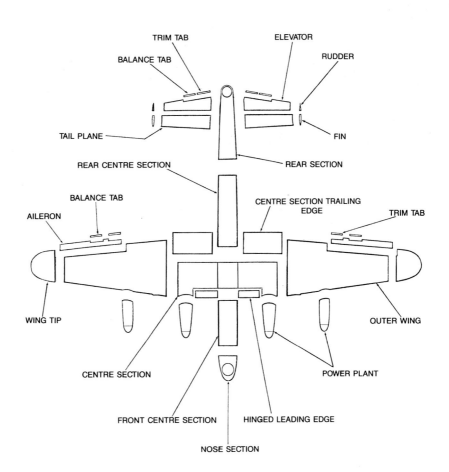

Some of the major components making up a Lancaster.

15 Starboard wing-tip
16 Port aileron
17 Starboard aileron
18 Port centre section flap
19 Starboard centre section flap
20 Port centre section trailing edge
21 Starboard centre section trailing edge
22 Port outer wing trailing edge
23 Starboard outer wing trailing edge
24 Port tailplane
25 Starboard tailplane
26 Port elevator
27 Starboard elevator
28 Port rudder
29 Starboard rudder
30 Port fin
31 Starboard fin

A Lancaster was made up of 55,000 separate parts, including such items as engines and turrets as one and excluding bolts, nuts and rivets. This required 500,000 manufacturing operations.[1]

The Lancaster was a large aircraft in those days, having a wingspan of 102 feet. The general specifications were as follows:

AVRO LANCASTER SPECIFICATIONS

— as a Mark B.I or Mark III, rather than a Mark X M.R./M.P.

DIMENSIONS

Wingspan 102 ft. 0 in.
Length 69 ft. 6 in.
Height (tail down) 20 ft. 4 in.
Wing area 1,297 sq. ft.
Wing loading 50 lb./sq.ft.
Length of bombbay 34 ft.
Weight all-up 65,000 lb. (29,484 kg)
Weight empty 37,000 lb.
Fuel 2,154 gals. (15,509 lb.)
Oil 150 gals. (1,350 lb.)

PERFORMANCE

Max. speed 272 -275 mph @ 15,000 ft. with full load, 287 mph empty, 245 mph @ sea level
Cruising speed 200 mph @ 15,000 ft.
Max. dive speed 360 mph
Stalling speed @ 50,000 lb. clean 110 mph, 92 mph dirty (flaps & wheels down)
Range 2,350 miles with 7,000 lb. load, 1,730 miles with 12,000 lb. load, 1,550 miles with 22,000 lb. load
Take-off run with full load 1,200-1,500 yds.
Service ceiling 24,500 ft. (MR), 19,000 ft. (B.1).

POWER PLANTS

Four Packard Merlin 224s, 1,640 hp with Hamilton A5/159 variable pitch, hydromatic 3-bladed propellers. KB700-774 fitted with Rolls Royce Merlin 38, 1,390 hp.

ARMAMENT

Two - .303″ m/g forward turret F.N.5., two - .303″ m/g mid-upper turret F.N.50 (later A/C KB855) were fitted with Martin 250/CE Type 23A electric mid-upper turrets with two - 0.5″, rear turret 4 - .303″ m/g F.N.20, early models one ventral F.N.64 1 - .303″ m/g.

Due to various management problems, the National Steel Car Company Aircraft Division was taken over by the government on November 5, 1942, as a Crown Company and renamed Victory Aircraft, which later became A.V. Roe Canada Ltd., or Avro Canada as it was commonly called after the war. The facilities are now occupied by McDonnell Douglas of Canada.

The first Canadian prototype, KB700, incorporated 150 modifications as it was built. It was fitted with Packard Merlin 38s and flown on August 1, 1943, by Ernest Taylor and his crew, 16 months after the drawings had arrived in Canada. It was named the *Ruhr Express* at an official naming ceremony on August 6, 1943.

In his book, *Canadian Aircraft Since 1909*, written with H.A. Taylor, Ken Molson recounts a rather amusing tale of why it was delayed in being flown to England after the ceremony:

"After the christening ceremony by Mrs. Power, the wife of the Hon. C.G. Power, Minister for Air, who wielded a specially made, thin-walled bottle of champagne, the crew from No.45 Group, R.A.F., captained by S/L R.J. Lane with P/O S. Boczar as second pilot and P/O J. Correre as navigator and with a complete complement of air gunners, bomb aimer and flight engineer, climbed on board and flew the aircraft away. Since it had been announced that KB700 was off to war, it could not return to Malton for completion of the electrical work, so a work party was sent to Dorval to complete the job, which inevitably took longer away from the Malton facilities. Then the British Ministry of Aircraft Production wired that since KB700 was the first aircraft from a new contractor, a full formal flight-test was required. A flight crew and engineering personnel were sent to Dorval and on 20 August, KB700 was loaded with sand bags and, flown by Ernie Taylor and crew, and with Ken M. Molson as engineering observer, took off for the test. An engine failed at 22,000 ft., the test was aborted and the aircraft returned to Dorval. No spare power-egg was immediately available, so it was not until August 31st that the test was completed. KB700 did not reach England until September 15th, probably two weeks later than it could have because of official interference and insistence that it had gone to war and therefore could not return to Malton."

Judging from the telexes in the archives Grant McLean of National Film Board tried very hard to have the *Ruhr Express* go straight off to war. Fortunately the higher command had more common sense, as the crew which the N.F.B. had demanded be Canadian was a scratch-seven man crew hastily gathered together from No.45 Group R.A.F. for the ceremony and the ferry trip to England. It consisted entirely of tour-expired airmen. The pilot, S/L R.J. Lane, D.S.O., D.F.C., was actually obtained from a Halifax bomber squadron. The newspapers also got upset with Ralph Bell, when he returned to Canada, for not informing the public honestly that the aircraft did not immediately fly off to squadron service, due to the delays already mentioned above. They all knew that the first aircraft off a production line, especially one as complicated as the Lancaster, would likely take some time to reach squadron standards. But the charade was maintained. This was

The crowd of Victory workers at the christening ceremony of Ruhr Express KB700 on August 6, 1943.

- *N.A.M.*

Sqd/Ld R.J. Lane's crew ready to fly KB700, the first Canadian built Lancaster to go to war.

- *N.A.M.*

KB700 Ruhr Express christening ceremonies official party in background.   - *N.A.M.*

From:- No: 20 Maintenance Unit, R.A.F. ASTON DOWN, Chalford, Glos.

Aircraft Type and Mark: Lancaster X.

Serial No: KB.726.

Date Received. 13-4-44.

    A copy is given below of a report by this Unit's Inspection Dept:
rendered following the inspection on receipt of the above mentioned aircraft,
and is forwarded in accordance with the instructions given in No:41 Group
letter 1103/1 dated 20th November,1943.

        1. DEFECTS.

1. Take off boost low on No:4.

2. All oil temperature guages unserviceable.

3. Locking pin missing from port upper inboard radius strut greaser.

4. Fabric stripping on M/P's around Bomb Bay and Engine nacelle.

5. Starboard fuel jettison flap requires hinging.

6. Fuel jettison handle to be lead wire locked.

7. "Press the Dot" fastener broken on flight engineers seat.

8. U/C selector quadrant to be painted red.

9. Aldis lamp stowage required.

10. Perspex blister starboard side of C/O fractured.

11. Acetate panel under pilots seat U/S broken in three places.

12. Hand pump operates flaps very slowly.

13. Beading round step inside F/U door broken.

14. Draught excluding doors near tail turret will not close.

15. Roof lamp glass broken.

16. Starboard green *Rec:* light smashed.

17. Bomb firing switch required and immersion switch.

18. Formation light switch requires adjustment.

        2. ESSENTIAL MODIFICATIONS OUTSTANDING.

   NIL.

       3. SPECIAL TECHNICAL INSTRUCTIONS NOT SATISFIED.

   NIL.

       4. EQUIPMENT REQUIRED TO COMPLETE TO CURRENT STANDARD

27D/2032.	Cover Cockpit	50A/26 Turret Fus.	8B/1588 Sight Reflector
" 2034	" Nose	" /86 " 50	5L/2269 Lamp Fil
" 2033	" Engine	"	
" 2035	"Mid Turret	" 118 " 120	6D/537 Regulator Voltage
" 2176	"Rear "	7H/2838 Tool Make & Break	27H/2026 Luminous D
" 1979	"Prop Hub	" 1667 Guns Browning	6A/1503 Holder Dev Card
" 2104	"Pitot Head	8A/1156 Unit Fire & Safe	6D/188 Switch Immersion
			10A/8940 Crystal Unit 6990

       5. ERRORS IN COMPILATION OF FORMS 700 AND 701

   NIL.

Snag list of KB726 when it arrived at 20 MU, Ashton Down. - *Nat. Archives*

further aggravated when the aircraft was sent to a Pathfinder squadron, where again the N.F.B. wanted the same crew to go on the first mission, to maintain the continuity of their story. Again the high command interceded and pointed out that the crew were not trained for Pathfinder duty and were also tour-expired. The records suggest that the N.F.B. still asked if they could have the original crew take-off and look as if they had gone on the first operation of the aircraft.

The *Ruhr Express* was the only Lancaster X to serve outside of No.6 (R.C.A.F.) Group, Bomber Command, where, probably for public relations reasons already mentioned, it was assigned to No.405 (R.C.A.F) Squadron, No.8 (Pathfinder) Group, near the end of October 1943. After only two missions, one aborted due to an engine failure and the other a successful raid on Berlin, it was withdrawn from operations and then reassigned to No.419 "Moose" Squadron at the end of April 1944. It saw 49 operations with this squadron, until January 2, 1945, when it hit a piece of earthmoving equipment in the overshoot area at the end of the runway and burst into flames, after returning from a raid. Fortunately, all the crew of this historic Canadian aircraft survived. The *Ruhr Express* is a story in itself.

The British were very impressed with the quality of workmanship and equipment on this first aircraft. The Permanent Secretary of the British Ministry of Aircraft Production sent a cable to Victory Aircraft saying that "KB700 was the best equipped aircraft ever to be received from the North American continent." This was to be confirmed by the arrival of KB705 shortly after. KB705 was used for interchangeability tests. These tests confirmed that all major components mated within the tolerances allowed between the Canadian-made parts and their British counterparts. It evidently surprised and pleased everyone on both sides of the Atlantic.

According to the records in the National Archives, KB726 was one of the early Lancasters to be fitted with 8,000 lb. bombdoors. It left Malton on February 26, 1944, and took 15 days to reach Prestwick, where it stayed for 33 days. It arrived at 20 MU Aston Down, Chalford, Gloucester, on April 13, 1944, where it spent another 46 days before being delivered to the squadron. The original snag list of this aircraft, when it arrived at the MU, is attached. It finally arrived at No.419 Squadron at Middleton St. George on May 28, 1944. It was to have a short life of 46 hours before it was lost over France on the fateful night of June 12/13, after only four operations, as described in the succeeding chapters. Its slow delivery was not unusual, as of the 120 aircraft delivered by September 30, 1944, only 90 had reached squadron delivery.

The installation of Packard Merlin 224s occurred on the 75th production aircraft. The original order was for 300 aircraft, which was later increased to 600. The first 300 aircraft were assigned manufacturer's numbers from KB700 to KB999 and were produced between August 1943 and March 1945. The second order was assigned FM100 to FM299 and was produced between March 1945 and September 1945. It was agreed to stop production at FM229 after V-E day. The last Lancaster X was produced in September 1945. In all, 430 Lancaster Mark X airframes were produced by Victory Aircraft before WWII ended, these aircraft included two converted to transports (KB702, KB703) for the Canadian Government Trans-Atlantic Service and six converted (KB729, KB730, FM184-187) for Trans-Canada Air Lines (T.C.A.) as XPPs. Also Victory Aircraft produced one Avro (694) Lincoln XV bomber and one Avro (685) York transport. During flight tests on September 10, 1943, KB702 achieved a top speed of 303 mph @ 19,000 ft. at 3,000 rpm with +8 boost.

All the aircraft that were ferried across to England arrived safely, and none were lost during air testing at Malton, as stated by Ken Molson. However, Greig Stewart in his new book "The Shutdown of A National Dream" mentions one lost in transit. This must be KB828, its loss was evidently due to the improper installation of a bracket on the fuel

Rollout of KB702 converted for Transatlantic Service, C.D. Howe 4th from left. First of two aircraft, with CGTAS. October 1, 1943.
- *N.A.M.*

Production line showing faired turret positions, KB819 at the back of the line.   - *N.A.M.*

100th Lancaster KB799, with a heavy wing load of workers. Note the paddled bladed props.

- N.A.M.

The large and small, Fleet Fairchild Cornell trainer beside a Lancaster at Malton, Fleet produced the outerwings sections of the Lancaster for Victory Aircraft.

- N.A.M.

Finished aircraft waiting to be ferried to England with faired turret positions. - *N.A.M.*

Forlorn Lancasters awaiting modification or disposal at the end of the war. - *N.A.M.*

control system. Later aircraft, KB855 onwards, were fitted with Martin 250/CE Type 23A electric mid-upper turrets with two 0.5 Browning machine guns, rather than two 0.303 in. in the original Frazer Nash 50, and positioned further forward on the fuselage. Also, the smaller 4,000 lb. bomb-bay doors were fitted, rather than the standard 8,000 lb. doors, and the H2S radar dome in place of the mid-under or ventral turret. The Canadian Lancasters with the two 0.5 in. gun type of turret were the only ones to see war service, as the British did not go ahead with modification in time for their aircraft to take part in wartime operations.

Production at Victory Aircraft Ltd. reached a peak of an aircraft a day during the first quarter of 1945, with a peak work force of 10,000 people.

All 430 airframes are listed in Appendix II by serial number starting with the FM series and finishing with the KB series. Every attempt has been made to keep the data as consistent as possible and to record the aircraft squadron service, identification letters, their conversion postwar, and final disposal. Those aircraft that were assigned to No.419 Squadron but which saw no operations with that squadron are indicated by an asterisk (*).

By the end of hostilities in Europe, 105 Canadian Lancasters had been lost due to enemy action or accidents, 288 Lancasters were taken back on strength by the R.C.A.F., including those that survived in England, which were selected to be flown across the Atlantic to Nova Scotia by their crews (160). There the Lancaster squadrons from No.6 Group, plus four more which had re-equipped with Lancasters Xs, Squadrons Nos. 405, 408, 431 and 434, began training for the proposed Tiger Force, which was to join the Far East war theatre against the Japanese. However, hostilities ceased before they could be deployed. The aircrews were demobbed and the aircraft put into storage.

"Roy Chadwick's Lancaster was indeed a shining sword placed through his genius in the hands of our Lancaster aircrews; a sword wielded with such effect as to become a major contribution to the final success of our arms." These compliments were paid to the designer of the Avro Lancaster, the late Sir Roy Chadwick, C.B.E., M.Sc., F.R.S.A., F.R.Ae.S., by the late Air Chief Marshal Sir Arthur Harris, G.C.B., O.B.E., A.F.C., L.L.D. (the WWII Air Marshal in charge of the R.A.F. Bomber Command, who earned the nickname *Bomber Harris*.)

Footnotes:
_____

[1] These sub-assemblies were to serve another useful purpose many decades later, in the restoration of FM213. It allowed components to be shipped various places for rework and new work to be done on them without heavy lifting equipment and jigs at the Canadian Warplane Heritage Museum, Mount Hope, whose facilities were limited.

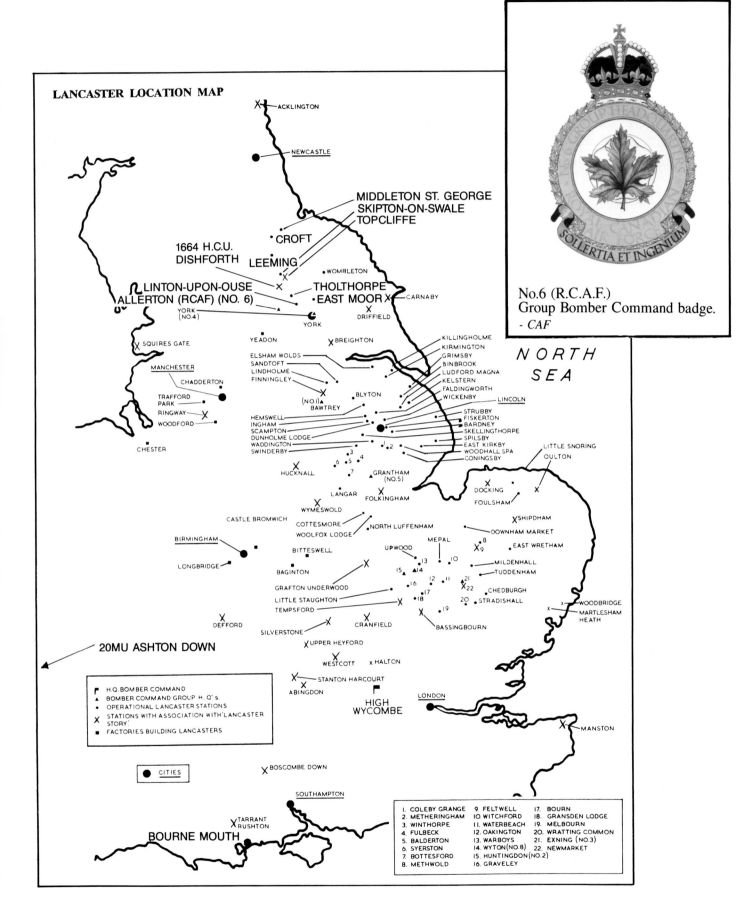

LANCASTER LOCATION MAP

No.6 (R.C.A.F.)
Group Bomber Command badge.
- *CAF*

Map of Bomber Command bases, showing No.6 Group's airfield positions.

30

II

CANADIAN LANCASTERS AT WAR

No.6 (R.C.A.F.) BOMBER GROUP

The Bomber Group No.6 of Bomber Command was unique in that it was a completely Canadian Group of Squadrons. It was created in 1942, when the headquarters unit was first formed on October 25, with temporary space at R.A.F. Linton-on-Ouse. By December 1, the headquarters had moved to Allerton Park Castle, east of Knaresborough. This property had been requisitioned by the Air Ministry from Lord Mowbray of Stourton, premier Baron of England. The estate had the Great North Road as its eastern boundary and on the south it touched the York-Harrogate highway. The 75-room Victorian castle was transformed into administration and operation offices for the Group. It was nicknamed "Castle Dismal" by the Group's public relations officer. Seven R.A.F. stations were initially handed over to the Group. These were Middleton St. George, Croft, Leeming, Topcliffe, Dalton and Dishforth, all in Yorkshire. They were all staffed by R.C.A.F. units. An additional seventh field at Skipton-on-Swale was under construction and would join later. The Group was also given the operation of 1659 Heavy Conversion Unit, which was in use by Canadian units. When No.405, the first R.C.A.F. bomber squadron to be formed in England, returned from Coastal Command to No.6 Group in March 1943, the Group consisted of 11 squadrons.

The Order of Battle was as follows:

	Squadron	Station	Aircraft
405	(Vancouver)	Topcliffe	Halifax
408	(Goose)	Leeming	Halifax
419	(Moose)	Middleton St. George	Halifax
420	(Snowy Owl)	M.S.G	Wellington III & X
424	(Tiger)	Topcliffe	Wellington III & X
425	(Alouette)	Dishforth	Wellington III
426	(Thunderbird)	Dishforth	Wellington III & X
427	(Lion)	Croft	Wellington III & X
428	(Ghost)	Dalton	Wellington III & X
	with two squadrons in No.4 Group		
429	(Bison)	East Moor	Wellington III & X
431	(Iroquois)	Burn	Wellington X

The Group was temporarily reduced by three squadrons when 420, 424 and 425 were detached and posted to Africa in April, to aid in the invasion of Sicily and Italy. This loss in strength was compensated by the formation of 432 Squadron in May with Wellingtons, and 434 Squadron with Halifax Vs in June. During that same year both 429 and 431 Squadrons joined the fold, with East Moor as their base and the new airfield at Wombleton. The first British Lancasters started to replace the Wellingtons in No.6 Group in 1943, with 424 Squadron being the first and the rest of the squadrons slowly changing their Wellingtons for Halifax IIIs and Vs. No.433 Squadron was then formed with Halifaxes but was not to become operational until November, and 420, 424 and 425 squadrons returned to the fold as their tour of duty in North Africa was complete.

With such a growth in the Group, it was organized into subgroups by area, for administrative convenience. Each subgroup had a major airfield and secondary or subsidiary fields. The first subgroup, known as 62 (Beaver) Base, covered the southern area of the Group, with Linton-on-Ouse as the main base and East Moor and Tholthorpe as substations. During 1944, 63 and 64 bases were formed: 63 Base being the central area, with Leeming as the centre and Skipton-on-Swale as sub. The northern area was centred at Middleton St. George, with Croft as a substation, though a further subgroup, No.61, was set up comprising the three Heavy Conversion Units (1659, 1664 and 1666) centred at Topcliffe, with Wombleton and Dishforth as substations. This did not last long, as they reverted to the R.A.F. Training Group later in 1944. The base stations of Linton-on-Ouse, Leeming, Middleton St. George and Topcliffe were all "permanent" stations built for the R.A.F. before the war began. The substations were all of wartime construction.

Unfortunately No.6 Group was never to have all the Canadian squadrons under its wing at one time. No sooner had 431 Squadron joined, when 405 Squadron was posted to the elite (Pathfinder) No.8 Group. During 1944 and early 1945 a number of the squadrons started to re-equip with the new Canadian Lancaster Xs, No.419 Squadron being one of the first. So by April 19, 1945, the Order of Battle for No.6 (R.C.A.F.) looked like this:

	Squadron	Station	Aircraft
408	(Goose)	Linton-on-Ouse	Halifax VII
415	(Swordfish)	East Moor	Halifax III
419	(Moose)	Middleton St. George	Lancaster X
420	(Snowy Owl)	Tholthorpe	Lancaster X & Halifax III
424	(Tiger)	Skipton-on-Swale	Lancaster I, III
425	(Alouette)	Tholthorpe	Halifax III
426	(Thunderbird)	Linton-on-Ouse	Halifax VII
427	(Lion)	Leeming	Lancaster I, III & Halifax III
428	(Ghost)	Middleton St.George	Lancaster X
429	(Bison)	Leeming	Lancaster I, III & Halifax III
431	(Iroquois)	Croft	Lancaster X
432	(Leaside)	East Moor	Halifax VII
433	(Porcupine)	Skipton-on-Swale	Lancaster I, III & Halifax III
434	(Bluenose)	Croft	Lancaster X

Only No.419 Squadron was to stay on the same base at Middleton St.George during the Group's lifetime. All these squadrons were financed by the Canadian government during their respective tours in Europe and North Africa.

The operational achievements of the Group were impressive and reached their peak in 1944, when the percentage of losses was lower than any other Group in Bomber Command operating four-engined aircraft. For example, in 1943, their first year of operations, 7,355 sorties were flown, dropping 13,630 tons of bombs, with the loss of 340 aircraft. In 1944 the sorties rose to 25,353, dropping 86,503 tons of bombs, with the loss of 377 aircraft. In the closing year of the war, 1945, 8,114 sorties were flown, dropping

25,989 tons of bombs, with the loss of 97 aircraft. Thus the Group flew a total of 40,822 sorties, consisting of 271,981 flying hours, during which a total of 126,122 tons of bombs were dropped, for the loss of 814 aircraft.

The Air Officers commanding No.6 Group were:

Air Vice-Marshal G.E. Brooks - 25 October 1942
Air Vice-Marshal C.M. McEwen - 29 February 1944
Air Commodore J.L. Hurley - 19 June 1945

After V-E Day three of the Group squadrons, Nos. 427, 433 and 434, had the happy task of ferrying ex-P.O.W.s back to England, many of these passengers were their own members. A total of 4,329 aircrew were airlifted back to the U.K. in three days, an amazing feat of logistics and airmanship.

After the cessation of the war in Europe, planning started on the amalgamation of forces against the Japanese in the Far East, called the Tiger Force. Eight squadrons from No.6 Group were earmarked to join this force and return to Canada for training. They were Nos. 405, 408, 419, 420, 425, 428, 431, and 434, all of which returned to Canada in June 1945 and all flying Mark Xs. Four other squadrons, Nos. 424, 427, 429 and 433, were to remain behind with No.1 Group Bomber Command to assist with the Armies of Occupation, where they ferried troops from Italy to England. No. 426 was posted to Transport Command to make trooping flights to India using Liberators. The remaining two squadrons, No.415 and 432, were disbanded within a week of V-E Day.

Therefore the proposed composition of the new No.6 Group (R.C.A.F.) on 10 July 1945, that would join the Tiger Force was as follows:

Commander Designate: A/V/M C.M. McEwen, later A/V/M C.R. Slemon

No.661 Wing: Nos.419 & 428 (B) Squadrons
No.662 Wing: Nos.431 & 434 (B) Squadrons
No.663 Wing: Nos.420 & 425 (B) Squadrons
No.664 Wing: Nos.405 & 408 (B) Squadrons
No.6 Group (Long Range) Transport Wing: Nos.422, 423 and 426 (T) Squadrons

By the end of August 1945 and the cessation of hostilities in the Far East, No.6 Group had ceased to exist and so the Canadian Bomber Group's career came to a close, with its members earning over 8,000 decorations for bravery.

No.419 "MOOSE" SQUADRON R.C.A.F.

Nickname: Moose
Motto: "Mossa Aswayita" (Beware of the moose.)

The motto is in the Cree Indian language. The crest represents a charging bull moose, as a fierce fighter indigenous to Canada.

This squadron was formed at Mildenhall, Suffolk, on 15 December 1941 as the third R.C.A.F. bomber squadron overseas. Its first C.O. was W/C John ("Moose") Fulton, D.S.O., D.F.C., A.F.C., from Kamloops, B.C., and it was from his nickname that the unit gained its name and the moose emblem on its squadron badge. He did his first tour of operations with No.99 Squadron and went missing on a raid on Hamburg in a Wellington bomber on July 28, 1942. Unfortunately he has no known grave, like so many of his compatriots.

The squadron was originally part of No.3 Group of Bomber Command and later No.4 Group, until it joined No.6 Group when the latter was formed on 1 January 1943. The squadron moved from Mildenhall, Suffolk, to Leeming, Yorkshire, in August 1942; to

King's badge No.419
Squadron.
- *CAF RE 20793-11*

A painting by F/Lt L.
Kenyon, R. Art F. of
W/C John "Moose"
Fulton, D.S.O., D.F.C.,
A.F.C. The first com-
manding officer of
No.419 Squadron, who
gave his nickname to the
squadron. He went miss-
ing in action in 1942.
- *Imperial War Museum*

Topcliffe, Yorkshire, in Aug. - Sept. 1942; and Croft, County Durham, in Sept. - Nov. 1942; before making its home base at Middleton St.George on November 10, 1942. It was the only squadron of No.6 Group to stay on one base all the time that the Group was in England.

It began operations using Wellington medium bombers (January - November 1942), later converted to Halifax heavy bombers (November 1942 - April 1944), and finally to Lancaster Xs (April 1944 - June 1945). On April 27, 1944, No.419 Squadron became the first squadron to operate the new Canadian-built Lancaster Xs, when eight Lancasters and five Halifaxes bombed an airfield at Montzen, Belgium. This operation was the only time the squadron flew into action with more than one type of aircraft on the same operation. The squadron then operated exclusively with Lancasters. The first enemy aircraft to be shot down by the Canadian Lancasters was a Ju-88 nightfighter. This action occurred on 7/8 June on a raid to Achères by the gunners of F/O W.J. Anderson's crew. The rear and mid-upper gunners were Sgts. W.F. Mann and P.F. Burton, who received D.F.M.s for their effort.

Over its three and a quarter years of war service, No.419 logged 354 operational missions, including 299 bombing missions and 51 mining excursions or "gardening ops," 3 leaflet raids and 1 diversion or "spoof." These missions involved 4,326 sorties and the delivery of over 14,000 tons of bombs and mines.[1] This was achieved with the loss of 154 aircraft. Ten were lost in training. The squadron record is broken down in more detail as follows in this information prepared by V. Elmer, 419 Squadron Historian, Prince Albert, Saskatchewan, March 8, 1987.

OPERATIONAL PERFORMANCE

Raids Flown
3 Group Wellingtons   - 67 bombing, 18 mine-laying, 3 leaflet
6 Group Halifaxes   - 105 bombing, 33 mine-laying, 1 diversion
6 Group Lancasters   - 127 bombing
Total - 299 bombing, 51 mine-laying, 4 other = 354 raids

SORTIES AND LOSSES

3 Group Wellingtons   - 711 sorties, 27 aircraft lost (3.7%) plus 2 over England on return from ops = total 29 plus 4 on training accidents.
6 Group Halifaxes   - 1,584 sorties, 68 aircraft lost (4.1%) plus 8 over England on return from ops = total 76 plus 3 on training accidents.
6 Group Lancasters   - 2,031 sorties, 42 aircraft lost (1.9%) plus 7 over England on return from ops = total 49 plus 3 on training accidents.
Total 4,326 sorties, 154 aircraft lost (3.0%) plus 10 in training.

The 419 squadron flew a total of 25,386 operational hours and 8,613 non-operational hours. The loss of 154 aircraft involved 1,404 aircrew, of whom 527 were killed in action, 167 missing in action, 204 P.O.W. and 52 evaded capture. Also, nine ground crew lost their lives. Their last operational sortie took place against the fortified island of Wangerooge when 15 aircraft plastered the target. When the last aircraft VR.X landed at 20:15 hrs, the navigator of this crew was F/O Bob Bodie (previously navigator of the Mynarski crew), who thus became one of the last flyers to land in a wartime operational Lancaster.

It is interesting to note that though No.419 was a Canadian squadron, it did have members from the R.A.F. and other countries. The commanding officers of No.419 Squadron during the war years were as follows:

W/C J. Fulton, D.S.O.,D.F.C, A.F.C.	21/12/41 - 28/07/42 KIA
W/C A.P. Walsh, D.F.C., A.F.C.	05/08/42 - 02/09/42 KIA
W/C M.M. Flemming, D.S.O., D.F.C.	08/09/42 - 08/10/43
W/C G.A. McMurdy	11/10/43 - 22/10/43 MIA
W/C W.P. Pleasance, D.F.C.& Bar	25/10/43 - 21/08/44
W/C D.C. Hagerman, D.F.C. & Bar	21/08/44 - 25/01/45
W/C M.E. Ferguson	26/01/45 - 05/09/45 DISB

No.419 Squadron carried out the most bombing raids and flew the most sorties of No.6 Group Lancaster squadrons.

The squadron members earned the following decorations:

1	Victoria Cross - Pilot Officer Mynarski
4	D.S.O.s
150	D.F.C.s and 3 Bars
1	C.G.M.
35	D.F.M.s
1	M.C.

During June 1945 No.419 flew its 20 Lancasters back to Canada, landing at Yarmouth Nova Scotia, to prepare for the Tiger Force, but with cessation of all hostilities the squadron was disbanded in September of that year.

The following is a record of the returning aircraft and their skippers:

AIRCRAFT	CAPTAIN	DATE
VR.A KB841	F/L F.G. Dawson	10 June 1945
VR.B KB721	F/O W.J. Smith	10 June 1945
VR.C KB881	F/L G.L. Smith	10 June 1945
VR.D KB839	F/L P.H. Tulk	10 June 1945
VR.E KB865	F/L E.G. Peters	12 June 1945
VR.F KB783	P/O D.G. Brown	10 June 1945
VR.G KB733	P/O D.E. Rickerts	16 June 1945
VR.I KB878	F/L B.A. Nichols	10 June 1945
VR.K KB884	S/L D.B. Hunter	10 June 1945
VR.M KB889	P/O D.W. Laubman	10 June 1945
VR.N KB857	F/L C.J. Widdicombe	10 June 1945
VR.O KB748	F/L W.G. Manning	10 June 1945
VR.P KB892	S/L J.W. Watts	10 June 1945
VR.Q KB921	F/L B.P. Wickham	10 June 1945
VR.R KB772	F/O R.E. Chambers	10 June 1945
VR.S KB746	F/L J.E. Short	13 June 1945
VR.T KB854	P/O D.R. Cushman	10 June 1945
VR.U KB823	P/O J.C. MacNeil	12 June 1945
VR.W KB851	W/C M.E. Ferguson	10 June 1945
VR.X KB732	F/L D.B. Lambroughton	10 June 1945
VR.M KB999	Transferred to No.405 Squad. to fly A.V.M "Black Mike" McEwen To Canada.	

The story of how the Victoria Cross was won by Andrew Mynarski in Lancaster X KB726 of No.419 Moose Squadron and his surviving crew's stories are an integral part of this book. The history and acquisition of the Lancaster FM213 and its restoration to flying condition, to represent KB726, and dedicated in honour of P/O Andrew Charles Mynarski

A/V/M C.M. McEwen with staff inspecting, KB732 "X-terminator" the oldest Lanc in No.419 Squadron which was transferred to No.405 Squadron to fly him home, 83 ops. - *CAF PL 43722*

Another old Lanc that survived, KB760 NA.P 72 ops. The inscription on the bomb says "P for panic hit old Jerry, in every conceivable place, the war in Europe is over, let's get cracking on that yellow race." Malton, Ontario, 1945.

- N.A.M. 6702

F/O Arthur de Breyne, pilot of KB726 VR.A. - *Pat Brophy*

F/Sgt James Kelly, wireless operator of KB726 VR.A.
- *Pat Brophy*

F/O Patrick Brophy, rear gunner of KB726 VR.A.
- *Pat Brophy*

F/Sgt Jack Friday, bomb-aimer of KB726 VR.A.
- *Pat Brophy*

F/O Robert Bodie, navigator of KB726 VR.A. - *Pat Brophy*

W/O Andrew Charles Mynarski, mid-upper gunner of KB726 VR.A.   - *Art de Breyne*

...) this story. The aircrews who lost their lives and whose heroism ... those who survived the war in Bomber Command, in particular ...., are surely represented by the Mynarski crew. The following ...cumstances which led to them becoming a crew, up to the fateful ... the Cambrai raid, and their survival until they were liberated.

...anadian Lancaster KB726 bearing squadron markings VR.A ...rt de Breyne, Navigator F/O Bob Bodie, Rear Gunner F/O Pat ...or W/O Jim Kelly, Flight Engineer F/Sgt Roy Vigars, Bomb-...and Mid-Upper Gunner W/O Andrew Mynarski. The original ...gt. Ken Branston.

...ASTER KB726 VR.A

...f the crew are woven around Art de Breyne's account of their ... survived to the present.

...r 1943 at No.24 Operational Training Unit at Honeybourne, ... consisted of 20 six-man crews. One hundred and twenty ... room, and in less than one hour they had formed 20 crews. ...oneybourne airfield was transformed into a turkey farm after ...ctors and crews at the O.T.U. may in jest think of it as an ...n certainly remember that the diet at that time included an ...ts, as that famous wartime vegetable seemed to grow in ...rs on after all these years.

...of the aircraft, Art de Breyne planned ahead to fill one or two key positions he considered vital. He had become friendly just a few days before with F/O Bob Bodie, who struck him as a serious-minded navigator then 30 years of age, and whose maturity he felt made him a man of sound judgement. Time proved this to be a remarkably accurate assessment. Bob's navigating skills never let the crew down.

Bob Bodie joined the R.C.A.F. in July 1942 and in May 1943 graduated from the Navigators School at Edmonton as a P/O. He was sent overseas, and after a session at Bournemouth and a battle course at Sidmouth, he proceeded to Honeybourne, where he met Art and the rest of the crew. While the crew learned to take Bob's ability for granted, Art, who had qualified as a navigator on a general reconnaissance course, truly appreciated how lucky they were.

Casting about for a rear gunner as soon as crewing up began, Art spotted F/O Pat Brophy, whose rank as a commissioned officer suggested that he must have displayed superior skills and come out close to the top of the class. As Pat was not yet committed, Art introduced him to Bob Bodie, not realizing that they already knew each other, and Pat agreed to join the group, making the nucleus of an excellent crew.

Pat was just turning 22 at that time. In 1942 he had tried to enlist in the Army and had been rejected, but he later enrolled in the R.C.A.F. Special Reserve as a 2nd class aircraftsman (the lowest form of human life in the Air Force). He attended No.3 Wireless School at Winnipeg, Manitoba, in 1942-43 and was promoted to the dizzy heights of leading aircraftsman shortly thereafter. He was promoted to sergeant at No.3 Bombing & Gunner School at McDonald, Manitoba. On graduation he was given a commission in the King's Air Force as a Pilot Officer. He arrived in England via the passenger liner *Queen Mary* and ended up at No.3 Personnel Reception Centre, Bournemouth, where P/O Bob Bodie, who was a navigator, became his roommate. Pat advised Art that he had a friend from his home town of Port Arthur whom he would very much like to fly with, as he was an excellent bomb-aimer. Not knowing any other bomb-aimer at the time, it seemed an excellent proposal, and so Jack Friday was acquired as the fourth man on the team.

Jack joined the R.C.A.F. in August 1942 and spent time in Edmonton, Calgary and Regina. He graduated from No.2 Bombing & Gunner School at Mossbank, Saskatchewan, and from No.7 A.O.S. at Portage la Prairie, Manitoba, as a navigator. He went overseas in August 1943, and after the normal session at Bournemouth, he was posted to Moreton Valence. Here he was rudely introduced to the R.A.F. On the first parade at this forlorn little station, the warrant officer in charge said he did not like Canadians and did not know why they were there, as the R.A.F. could do the job without them. Fortunately, No.6 Group and No.419 Squadron in particular were to prove him wrong.

At that time Gloucester Aircraft was using Moreton Valance airfield to test fly the secret new Gloucester Meteor jet fighter aircraft. The men were not supposed to look at the aircraft as it went whistling by, as it was top secret.

Jack soon went on to O.T.U., where he met the rest of the crew. The process of selection now became a team effort. Pat was friendly with another gunner from Toronto, Ken Branston, and before Art knew it, a mid-upper gunner had joined them.

Ken had joined the R.C.A.F. on November 13, 1942, and was posted to Manning Pool, Toronto, then to Laval University, Quebec City to take part in the Wartime Emergency Training Plan, thence to "tarmac duty" at Mont Joli, P.Q., after which he was posted to Little Norway, Toronto. There he flunked the Link Trainer course, remustered as air gunner and was posted to Trenton for Air Gunner's Ground School, where he graduated.

His association with Pat Brophy began at No.3 Bombing & Gunnery School (B&G) at McDonald. Of 132 men on course No.59 there were 11 commissioned on graduation and Pat was one of them. On several 48-hour passes Pat and Ken had visited Winnipeg and enjoyed the hospitality of that city. After a pre-embarkation leave, Ken reported to Halifax, Nova Scotia, for posting overseas. He subsequently sailed from New York on the liner *Queen Mary* in October 1943, arriving at Bournemouth, which was the central depot for incoming R.C.A.F. personnel. After a few days he was posted to the Operational Training Unit at Honeybourne.

In turn the N.C.O.'s were friendly with another Torontonian, who lived in Winnipeg and was a wireless operator. Jim Kelly was a roommate of Jack Friday. Jim was already a married man, though just turned 19. Jim had joined the R.C.A.F. in April 1941 in Toronto. Georgetown was his home. He took his wireless training in Winnipeg and Air Gunnery in Dafoe, Saskatchewan. In addition he spent eight months on staff at the Navigation School, Malton, Ontario after which he went through the Operational Training Unit at Greenwood, Nova Scotia (Coastal Command). He was posted overseas as a Flt/Sgt W.O/A.G. in August 1943, ending up at Honeybourne for O.T.U. Jim was welcomed to complete the crew. Thus, each crew member had some prior association with another member of the crew, thereby making a bond which would weld them together. So Art de Breyne as the pilot, ended up with Bob Bodie as navigator, Jack Friday as bomber-aimer, Jim Kelly as wireless operator, Pat Brophy as rear gunner and Ken Branston as mid-upper gunner. Everyone seemed happy with the outcome, yet the whole process had probably been completed in only 15 minutes. Pleased with their accomplishment, they duly registered themselves as a crew and went off to have a few beers together to get better acquainted.

At the end of that day Art sat down in a corner of the mess and began to reflect on his role and responsibility. He had left college at the age of 20 to join the R.C.A.F. at the same time as Pearl Harbour, though he was not activated until January 1942. He did his elementary training on Tiger Moths at No.4 E.F.T.S, Windsor Mills, his service training at No.8 S.F.T.S, Moncton on Harvards and graduated on Ansons. Until now, he had been a student pilot. Suddenly he was the captain of a six-man crew. He was 22 years of age and one of his crew was considerably older than him. He had already been addressed as Skipper, which implied to him that he was looked upon for leadership. As he contemplated, the realization of all this became an added weight on his shoulders. He had one asset: he was still a stranger to his crew. They knew nothing of his weaknesses or lack of experience. He had to give them the impression of being a highly qualified pilot on all types of aircraft, with the greatest confidence in his skills. The fact that he had not yet even seen a Whitley V, in which they were to fly, did not matter.

He was quite aware of his lack of experience and limitations. His training in Canada on Tiger Moths, Ansons and Harvards, mostly in daylight, had taught him the basics. What skills he had were acquired on Airspeed Oxfords at Kidlington, which he had flown for three months and on which he had learned to fly on instruments.

It was clear they were destined for night flying. After three weeks of familiarization at Advance Flying Unit, his training was moved to Feltwell in Norfolk for a landing beam approach course. Fog rolled in every morning off the Wash estuary and the area was covered with it, up to 300 feet (Harry Clampers - weather clamped right down to the ground), making for ideal blind approach flying, even in daylight. The last month of the course was night flying at Kidlington, near Oxford, and they put into practice what they had learned on the beam approach course.

Now at Honeybourne, they were graduating to Whitley Vs. Art knew nothing of this aircraft beyond the fact that it was much bigger than anything he had yet flown. It looked like a boxcar with a long fuselage and a catwalk under the mainspar to communicate with the rear. It had a wingspan equal to the Lancaster, with a much thicker wing and two good Merlin engines where it needed four. It was jokingly referred to as the four-engine bomber on which they forgot to put the two outboard engines for economic reasons. It climbed 300 feet a minute and its lack of power made it dangerous, as it had nothing to spare.

On November 22, 1943, training began. Their designated instructor, F/O Storey, flew with them for two and a half hours and instructed Art in all the emergency procedures. He somehow omitted single-engine flying. After landing, Art went into the flight room and the instructor immediately checked out the group as a crew, much to Art's surprise. For the next two weeks the crew flew without an instructor. Taking off and landing this big crate was like flying an Anson all over again, with one exception: it was a heavy aircraft and failure of one engine could be disastrous. This familiarization period did much to establish confidence in all members of the crew, a confidence which never left them.

The one thing that this crew had in common was that they were all Canadians determined to strike a blow for freedom. They came from widely separated parts of the country, each with little or no knowledge of the others' home towns. Bob Bodie had worked in a paper mill at Ocean Falls, on the B.C. coast. The four junior members of the crew struck Art as fun-loving youngsters, not long out of high school and always ready for a good party. Art decided that they would adhere to one strict rule, that the business of flying was serious and exhilarating, but only when on the ground could they enjoy themselves, as he did not want them playing silly-buggers in the air.

Once they became familiar with their duties on the Whitley, practising daylight bombing on the range and fighter affiliation, they graduated to night flying. In November and December the English countryside near the Welsh border is pea soup country, foggy and cloudy, and after take-off, the ground was seldom seen again until landing. Being a training aircraft, the Whitley had no radar equipment. The one reliable navigational instrument which Bob Bodie had learned to use was the bubble sextant. The problem was that on cross-country trips they could not get above 15,000 feet and often went considerable distances before being able to sight a star to shoot. When they did, they were able to fix their position within three or four miles. Pat Brophy used to bet with Art on every flight that he would give him a penny a point for every three-point landing — this appeared to work and saved Pat from being jolted out of his seat in the rear turret.

Towards the end of their O.T.U. training they were given an exercise delivering the mail or nickels (propaganda pamphlets) to Paris, their first sortie over enemy territory. On the outward journey they crossed the French coast at 14,500 feet and drew a little flak but were not hit. They had a strong tail wind and, in spite of their 160 mph airspeed soon found themselves over Paris, where they proceeded to release their load of pamphlets. Jim Kelly had crawled down the catwalk to drop them down the flare chute. As he emerged from the catwalk up front again, he was still on his knees when they were attacked by an FW190. Pat Brophy gave Art the command to corkscrew to port, and as he pushed forward on the control column and banked, something brushed against his sleeve. He turned his head, and there was Kelly in mid-air alongside him with a surprised look on his face (due to the negative G-force). The situation was corrected when Art pulled back on the control column. The closing speed of the FW190 was so great, because of the exceptionally low speed of the Whitley, that it skidded across their tail without getting in a shot and then was lost to them.

Setting course for home they were now bucking the wind that had been so helpful in getting to the target. Their ground speed was 70 mph and they settled down for a long trip. The total time was nearly six hours. They celebrated Christmas and New Year's Day while they were at Honeybourne.

The training of a bomber crew covers many phases. From O.T.U. the crew went to No.61 Base at Dalton, in Yorkshire (Dalton-in-the-Mud) for an escape and evasion course, in case they should be shot down. They were duly impressed by the statistics quoted to them that two out of three men would eventually put to good use what they had learned there. It was a grim realization, yet everyone was sure he would be part of the lucky one third. They did not know then that months later four of them would put to good practice the training they had received.

After one month at Dalton, they went on to No.1664 Heavy Conversion Unit (H.C.U.) at Dishforth, not far away, to convert to Halifax four-engine bombers. About this time they had to say goodbye to their mid-upper gunner, Ken Branston, who suffered an off-duty accident and would spend two months in hospital.

The story behind this incident is that when they arrived at the H.C.U. several of the crew went to the local pub to celebrate. After imbibing and much hilarity they returned to base. Ken was more than a little inebriated and Pat decided to put him to bed. As Ken lay on the bed, Pat attempted to take off his trousers, and Ken playfully tapped him in the stomach with his feet. After a while Ken got up and, facing Pat, started to tease him. By this time Pat had decided that this was more than enough nonsense and he planted a hard shot to Ken's jaw (docked his clock). Instantly Ken saw stars, and they then commiserated with each other in an inebriated way and went to bed. When morning dawned, Ken awoke with a tremendous pain in his jaw, which appeared to be somewhat misaligned. After reporting to the M.O. (Medical Officer), it was discovered that he had a double fracture of the upper jaw. Ken was consequently shipped to the Queen Victoria Hospital at East Grinstead, where he was wired up and kept until the end of April 1944. On discharge from hospital he returned to No.1664 Heavy Conversion Unit and crewed up with Lorne Frames' crew, which was subsequently posted to No.419 Squadron, where his first crew had already been posted.

On the night of July 3, 1944, there was a stand down due to poor weather, and so, with other members of Frames' crew, Ken went into Middlesbrough for a little relaxation. During the night's fun and games he injured his leg (not from playing High Cock A Lore 'em, as was first supposed, as this was exclusively a R.A.F. officers mess game) and had to be taken to Base Hospital. On the afternoon of July 4 the crew came to visit him and said they were "on" for that night. The next morning, when the orderly came around, Ken asked for news of the "ops" from the previous night and was told that three crews were missing and among them were F/O Frames' crew. They fortunately all survived though three of them became prisoners of war. Ken was returned from hospital to Middleton St. George in October and was posted to No.428 Squadron to replace a mid-upper gunner who had been killed in F/O Miller's crew. Ken completed his tour of operation on February 2, 1945.

Art de Breyne's crew were sad to lose Ken but had no choice in the matter and had to say goodbye. A new man, Andrew Mynarski, who had previous experience as a gunner, was assigned to the crew as the replacement mid-upper gunner.

Andrew Charles Mynarski was born in Winnipeg, Manitoba, on October 14, 1916, being the second son of Polish immigrant parents. When Andrew was 16, his father died, and in 1935 Andy obtained a job as a chamois cutter with a local furrier to supplement the family income. This additional income was most welcome as his mother had been left with three sons and three daughters to raise on her own. Andy proved good at his job and his employer considered him his best cutter. His natural skill with his hands showed up in other ways, as in the wooden furniture and model aircraft he built in a small workshop in the basement of the family home, where he also painted pictures.

In 1940 Andrew Mynarski had his first experience of military life when he joined the Royal Winnipeg Rifles (Non-permanent Active Militia) with whom he served for a short period. Just before his 25th birthday, on September 29, 1941, he joined the R.C.A.F. at a Winnipeg recruiting centre, and a week later was at No.3 Manning Depot in Edmonton, Alberta. He was posted to No.2 Wireless School at Calgary, and after experiencing difficulty in mastering Morse code (dit dah), he was transferred to No.3 B & G School at MacDonald, Manitoba, on October 12, 1941, where he earned his air gunner wing just before Christmas. On New Year's Day 1942 he found himself as a temporary sergeant at the Embarkation Depot, Halifax, Nova Scotia. By mid-January he was awaiting posting at No.3 Personnel Reception Depot in England. In March he was sent to No.16 O.T.U. for gunnery training on Wellington aircraft and then on for training on Halifax (Hallibags) at No.1661 H.C.U., where he was promoted to flight sergeant on June 18, 1943. His first operational unit, at which he arrived on October 31, 1943, was No.9 Squadron, equipped with Lancasters. A month later he was posted to No.1668 H.C.U., then to "R" (Replacement) Depot and later to No.1664 H.C.U. at Dishforth, Yorkshire, arriving in March 1944.

A four-engine Halifax bomber also required a flight engineer and a young Englishman freshly trained for the job took on this duty. This was Roy Vigars of the R.A.F., the only non-Canadian in the crew. Roy had served an apprenticeship as a railway engineer, had just turned 20, and though he had no experience was as keen as "Punch." Roy joined the R.A.F. in June 1943 at the Air Crew Reception Centre (A.C.R.C. - Arcy Tarcy) at St.Johns Wood, London. Roy's memories of those days are described in his words.

"All aircrew trainees were billeted in the surrounding hotels and blocks of flats, with our main parade ground on the hallowed green of British cricket, Lords Cricket Ground.

"I was posted, in the middle of June, to No.21 Initial Training Wing (I.T.W.) at Torquay, Devon, to enjoy summer weather square bashing and learning the rudiments of airmanship. Then on to the Engineer School of Technical Training (E.S.T.T.) at St. Athans, South Wales.

"The six-month course passed all too quickly. On passing out, I was a fully qualified flight engineer for a Handley Page Halifax Mark III bomber. Strangely enough I never did fly in a Mark III. After leave earned for passing out, I was posted to No.1664 H.C.U. at Dishforth. On March 13, 1944, one day before my 20th birthday, I reported to the Engineer Officer and, along with other engineers from the course at St. Athans, was taken into a large hangar where other crew members were gathered. We were given an introduction to a group of pilots who were looking for flight engineers for their conversion to four-engine aircraft. The engineer leader's introduction was brief and to the point: 'Here are the engineers.' With that he left the proceedings.

Bombing up a Halifax VR.W JB965 with 2,000 pounder and incendiaries. The ground crew are L.A.C. J.A. White, Toronto, L.A.C. R.H. Wilson, Vancouver, L.A.C. Hall, Moose Jaw, L.A.C. M. Brouillard, London, Ontario. Infamous NAAFI wagon far right.   - V. Elmer, CAF 32562

The now famous picture of the whole crew together in front of a Halifax II Series 1a, which they had just air-tested. Front row: Pat Brophy, Roy Vigars, Andy Mynarski. Back row: Jim Kelly, Art de Breyne, Jack Friday, Bob Bodie.   - R. Bodie & Art de Breyne

"A very tall pilot came over to me and said, 'I'm de Breyne. Would you like to join my crew'? I replied, 'Yes please, Sir,' and gave a R.A.F. parade ground salute. With that my pilot said, 'Take it easy. My name's Art. What's yours?' This was a bit different than how I had been taught to address officers so far. After this Art said, 'I'll introduce you to some of the crew. See those two mad-brains over there' (referring to two chaps playing dirt track on bicycles). They were Pat Brophy and Ken Branston."

The course was very intense. The sole object was to familiarize the crew as quickly as possible with the Halifax they would be flying on operations. Replacement crews must have been needed on squadrons. In a two-and-a-half-week period they put in 27 hours of day and night flying, mostly without an instructor. It was probably during this period that the navigator, Bodie, refused to go with them on purely training exercises that did not require any significant navigation. The reason for his refusal to fly on unnecessary flights was a trick quite common among bomber crews. When any member had to go to the Elsan (chemical toilet in the back of the aircraft) to relieve himself, someone would signal to the pilot at the appropriate moment to push the stick forward, causing the fluid in the toilet to fly out under negative G-forces catching the individual in a shower of "Sweet violets." "Covered all over from head to foot in Sweet violets," as the song goes. Evidently this happened to Bodie and he swore he would not fly with them on any future exercises unless it was an "op" or they were serious! Bodie did retaliate on one of their trips by asking the pilot to change course "Starboard 90," then "Port 90," then "Port 90," and finally "Starboard 90." At this point Art asked, "What in hell is going on?" Bodie's reply: "You have just flown around the cigarette case sitting on my map!"

They made their first flight as a crew on March 26, 1944, in a Halifax.

On April 10,1944, they arrived as a new crew on No.419 Squadron at 5 p.m. Art was told to report immediately to the briefing room, and three hours later took off on his first bombing trip to Ghent marshalling yards in Belgium as second pilot with P/O McLean's crew, in a Halifax II. Two days later he was given a similar second pilot experience on a mine-laying or "gardening" sortie off the Danish coast (Heligoland) with P/O Patterson, in a similar aircraft JP130. The crew's training was now complete.

Their first operation as a crew was a bombing attack on the railway marshalling yards of Laon, in eastern France, a six-hour trip which was relatively uneventful for them, but considerable fighter action was observed involving others. That was their one and only operation in the Halifax Mk II HR925.

A now famous picture of the crew in their flying suits and parachutes was taken in front of a Halifax II series 1A after a daylight air test. The aircraft went missing that night, but fortunately they were not aboard.

The new Canadian Lancaster Mark Xs arrived on the station from Canada and the next few days were taken up in getting the feel of them. KB726 arrived on the station from the 20 M.U. on May 28, 1944. To Art, flying one was like graduating to a fighter plane, as the Lancaster was light on controls and had a landing speed of 20 mph less than the Halifax, and no tendency to swing on take-off and landing. They flew Lancasters KB701, 711, 712, 715, 717, 718, 719, 724, 726, 727, 736, and 738 during their familiarization training and on operations.

The newest members of the crew by this time had integrated very nicely. Roy Vigars, the flight engineer, with whom Art had to work most closely, was completely familiar with all controls even in complete darkness. Andy Mynarski was far removed from Art physically in his mid-upper turret and their only contact was by intercom. Social get-togethers with the crew while on the squadron took place every two weeks or so, when they had occasion to treat the ground crew to a few beers at the Cavendish Hotel, overlooking the Tees River. This was a lovely setting in springtime. The N.C.O.s in the crew became a very close-knit group, and Andy Mynarski, Art believes, felt a new sense

Canadian Lancasters of No.419 Squadron lined up ready for their first operations, with ground crew chatting to the rear gunner. KB711 was one of the aircraft in which the Mynarski crew trained.
- CAF PL 29474

No.6 Group Commander Air Vice Marshal "Black Mike" McEwen inspecting a Lancaster bomb load. Note: 4,000 cookie and 1,000 lbs. Bombs tail armed and stacked.
- CAF PL 43699

1,000th sortie by "The Moose Men" with 4,000 lbs. Cookie and the hard
working ground crew.   - Art de Breyne

A clear photo of daylight bombing of railway lines in France.
                                                          - CAF PL 43555

Crew during debriefing, Pat Brophy, Jim Kelly, Art de Breyne sleepy as usual, Roy Vigars.

- Art de Breyne

The only surviving photograph of a bombing raid of F/O Art de Breyne, of the raid on Bourg-Leopold camp 27/28 May 1944.

- Art de Breyne

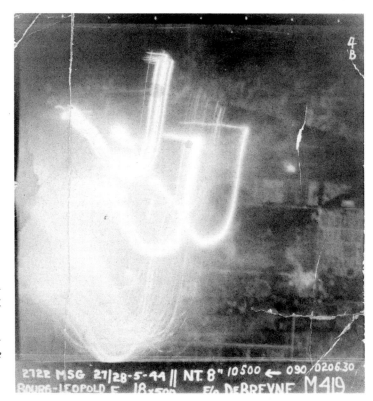

of identity within it. Their favourite pub was the "Unicorn" in Stockton-on-Tees which was easily reached by train. The four mad-brains were Pat, Jim, Andy and Jack, and they had many hilarious times together.

Their arrival on the squadron coincided with the start of the softening-up operation designed to destroy all railway communications in preparation for the invasion of Europe. These targets consisted mainly of marshalling yards, which were mostly in friendly countries, necessitating low-level bombing from 1,500 to 2,000 feet to improve the bombing accuracy and limit the damage to the civilian population. This meant that the approach to the target concentrated the stream within about 1,000 feet difference in elevation as the target was approached, making it very easy to track from the ground and to direct nightfighters to the bombers, who were vulnerable to these attacks. Losses were heaviest at this point.

Spring had arrived at Middleton, and while the war went on what leisure time the crew had was very pleasant. They enjoyed the English countryside and even managed to get in the odd game of golf at the Middleton-One-Row course. Bob Bodie and Art made a quick trip to Scotland, on one of their leaves, which was very relaxing, and they did some hill-climbing. Bob was a keen cyclist and mountain climber. He didn't think twice of cycling off to parts unknown whenever he got a chance. The rest of the crew headed for London in the fast lane and achieved the same result.

Things were going well for the crew, probably too well. They had done a number of operations without serious incident and had not caught too much flak. Their first operation in the new Lancaster KB718 VR.J (this aircraft went MIA on 4/5 July near Villenueve St. Georges with another crew) was a raid on St. Ghislain marshalling yards on May 1,1944. According to Art's logbook, it was "Bang On" D.C.O. (duty carried out). Future raids took them on trips to Belgium, France and Germany. The targets of these raids were Ghent, Boulogne and Louvain marshalling yards. On the raid of Louvain, they did not drop their bombs, as the target was obscured by smoke, and as that city was an old university town, Art told Jack Friday to hold off just as he was about to press the bomb release "tit." They returned and landed very gently with their full load of bombs aboard.

The only German city that they bombed was Aachen. The raid on Bourg Leopold was very successful and was against a German military camp in Belgium. They evidently caught the Germans napping, and though the raid only lasted from 02:05 to 02:08 hrs, they achieved heavy casualties, according to reports received later from the Belgian Underground. They bombed Mt.Couple, a German radar station near Cap Gris Nez and they flew Lancasters KB712, 715, 718 and 736 on these raids. During this time their squadron suffered the loss on average of one plane per raid and the flight roster had new names continually added to it.

Pat has mentioned in his reminiscing that he would always confound the equipment officer, as he always came back from a raid minus either one or both of his flying gloves. His explanation was that when you are back there cramped up in the rear turret, you cannot afford to leave it thereby putting the aircraft in an undefended condition. You have to find some solution if you need to relieve yourself. His unique solution was to piss into the gloves when the aircraft was at a low enough altitude on the way home and throw them overboard!

D-day came and they were called upon for a maximum effort, three nights in a row. The first was the bombing of heavy coastal guns at Longues, five miles west of Arromaches (later a Mulberry Port), where they bombed through a low layer of cloud from 1,500 feet at 4 a.m. just before the landings on June 6. Very shortly after the bombing and on their way back to base, the bulk of the invasion fleet became visible to them with the first light of day. A most magnificent sight to behold. They had to divert to a base at Colerne, near Bristol, due to bad weather at Middleton St. George. This was the first of four operations

"Early Morning Arrival" landing at Colerne, after KB726 first operational raid on D-day morning June 6, 1944. Painting by Robert Taylor.

- *Mike Johnson*

they would make in their brand-new Lancaster KB726 with the squadron code VR.A which had only 25 hrs on it. The next night they took out the bridge and crossroads at Coutances, in west Normandy, from 1,200 feet, to slow the advance of tanks heading north to the beaches. On the third night they raided the Achères marshalling yards on the western outskirts of Paris. Each of these raids lasted about 4 to 5 hours, so the aircraft had only 46 hrs on the airframe when it went down on their final mission.

Their fourth and final operation on June 12, in KB726 (their 13th operation as a crew and the 15th for Art) had all the indications of being a repetition of previous railyard attacks. They had done a fighter affiliation and radar test flight of 1.25 hours duration, that day with Lorne A. Rolston (A.K.A Rostein) as radar instructor. He was the navigator of W/C Bill Pleasance D.F.C. crew. Bill was the commanding officer of No.419 Squadron at that time.

But now, one week after D-day, the German nightfighter squadrons had moved to northern France in force and accounted for most of the losses that night. This operation was to be against the railway marshalling yards at Cambrai, France, and provided more action than they bargained for.

Roy Vigars recollects that things had gone well for them on their ops and they had nothing serious to report. On this op, like many previous ones, they would sit around the kite joking with their ground crew, waiting for the word to climb aboard and take up their traditional positions and duties. When they finally took off at 21:44 hrs, he remembers never having seen so many planes in the air at the same time.

Pat Brophy remembers sitting on the grass by their Lancaster bomber, waiting to take off for France, after being briefed a few hours earlier. It was to be their 13th operation and the next day was the 13th of June. Andy Mynarski found a four-leaf clover in the grass and offered it to Pat as a good-luck token. Pat and Andy had become close chums, even though the difference in their ranks held them apart, and Pat nicknamed him Andrew O'Mynarski. They made up for their disparity in rank after a mission, at celebrations such as pub crawls, where rank did not count. It became a ritual on splitting up after these events, with Pat slapping Andy on the back and saying, "So long, Irish." Andy would stiffen into exaggerated attention, salute, and reply with a hint of a Polish accent, "Good night, Sir."

Pat found out he could always count on Andy when in a tight spot. An example of this occurred while on one of their leaves together with two other crewmates. Pat, who was known to get into scraps, ended up in a police station one night and phoned the crew for help. They laughed and said that a taste of jail overnight would teach him a lesson. While the others went back to sleep, Andy got up and went to the police station to bail Pat out.

There was something that Andy would never do and that was to trade places with Pat for the rear turret position. He, like most air gunners, hated the cramped and isolated conditions of those rear turrets (rear-end or arse-end Charlies). He would remark, "Back there, you're completely cut off."

At this point in the story, the record is best obtained from members of the crew as each remembers that night, after all these years.

The tragic outcome of the attack on their plane and the loss of the life of a most heroic teammate brought home to everyone the value of his closest companions, and indeed of all the men and women that made up the Canadian No.6 Bomber Group force. To volunteer for the task that they undertook made them a breed apart. In the face of frightful odds they saw it through to the end, the task of bombing out of existence the Nazi war machine, through four very long years.

The first story is told by Pilot F/O Arthur de Breyne, who recorded and originally presented his story to the Royal Air Force Escaping Society annual meeting of the Canadian Branch.

Lancaster taking
off in daylight.
- *CAF PL 44667*

Pat Brophy's rear turret
position. Note: no perspex
in front of gunner for
better visibility, but a
lot colder.
- *CAF PL 43723*

Andrew Mynarski's mid-
upper gun turret position.
- *CAF PL 43724*

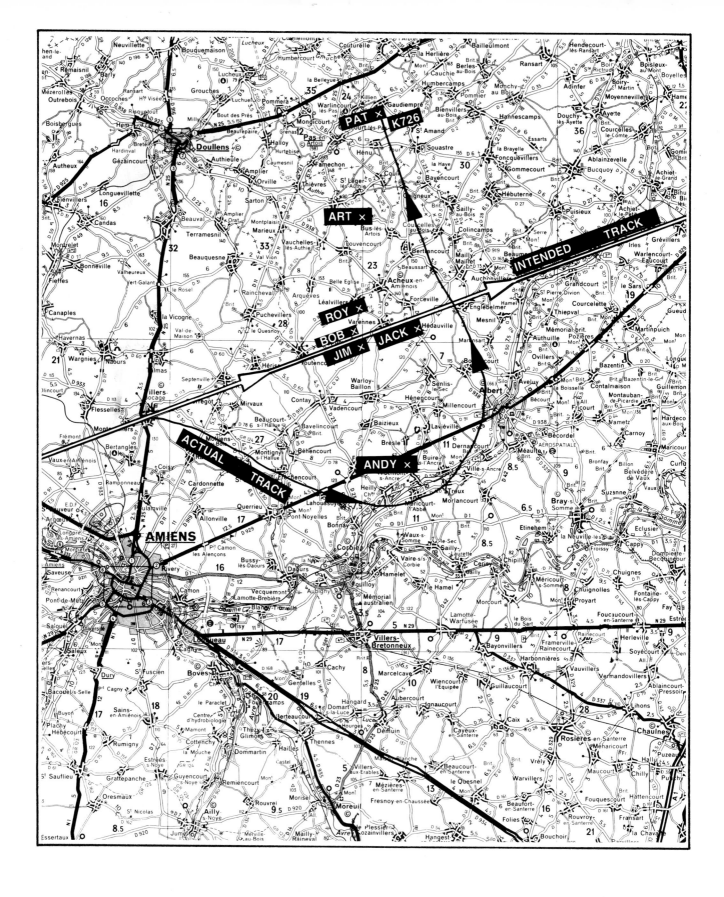

Map of France near Amiens showing the landing positions of the crew; the intended and actual track of the aircraft.

- R.D. Page

THE CAMBRAI RAID - JUNE 12/13, 1944

ART DE BREYNE

"It was shortly after midnight on June 12/13, 1944. I was lying in a field of tall wheat ten miles from Amiens in Northern France. I was a little shaken up but, thankfully, still in one piece. Three or four minutes earlier I had been piloting a Canadian Lancaster, VR.A KB726, and getting ready to bomb the railway yards at Cambrai, 25 miles ahead. We had been coned by searchlights shortly after crossing the French coast. After putting the aircraft into a banking dive, followed by a climb, I was able to evade the searchlights, and shortly afterwards we started to descend to our low-level bombing height of 2,000 feet from 5,000 feet.

"Our ordeal started with an attack by a Ju-88 nightfighter. The tail gunner, Pat Brophy, had observed for a fleeting moment a twin-engined fighter and lost sight of him. It then approached unseen from below and was spotted just as it was about to open fire. No sooner had I initiated a corkscrew manoeuvre to starboard from 5,000 feet, when three exploding cannon shells rocked our plane. Two hit the port wing, knocking out both engines and setting the gas tanks between them on fire. The third, I learned later, burst between the rear and mid-upper turrets and also started a fire associated with the hydraulic fluid for the rear turret. The intercom went dead and my instrument panel turned black. I was down to approximately 3,000 to 4,000 feet at the bottom of the corkscrew and with the loss of power was forced to keep losing altitude. With a full bomb load, it was clear the plane would crash in a minute or two, and I immediately ordered the crew to bail out by signalling with my hand to the flight engineer at my side and signalling a 'P' by Morse code on the red light in the gunners' turrets.

"The progress of the four crew members in the forward area in jumping from the plane was painfully slow and I could not understand why. The answer to that I learned three months later on my return to England. Jack Friday, the bomb-aimer had pulled up the escape hatch in the nose of the aircraft and the force of the airstream had blown it up and struck him above the eye, knocking him out. Even today, he remembers nothing of the trip except the briefing."

ROY VIGARS

"I made my way down to the bomb-aimer's position and found Jack Friday slumped on the floor, unconscious, as if having a nap. He had a gash over his eye. I rolled him over, clipped on his chute pack, and slid him over to the escape hatch and dropped him through the opening while holding on to the ripcord. This was a risky manoeuvre, as pulling the ripcord too soon, the parachute could wrap around the big tail wheel of the Lancaster, which was non-retractable. But Jack made it O.K."

He floated down in a state of slumber, landing beside a chateau at Hedauville.

ART DE BREYNE

"While all this took about a minute, it seemed like an eternity to me, and I could only guess how close to the ground we were. I had to gauge my descent by the sound of the wind and was able to keep my port wing up with the help of my only visual aid, a searchlight some ten miles away at ten o'clock off the port wing. I applied rudder and elected to keep it in that position to keep the port wing high at all times. I was tempted to turn towards it to use it as a rate-of-descent indicator, but I might then have dropped the port wing — something I could not afford to do and still keep the aircraft under control, as it may stall. I had to judge my speed by the sound of the airstream past the aircraft."

Before Roy Vigars could finally jump, he had to remove the escape hatch, which had become jammed in the opening after he had dropped Jack. It evidently took some time to kick it out. It seemed ages, but it was probably only seconds. While he was trying to kick the escape hatch free, he remembers that Bob Bodie was behind him and patted him on the back in a way of encouragement. After Roy finally jumped, he was followed closely by Bob Bodie, the navigator, and Jim Kelly, the wireless operator.

"When I saw the last one go, I throttled back the starboard engines to keep an even keel, plunged through the escape hatch and immediately pulled the ripcord. After a couple of swings the ground came up to meet me before I expected it. A wheat field was a perfect place to land and the cushion on my seat pack helped soften the impact.

"I rested a while in the field to recover my senses. My thoughts turned to my crew. I knew the four up front had jumped before me and could only hope my gunners had made it out successfully. I knew the P (.--.) I had flashed was received, as my own light lit up.

"Lying there on the ground, I could observe the bomber stream ahead as it descended towards the target. Bombing altitude was 2,000 feet. I was amazed at the action taking place. Since my landing, four more planes had plunged to the ground in quick succession. I could only hope a couple were Ju-88s. On returning to England I learned our losses in northern France that night were 42 planes."

Later Art was to learn that as he throttled back the starboard engines to keep the aircraft on an even keel while he jumped, he helped save the life of the rear gunner F/O G. Pat Brophy.

PAT BROPHY

This is Pat Brophy's account of what happened as they approached the target, as told to David MacDonald of Reader's Digest and edited.

"As we crossed the French coast, I saw enemy searchlights sweeping the sky, then lazy puffs of smoke and deceptively pretty sunbursts of sparks. 'Light flak below, Skipper,' I reported.

"Suddenly, with a blinding flash, a searchlight caught us. Other searchlights quickly, converged, coning the aircraft. 'Hang on' called Art de Breyne. 'We're coned!' He threw the Lanc into a banking dive, then swung upwards, trying to squirm away from the deadly glare. Then, just as suddenly, we were in the dark again.

"We'd escaped — or had we? The Germans sometimes allowed a bomber to shake loose once their nightfighters had got a fix on the aircraft. It was too soon to tell.

"Once past the coastal defences, we began a slow descent. This was to be a low-level raid from 2,000 feet. We were down to 5,000 feet when I caught a fleeting glimpse of a twin-engine fighter. 'Bogey astern!' I yelled on the intercom. 'Six o'clock!' Instantly, as he'd done to evade the searchlights, Art de Breyne began to corkscrew. Seconds later I saw a Ju-88 streaking up from below: 'He's coming under us!' As I rotated my turret around and opened fire, the white-bellied Ju-88 flashed by with its cannons blazing. Three explosions rocked our aircraft. Two rounds knocked out both port engines and set the wing tank between the two engines on fire. The third tore into the fuselage, starting another fire between Andy's mid-upper turret and mine.

"I sensed we were losing altitude fast. I listened for orders on the intercom, but it was dead. The red light that was supposed to flash in my turret in Morse code the letter P (.--.), the signal to bail out, was silent, as all circuits had been cut by the explosion of the shell. I could tell by the fire in the fuselage that was sweeping towards me, due the air drafts in the fuselage, that our aircraft A for Able had had it. For some reason, I glanced at my watch. It was 13 minutes past midnight, June 13, on our 13th operation! And if I did not do something fast I was going for a Burton with it.

"As recounted by Art, when he finally jumped — from barely 800 feet — he felt sure that both Andy and I had already left the aircraft by the rear fuselage side hatch.

"Unfortunately, he was wrong. To fire my guns I had traversed my turret to port. Now I had to straighten it out so the guns were pointing aft, so I could open the turret doors to get back into the aircraft fuselage for my parachute and then jump from the rear hatch. There is no room in the rear turret to stow a parachute pack. I pressed the rotation pedal and nothing happened. The hydraulic system had been shattered by the cannon shell explosion, locking my turret at such an angle that I couldn't get out. Meanwhile, from inside, the fuselage flames were sweeping towards me.

"I remember telling myself 'Don't panic. There's still another way out.' I managed to pry open the turret doors a few inches, reached in for my parachute and clipped it on to the harness on my chest. I then tried to hand-crank the turret to a beam position, where I could open the doors and flip out backwards into the slipstream. To my horror, the rotating gear handle broke off in my hand. Now there was no way out. At that moment, imprisoned in the mortally wounded Lancaster, I remembered Andy Mynarski's words: 'Back there, you're completely cut off.'

"Then I saw him. Andy had slid down from the mid-upper turret and made his way back to the rear escape hatch, about 15 feet from me, having received the same P signal to bail out from the skipper. He opened the door and was just about to jump when he glanced around and spotted me through the plexiglass part of my turret. One look told him I was trapped.

"Instantly, he turned away from the hatch — his doorway to safety — and started towards me. All this time the aircraft was lurching drunkenly as Art tried to keep it on an even keel without instruments. Andy had to climb over the Elsan chemical toilet and crawl over the tailplane spar, as there is no room at that part in the fuselage. These cramped conditions forced him to crawl on his hands and knees — straight through the blazing hydraulic oil. By the time he reached my position in the tail, his uniform and parachute were on fire. I shook my head; it was hopeless. 'Don't try!' I shouted, and waved him away.

"Andy didn't seem to notice. Completely ignoring his own condition in the flames, he grabbed a fire axe and tried to smash the turret free. It gave slightly, but not enough. Wild with desperation and pain, he tore at the doors with his bare hands — to no avail. By now he was a mass of flames below his waist. Seeing him like that, I forgot everything else. Over the roar of the wind and the whine of our two remaining engines, I screamed, 'Go back, Andy! Get out!'

"Finally, with time running out, he realized that he could do nothing to help me. When I waved him away again, he hung his head and nodded, as though he was ashamed to leave — ashamed that sheer heart and courage hadn't been enough. As there was no way to turn around in the confined quarters, Andy had to crawl backwards through the flaming hydraulic fluid fire again, never taking his eyes off me. On his face was a look of mute anguish.

"When Andy reached the escape hatch, he stood up. Slowly, as he'd often done before in happier times together, he came to attention. Standing there in his flaming clothes, a grimly magnificent figure, he saluted me! At the same time, just before he jumped, he said something. And even though I couldn't hear, I knew it was 'Good night, Sir.'

Now Pat Brophy was alone in the Lanc, going down less steeply than before, but he knew it would hit the ground in a matter of seconds, with five tons of explosives barely 50 feet from where he was trapped in his turret. He remembers bracing himself in the prescribed position for a crash landing and waiting for the impact.

In his words: "Time froze while I was struggling inside the turret and Andy was fighting to get me out alive, a minute or more had flashed by like a second. Now the last agonizing seconds were like eternity. Prayers and random thoughts raced through my mind. Hail Mary, full of Grace ... I hope Andy got down okay . . . Pray for us sinners . . .

The boys back at the squadron would probably say, 'Brophy? Oh, he went for a Burton over Cambrai.'

"Suddenly time caught up. Everything happened at once. The ground came up, the aircraft slammed into the earth, like the sound of a thousand sledgehammers and the screeching of ripping metal. Just as the Lanc went bellying into a field, it hit a thick tree with its port wing, which tore off the flaming wing and engines and spun the aircraft violently to port or left — in one final lurch. This violent impact with the tree and the ground, the resulting whiplash effect on the tail of the aircraft, snapped my turret around and the doors flew open, freeing me from my potentially explosive and flaming prison. I came to rest against a small tree about 30 to 50 feet from the remains of the aircraft. That is when I heard two explosions close together. Only when I felt solid earth tremble under me did I realize that the crash was over, and somehow I was alive.

"Slowly and reluctantly, I moved my arms and legs, as you always think that you will not be able to move them and do not want to know, but the force of life makes you nevertheless. Much to my surprise, nothing hurt. I sat up and found I wasn't even scratched! It was as if some gentle, unseen hand had swept me out of my turret, now somewhere in the twisted and blazing wreck of our aircraft less than 50 feet away. Incredibly, and lucky for me, only two of the Lanc's 20 bombs had exploded.[2] But fear had left its mark: when I hauled off my helmet a patch of my hair came with it." Pat suffered a scalp condition which caused him to lose patches of his hair. Today Pat has not a hair on his distinguished head. He set the fashion long before Yul Brynner and Telly Savalas did!

JIM KELLY

"I was the radio operator and my duties demanded that I monitor the radio messages to catch any that may refer to our operation.

"I therefore did not know what was going on around me, as I was listening to the radio, rather than the intercom.

"The first inclination I had that something was drastically wrong was when the aircraft took violent evasive action for the second time. I took off my earphones when I felt the shudder of the bullets hitting the aircraft. I could smell smoke and looked outside to see that the wing was on fire. When I saw what was happening up front as the others prepared to bail out, I clipped on my parachute and made my way forward, past Art, and jumped, after Bob Bodie. I remember with a shudder the tail wheel whipping by over my head. My next recollection was landing on my back in a grain field, where I just sat.

"My first sensation was of quiet, after the roar of the plane engines. I could still hear the steady hum of aircraft high overhead, remote from me now, and I remember thinking that they would be home in four hours, but that I certainly would not. I could see in the distance the flames of Amiens. The explosion of bombs were still bursting and searchlights were still trying to pick out the bombers. Over on my left Arras was burning too. It had all happened so fast I was still a bit confused. I roused myself finally and started to empty my pockets and bury the contents in the ground. I wasn't wearing a revolver. Most of us didn't in those days.

"Suddenly I remembered my evasion tactics and realized I'd better not hang around there too long. I buried my parachute as best I could under some trees and began to crawl across a road and into another field, and then started walking to the darkest part of the sky.

"After a number of hours I heard someone walking towards me. I could see that this person was not wearing a helmet or a hat and did not appear to be armed. I picked up a stone as a weapon just in case, and called to him — it was Bob Bodie, my navigator. What luck! We were indeed fortunate, as we were to spend the rest of our time in France together."

58

BOB BODIE

"As we were approaching the target area at Cambrai, I heard Pat Brophy's voice on the intercom, 'Fighter below.' Then I heard cannon shells striking the fuselage. Next thing I knew we had received orders from our pilot to bail out because the aircraft was on fire. With some apprehension, I clipped on my parachute pack and made my way forward to the escape hatch in the nose. There I found Roy kicking the jammed escape hatch door. When he went out I followed through the opening and felt very relieved when my chute opened. The sky was full of flares, creating a spectacular background. Below all was in darkness. A sudden bump told me I had landed, fortunately on a soft field.

"The first chore was to hide the parachute. I found a dirt bank where, with much effort, I managed to dig out a hole for the chute. I started to walk towards some trees outlined against the sky, when I was startled by a shadowy figure. Imagine my joy to find it was our radio operator, Jim Kelly, who had bailed out behind me."

ROY VIGARS

"As I went out, I did not know what height we were, so I pulled my ripcord as soon as I thought it was safe to do so. I soon hit the ground, so we could not have been at any great height. I landed rather heavily on my left side and twisted my hip, but otherwise was O.K.

"I had evidently landed very near to a German airfield, as I saw some Me 110s (twin-engined nightfighters) taking off. Not wishing to meet any airfield defenders, I crept into a clump of bushes and slept until dawn."

The seven members of the crew were now on the ground, scattered across the countryside: Art de Breyne, the pilot; Jack Friday, bomb-aimer, unconscious; Roy Vigars, flight engineer, with a sore hip; Jim Kelly, wireless operator; Bob Bodie, navigator; Andrew Mynarski, mid-upper gunner, mortally burned; and finally Pat Brophy, unscathed in the only landing he made by himself. Pat was to learn about Andy's death later, on September 13, from his wireless operator, Jim Kelly, when they returned to England after evading the Germans. Not long after Jim was hidden in a barn by a French farmer another Frenchman arrived. In halting English, he spoke of finding a parachutist who had landed alive with his clothing on fire, only to die soon after from the severe burns to his body. The Frenchman then held out a flying helmet which had Andy's name on it. Evidently, from the position where Andy had landed south of Bresle relative to the rest of the crew, he had been the first to bail out. The rest were delayed by the struggle to get Jack out and unblock the escape hatch. They would not be able to know this or tell their tales until they were all liberated and returned to England many months later.

No.419 Squadron sent out 16 aircraft that night and lost three. The two other crews who were lost on the Cambrai raid were F/O F.N. Wilson and his crew in KB714 VR.V, all of whom perished, also F/O W.M. Lacey and his crew in KB731 VR.S, of whom only two survived, one as a P.O.W. and one evaded.

All that can be said of the actual attack on Cambrai marshalling yards was that it was anything but a smashing success (seeming to be generally disorganized), and what limited success it did have failed to justify the comparatively heavy losses inflicted on the attacking force, which attacked Arras and Amiens as well as Cambrai.

Art de Breyne noted that another airman had a spectacular escape from death at the same time but away on the other side of the world. Ensign Donald C. Brandt was flying Hellcats from the USS Hornet on a pre-invasion mission on June 13, 1944. He was flying aircraft No.13 on his 13th mission when at 09:13 hrs he was hit by flak. He bailed out, and though he had broken ribs and a damaged hand from shell fragments, he was able to climb aboard a dinghy dropped by one of his fellow airmen. He was under fire from the Japanese guns ashore, both light and heavy. The submarine USS Stingray rescued him on the fourth try by having the pilot lasso the periscope and tow him out to sea, out of range of the guns.

An amazing coincidence of dates and thirteens.

THE FOUR EVADERS AND TWO P.O.W.s

The four members of the crew that evaded capture by the Germans and the two that didn't all had different stories to tell.

ART DE BREYNE

"Having pulled myself together, I sat there assessing my new predicament. I resolved there and then not to fall into enemy hands. I knew exactly where I was, had a good map and possessed the greatest advantage over my fellow airmen — I spoke French. The next day or two would be most critical. I had to get civilian clothes. I decided to travel on my own and head towards southern France. It was summer and I would try living off the land. I decided to set out immediately to get out of an area where probably 100 airmen had landed that night.

"The night was clear, so navigation was no problem. I lined up the north star and headed roughly southeast to cross any rivers to the east of Paris, where they were not wide. I walked along the edge of the wheat field to keep out of the tall wheat, which was covered with dew, but my feet and pants became soaked nevertheless. I came to a back road, which I followed for some time, as it led in the right direction. I shortly came upon my first road sign, which read: Acheux-en-Amienois - 3 km. I made a mental note of it for future reference.

"I was soon startled by an aircraft which passed almost directly overhead at less than 100 feet altitude. It must have just taken off. It was very different from any plane I had ever seen. I could tell from its outline that it did not have a propeller, was small and trailed a flame about ten feet long. It had a pulsating sound somewhat like an outboard motor. It gained altitude slowly and disappeared in the distance.[3]

"It was risky to be out after curfew close to an airfield, but I chose to keep going to reach safer territory. I changed my direction across pasture land and headed due east, cautiously stopping at intervals to listen for any activity ahead. After about an hour I resumed my original southeast course. I was wet and not at all sleepy and anything was better at this time than lying on wet ground. Adrenalin was probably keeping me going.

"As dawn was about to break, I could hear a motor vehicle in the distance, stopping at about 30 second intervals until it faded away in the distance. I imagined it to be an Army vehicle dropping off soldiers to patrol a road, and as it was in the direction I was heading, I decided to go no further till it got light. When dawn broke I could observe in every direction a treeless landscape of farmland. I was within a quarter of a mile of a small village.

"Soon a man appeared to fetch the cows for milking. I walked towards him, and as I got closer he noticed my uniform and motioned me with his hand to head towards the wheat field. He was somewhat surprised when I addressed him in French, but he did not stop walking and I followed him into the tall wheat, and we both crouched down out of sight. He stayed just long enough to tell me there was a German observation post some two kilometres away and not to stand up, and that he would come for me after dark.

"June 6th is remembered by armies on the Normandy beaches as the longest day. For me it was June 13th. It was probably the most uncomfortable day of my life. It was five o'clock in the morning. I had the choice of crouching down or lying on the wet ground to

60

keep out of sight. By noon the hot sun had almost dried me out and I was almost wishing for the cold damp ground again. I was thirsty and hungry and ate a chocolate bar I had in my escape kit. The heat only grew worse as the day wore on. The sun set around nine o'clock and around ten my benefactor reappeared.

"He was an 18 year-old-boy. His name was Raymond Letoquart. He led me to his father's house on the edge of the village. After drinking two big glasses of water and washing up, I was served hot soup, meat and bread. They could not wait to be brought up to date on the progress of the war. Did we think our armies could hold on to the beaches, and when did I think they would be liberated? I assured them that after a week in Normandy our forces had grown considerably and if the Germans had not been able to throw them into the sea in the first week, it was not likely they could defeat the present force, which was strengthened with each day that passed. They offered to hide me, but I declined the offer, as I considered the area a most insecure hiding place, far from any wooded area in which to take refuge. The risk to them would also have been very great. Realizing I would need clothes, Raymond had visited a friend in the next village and brought back a complete outfit, which almost fitted, but not quite. Mr. Pannier had much shorter legs than I. I changed into my new clothes and was amazed how much like a Frenchman I looked when I put on my beret.

"Along with my uniform, I gave up my revolver, which I did not want to carry. We chatted on till after midnight and they asked a million questions. I finally bid them all good night and goodbye and left to sleep in the barn, as I wanted to get an early start during the night to cross the patrolled highway, which it turned out was one of the most used transportation routes to the front. Around three in the morning I woke up and took off slowly down the road and was able to cross the highway, which did not seem to have any patrol that night.

"Day 2 was relatively uneventful. The same bright sun beat down, but I had some protection with my oilskin raincoat and beret. I carried a hoe on my shoulder, parading as a Belgian farm worker. I was told that a good number of labourers came from Belgium at this time of year to work in the beet fields. I followed the river Somme on the north shore for quite some distance, looking for a place to cross.

"At Bray-sur-Somme I walked into the village and through towards the river, trying to look as casual as I could with my short pants. It was then that I realized my shoes were much too new and shiny. I later covered them with dust and rubbed some of it in. I was glad I had not worn my issue flying black boots which had a small knife in a pocket on the side to cut off the top of the boot. The ragged edge would have been a dead giveaway.

"Once over the river, I soon disappeared off paved roads onto the paths and back roads. Covering another ten miles, I approached a farmhouse to see if I could get some food. They accepted me as a Belgian farm labourer and readily offered me food and gave me a bottle of water to quench my thirst along the way. It later occurred to me that I might not have fooled anybody, as they were very kind to me and did not ask many questions.

"Around 8 p.m., after eating a sandwich I had been given, I started looking for a spot to bed down for the night on the edge of a woodlot. I laid my coat on a bed of hay and slept quite well, but when I woke up I was cold and then used the coat to cover myself. I became very grateful for that oilskin as the days went by.

"Day 3 was much the same as the previous one. I passed Meharicourt and Omiecourt and saw a great many World War I cemeteries, mostly Canadian and British. Every third grave was that of an unknown soldier, which said something about the kind of war it was. These men were probably blown to bits by exploding shells and were no longer recognizable. Poppies, for some reason, were more plentiful in the cemeteries along the stone walls than outside, yet they grew wild.

"Food was easy to come by. I had not yet been refused and not yet revealed my identity. As the weather was clear I again chose a similar place to spend the night, but things turned out differently. I was awakened by the sound of a snorting pig.

"I remembered then that there were wild boars in these woods and it was probably not the best place to be at night. I started walking again, but had not gone far when the heavens opened up and the rain came down in buckets. I took refuge under a large oak tree, but it was not long before it rained just as much under its branches. I became completely soaked and was glad when the early morning sun reappeared and I was able to wring out my wet clothes and attempt to dry them in the sun, which took most of Day 4. I by-passed the large town of Nesle that day and came upon a farm where the people were particularly nice to me, fed me well and even had a couple of glasses of red wine for me. I revealed my identity to them and they offered me shelter in the house, which was very tempting, but I preferred to sleep in the barn, where they would not be implicated should I be discovered. When I asked to have my bottle filled, they filled it with wine, but I would have much preferred to have water during the night when I developed a thirst. This was my first uninterrupted night's rest, and in the morning the farmer came in with his son carrying a pitchfork. Their manner and attitude were suddenly very cold and businesslike, even hostile.

"I sensed something was wrong. They told me they offered hospitality to all passersby without distinction and I was no different. When I pressed them for an explanation, they wanted to know if I was German. I showed them my dog tags, which reassured them somewhat, and they told me that Germans parachuted men near a neighbouring village in R.A.F. uniforms. I showed them the label inside my shoes, which were Canadian, and they seemed reassured. I explained that this was really no proof of my identity and they would have to trust me. If I were German, certainly other Germans would know about me being here. They seemed quite convinced I was genuine and after a good breakfast in the kitchen, I set out on a full stomach and feeling the best I had felt in a while.

"I was approaching the Oise River, which I had guessed might be 50 feet wide. I decided to head for the town of Noyon, a medieval town of about 30,000 people, which I thought would be a good place to cross unobserved and not be challenged. Arriving in town about 11:30 a.m. I walked up and down a street in full view of a bridge, which had a sentry at each end. People seemed to be stopped at random for identification. I did not like to take the risk and was considering going elsewhere when the noon whistle blew. Workers appeared from all directions and many headed over the bridge. I joined in the crowd and crossed unchallenged with the greatest of ease. Once over I headed for the countryside and the back roads. I covered a good eight miles, I estimate, mostly through bush country, till I reached the village of Carlepont. I stopped a passerby to inquire what villages lay ahead and to find out what I could about them, as I was running off my map. One thing led to another until I became aware the man certainly was not a German sympathizer and had already guessed who I was. He warned me not to stop at a certain large farm four or five kilometres down the road, as the chap was a collaborator. I was also warned of the danger of travelling through the country without any identification, a fact of which I was well aware. He suggested I stop for a few days and he might be able to obtain an 'I card' for me. This seemed too good to pass up and I accepted. After my best meal yet on pork chops, I had a good night's sleep in a shed next to the house, on a comfortable folding bed.

"He escorted me the next day to an isolated farm called Bellefontaine some ten kilometres away, owned by Monsieur Lemaire, an elderly gentleman who received us warmly and told me I was welcome to stay there. I was billeted in an old chapel monastery ruin of some 700 years, on one corner of the farmyard. As a companion I had a French *refractaire* who was supposed to be working in Germany but had skipped off before being sent. I was visited the next week by my good friend, the Marquis de Broissia, who has since, twice, visited us in Canada. He interrogated me at length and had lots of good questions to trip me up, to many of which he did not know the answers, and I was able to fill him in. My stay at Bellefontaine was for three uneventful weeks. Food was plain but good. I spent many pleasant afternoons picking delicious big strawberries and kept away from the farmhouse as much as possible during daylight hours.

"Around the 1st of July, a drop of small arms was made on the plateau a couple of miles above the farm and it was feared we would be raided. I was moved to a new location some ten kilometres away to stay with a childless couple in their forties, Mr. & Mrs. Marcel Bonneton, in the village of Tracy-le-Val. I moved in on the Sunday morning in the early hours. My friend Jacques, with whom I had lived in the chapel, was rounded up by the Germans and was shipped off to Dachau concentration camp and came back a year later some 60 pounds lighter.

"My new home with Mr. & Mrs. Bonneton was located some 200 yards from Max de Broissia's chateau, which lodged some 100 German troops while he lived in the gardener's house a hundred yards away. Most of the troops served on guard duty at strategic points. Fruit and vegetables were abundant in the Bonneton's garden during the summer, and life was pleasant.

"Max took my picture, and in a few days returned with an identification card. I received it at 11 a.m. and at 2 p.m. that same day I met a German company of troops with a sergeant in charge who asked for my papers. As soon as I said something in French, I was handed back my card, and that was the only time I was asked for it.

"On a few occasions after that I ran across Germans but was never asked to produce identification. I had to be more careful not to be seen by the people of the village. I was a stranger in their village and there were a few loose tongues, one in particular being an old lady living next door. Wheat sheaves along the fence prevented her from ever seeing me in the Bonneton's garden over a two-month period.

"The Bonnetons were wonderful friends. They visited us in Canada and Mr. Bonneton worked in Canada for several years. As a fugitive in an occupied country, I consider I probably enjoyed greater hospitality than anyone could hope for. I enjoyed many a lavish meal at Max de Broissia's, in the company of some of his friends to keep me from being conspicuous. Max had an extraordinary wine cellar. The quality of the wine only got better as the cellar became depleted, and we deplored this happening, but the youngest wine was, at the end, of 1929 vintage, I believe.

"Early on the morning of September 2, the last of the Germans pulled out, and very soon after, American First Army tanks rolled in and celebrations began. I was invited by the priest to ring the liberation bells. He then served me two generous glasses of cognac which he had kept hidden for this day. This started me off in good spirits, but I must say a great many felt no pain at all on that day of rejoicing.

"After a couple of days to say goodbye to all, I was driven to Paris in a charcoal-fuelled car owned by Max's mother-in-law. I later went to Arras for interrogation and returned to Paris twice, once by truck and once by Auster aircraft, before leaving France. I arrived back in London on September 13, three months after being shot down."

JIM KELLY AND BOB BODIE

"We walked the rest of the night. As daylight approached at 5 a.m. we reached a village set flush against the road. We ran across the road and hid in a small woods at the other side of the village. It was cold and damp under the trees and our battle dress and flying sweaters weren't quite enough to keep us warm. We felt the cold right through us, but settled down to prepare ourselves as best we could for our stay in France. We cut off all badges and rank identification, but tucked them away safely in case we were taken prisoners by the Jerries and had to prove we weren't spies. Bodie lacked not only his escape kit but his identification tags (dog tags)!

"I had my escape kit complete, including a handkerchief map, French and German money, one chocolate bar, chewing gum, a tube of condensed milk that had broken and spread over the rest of the kit, a file, a saw, and several compasses. I had my dog tags — and very fortunate it was too, as it turned out later.

"We waited till dark in hopes of locating ourselves but didn't dare venture out. Next day, as we continued to huddle in the woods, we saw several German soldiers for the first time as they passed on motorbikes. Both of us were impressed by how much they resembled the popular Hollywood version, in fact we still hadn't really accepted the fact that we were behind enemy lines. It was too much like the movies.

"Around dusk we saw Ju-88s take off, and as we continued to crouch in the woods for another night, it became apparent that this was a regular routine for this area. Just before dark each evening, off they'd go.[4]

"We must have grown weary and a bit careless from hunger, because on the second day, we were surprised by a French lady who had come to work in the fields nearby and saw Bob, and made contact with us. (Mme. Dupont.) With the aid of the French phrase book provided in the escape kit, we learned that the nearby village was Varennes and that there were no Germans billeted in the village.

"She appeared to be nervous as we talked to her and soon left us, which was understandable, as anyone found helping airmen to escape was shot. We talked it over and decided to wait until dark to slip away. However, that evening she reappeared accompanied by a teenage boy, who turned out to be her son. They gave us black bread and wine. The bread was hardly palatable, as it had been made with the sweepings of the local flour mill and wine, we found out later. The yeast factory had been bombed by the British and wine was the best substitute available.

"The boy couldn't speak English either, but with the phrase book we learned that they wanted us to stay put. The woman came back later in the evening with the boy and led us to a farmhouse in Varennes owned by Hector and Louise. There we were interrogated by Toto and another Frenchman, neither of whom could speak English. One of them, we learned later was the local leader of the French Underground. The two men took us aside and questioned us very closely, which was difficult because of the language problem. Later we realized that they had to be sure that we weren't German agents disguised as downed Allied airmen in order to infiltrate the Underground network. This made it rather difficult to convince them that we were not German impersonators of Allied airmen. But a snapshot of my wife Lee convinced them we were for real.

"In the house, unknown to us, was another airman, and we were surprised by the number of people in the household. The household consisted of Grandma, Hector and Louise, then Toto and Bebe, which with the other airman made our accommodation and food supply difficult. We didn't appreciate this at the time. We were then led to a barn remote from the farmhouse, where they again left us. It turned out that the barn was a safe place to hide because it was owned by the village 'quisling.'[5] We hid in the hay.

"In the morning these new friends returned with a razor and cold water, but without soap, and left us to our shaving. The razor was a familiar American make.

"Without thinking very carefully we went out into the village and knocked on the door of one of the houses. I believe the intent was to locate the owner of the razor, but I don't recall anyone answering the door. While we were doing this, we saw a German staff car go past, and we sobered up rather quickly and dashed back to the barn.

"The next day the people from the village came to look at us. They brought a dozen cold boiled eggs, and in the evening gave us some hot soup — our first hot meal since we had left England. One kettle, two spoons and a dozen smiling women, but we ate with a will.

"The following evening we were taken back to Toto's house and given old clothes to replace our uniforms, which were duly burned. And later we were given new identities with appropriate ID cards showing our pictures; they would not accept the ones supplied in our escape kits, as they were not French.

"The following night we were taken to a house in another nearby village. It turned out to be the home of Mme. DuPont, the person who had first contacted us. She, her teenage son and a younger daughter occupied the house. Her husband worked in an aircraft factory in a town some distance away and only returned on weekends. Upon his return he was not too pleased to see us because of the fear of reprisals by the Germans should we be discovered.

"We were moved at night back to Toto's house, where we had been interrogated. Here we met a New Zealand fighter pilot, Noel, who had been shot down ten months previously, and later an R.A.F. P.R.U. (Photo. Recon. Unit) pilot joined us. We stayed in the house for about three weeks. Food was scarce, as it was rationed, and ration cards were only available, for bona fide residents, which made it very difficult for our hosts. Black market supplies were available, but the cost of these was far too high.

"During this period M.deFlond, who had knowledge of airmen being hidden in the area, was picked up by the Gestapo, so we had to leave just in case he was forced to divulge our present hiding place. Unfortunately he died at the hands of the Gestapo, but he did not divulge our whereabouts. We were taken to hide in a grain field, where other downed airmen were congregated. We became a group of six or seven and food was supplied to us once a day by our individual hosts (Toto came out several times a day with hot soup). We stayed together for about a week and then we were dispersed and returned to our safe houses.

"We had to move again, probably because of the desperate food situation. The man who had interrogated us guided us again, by daylight, to another village, named Hennencourt, some distance away. He instructed us to follow some distance behind him as he walked his bicycle along the road. We were not to acknowledge that we knew him, and if he were to be stopped by anyone we were to keep on walking. Likewise, if we were stopped he would continue on his way. We had been supplied with some garden tools, a hoe and a rake, I believe, on the understanding that if we heard vehicles approaching we were to saunter into the fields and appear to be working.

"We were led to a house in the centre of Hennencourt. The family of Sagez consisted of father, mother, six children and a grandmother, who were very friendly, and we were taken in as part of the family. We ate comparatively well. The family would invite their friends to visit and the friends would usually bring food for us. We became very concerned when we realized that there was a small German military transport detachment stationed in a building only 200 yards from our refuge.

"During this time we saw many fleets of bombers pass over; the Americans by day and the British/Canadians at night. By day we could see the black puffs of anti-aircraft fire near the aircraft. We could also hear the V-1 rockets taking off for targets in England.[6]

One day we saw parachutes from an American bomber, and this seemed to cause some activity on the part of the German soldiers and also the French villagers. The Germans rode motorcycles while the French rode bicycles, appearing to race after the parachutists.

Later that day the head of our household returned to show us a set of silver wing insignia of the U.S. Air Force. We learned that the Germans and the villagers had raced

Madame J. Serant's chateau in Senlis-le-Sec where Bob and Jim lived on the second floor. Note - the wrought iron gate and the surrounding brick walls of the garden. German troops were accommodated on the first floor. *- Art de Breyne*

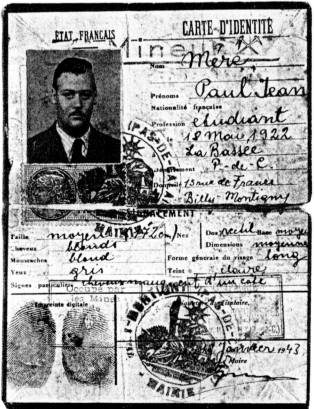

Jim Kelly's forged I.D. card. *- Jim Kelly*   Pat Brophy's forged I.D. card. *- Pat Brophy*

Bob, Collete the school teacher, Jim and Mrs. Serant in the attic of the chateau where they had to hide sometimes when the Germans got nosey. Taken in 1981. *- Jim Kelly*

Mrs. Serant demonstrating to Rose Bodie, the ruse she used to embarrass a German officer who tried to investigate Bob and Jim's hiding area. *- Jim Kelly*

each other to be first to locate the downed airmen. The French, being more familiar with the territory, arrived first. One Frenchman removed his clothes while another stripped the airman so that they could exchange clothes. The villager, now in uniform, knowing the terrain, disappeared from view while the local villagers gathered around the American as the Germans passed by, still searching.

"Unfortunately, M. Sagez, while drinking in the neighbouring tavern, bragged about hiding some airmen. Soon thereafter a priest visited the house and told us that he had made arrangements for us to be flown to England. We said our goodbyes to our adoptive family and accompanied the priest. After we had gone some distance he shattered our illusion by telling us that we were not going home but rather to a safe house in another village. He explained that too many people knew where we had been hiding.

"Colette, a schoolteacher, moved us to a house in another village, called Conty, occupied by a very frightened elderly couple M. & Mme. Duboille, who eked out a living weaving baskets. They insisted that we stay in our room 24 hours a day. When the Germans conducted a mock battle, they hid us in the attic. We only stayed a week before being moved again by Colette to another village, named Senlis le Sec, with the usual bicycle routine and hoes. This house was really a chateau with about 20 rooms. It was surrounded by lawns and flower beds. It was enclosed by a high brick wall and had a beautiful large wrought iron-gate. It was occupied by Madame Serant and her two young daughters, Evelyne and Nicole, aged nine and six. Her husband had died in 1940. We lived here in comparative comfort for six weeks, until we were liberated. We were given a nice room on the second floor.

"We were able to go out each day and walk around the large, lovely garden, because of the high wall and the gate on which was a bell which would ring if the gate was opened.

"During the time we were in hiding we played a lot of cards. Hearts was our favourite game, but we spent most of our time talking about our home lives and our dreams and plans for the future. We learned sufficient French to be able to converse with our hosts, and they told us about their lives before the war and their experiences during the invasion and occupation. We did have access to books and magazines, but they were all written in French. The only radio we heard was the relaying of daily coded messages on the B.B.C.

"The young lady schoolteacher, Colette, who had been involved in some of our moves, visited us quite often and kept us in touch with the New Zealander whom we had met earlier. She also took us cycling a couple of times when she borrowed a bicycle for us. We were able to work in the fields in a few instances.

"This house, being so large, was of interest to the Germans as a command post during their retreat in August, and one day early in September two German officers visited the house and asked to be shown around. Bob and I had gone to our room when they came to the door. They were shown through the main floor, and as they mounted the stairs to the second floor, the children guided us down the back stairs to the wine cellar. After they left, Madame Serant told us that German troops would be billeted on the grounds and the house would be the officers' living quarters and operations centre.

"The procedure appeared to be that a unit commander and staff would move in and stay a few days to regroup his troops. He would then move on and another would take his place.

"At first these were service rather than fighting units. Apparently they had been stationed for some time in France, and as they were conversant in the language, most of them would speak French with Madame Serant. She was therefore able to explain to them the living arrangements, which were that she and her daughters had bedrooms, also that two men boarded at the house but were away all day at work in a nearby town. This seemed to explain our presence and so we hid all day in the wine cellar and at night moved up to our room, where she would provide us with food. Once, one of the German officers came into the chateau where we were hidden on the second floor and decided to use the second-floor toilet just as Madame Serant was bringing food to us. With quick thinking she rushed behind the door and sat on the bidet, embarrassing the German officer, who rushed away apologizing profusely.

"Madame Serant was able to extract some ideas from the officers as they left as to when she was to expect the next contingent. This usually gave us a day or two to relax.

"During this period we were able to witness the retreat, as all day and night there would be a steady stream of tanks, trucks and other military equipment moving along the roads. There were men on bicycles, horses and wagons, civilian cars and many on foot. They were harassed by Allied aircraft with machine guns, cannons and rockets. The attacks took place in open country, as if to protect built-up areas.

"We were concerned that as the front approached the character of the troops would change from comparatively friendly to decidedly unfriendly.

"Finally one night an S.S. unit showed up. The Commander disregarded the explanation about the rooms reserved for the family. Bob and I knew from the commotion that we had better hide. We jumped out of bed and hid in the linen closet in Madame Serant's bathroom, and we didn't have our clothes with us.

"We hid in the closet for the rest of the night and all of the next day, as I recall. Madame Serant could not approach us because the Commander had taken over her bedroom, which adjoined the bathroom.

"Eventually she managed to bring us our clothes. We dressed and on her instructions we left the bathroom with her when the coast was clear. We walked with her down the stairs, through the house and out the kitchen door. All of that time she kept up a conversation with us. We looked only at her and pretended that we understood all that she said. We were able to pass the German officers who were living in the house without ever being questioned. Madame Serant stopped at the back door, talked to the sentry and waved to us as we walked through the yard and out of the gate. She had directed us to the village cemetery, where we were to hide in the family crypt.

"Later in the day someone came for us and we were taken to yet another house, which belonged to the local village gendarme and that evening we heard by radio that the Allies were in Amiens. The policeman duly dug champagne up from his garden, where he had been keeping it for such an occasion. The next morning we were liberated. It was during this period of celebration and confusion that Bob and I nearly got shot, as the local F.F.I. gave us armbands and a German Luger and asked us to come and help them take some Germans prisoner. When we arrived some tanks had taken position on the road on top of the hill and in the ensuing gunfire we were nearly hit. When the firing stopped, we found we were the only ones there. So we carefully approached the tanks, indicating we were friendly.

"We returned to Mme. Serant's house, after sobering up, to find that it had been taken over by the local Maquis, the leader of whom turned out to be a British agent! He took us to Paris and Le Bourget airport in a commandeered truck that a farmer had carefully hidden during the long years of the occupation. We were then flown home to England in a Dakota."

Jim and Bob were given survivors' leave in Canada. Bob returned to Middleton St. George and completed three more trips over Germany. Jim returned later and completed another H.C.U. course, but by that time the war was over. Both of them flew back to Canada in Lancasters to prepare for the Tiger Force, but the Japanese war was over and the squadron was disbanded.

JACK FRIDAY

He was found by two farm workers, near the chateau, early in the morning. He was to find out about this later, after the war from members of the French Underground. The farm workers took him to a doctor in a nearby village for medical help. The doctor feared that he was seriously injured and turned him over to the Germans, where he felt that he would receive better medical attention. The doctor also feared for his own life by attending to an enemy of the German Occupying Forces, since many people were shot for helping Allied airmen if they were caught. Jack's first memories were of waking up in an Amiens prison cell, on June 17, four days later, with a nasty cut above his eye, the scar of which he still carries. He remembers asking the American airman who shared his cell to lift the bandage over his eye and tell him if he had lost his eye. Evidently the Germans had not stitched his wound, as the American told him the skin flap was hanging down over his eye and that was why he could not see with that eye.

After the Germans decided he was fit enough to travel, he was transported to an Amiens prison in preparation for going to Dulagluft Interrogation Centre. The first vivid memory he has after recovering consciousness, as to this day he can't remember anything after the briefing, was the bright sunlight at the railway station, where much to his surprise he saw his flight engineer, Roy Vigars. He travelled with Roy to Stalagluft 7 in Silesia, via Brussels and Frankfurt.

ROY VIGARS

When Roy woke up the next morning, after sleeping in the bushes, he continued his journey.

"I made my way away from the airfield and came to a small village called Varennes. (The same place Jim and Bob found.) I knocked on the door of a house on the edge of the village. The door was opened and I was pulled very quickly inside. The lady of the house could not speak English and I could not speak French, so a lot of hand signs were used. An older man later appeared and he could speak English of sorts. He had served in the 1914-18 war and picked up the language from the British Tommies. The woman was his daughter and her husband was a French Army P.O.W. in Germany. After giving me some food, they showed me into their best bedroom and I slept for about five hours, after which more food was produced.

"As they had no contacts with helpers of the Underground, I told them I would be on my way so as not to endanger them. A suit of overalls, beret and a haversack with some food were produced, and they were disappointed when I insisted that I have some water for my water bottle, instead of wine. I offered some money from my escape kit to compensate them, but all they wanted was the box of matches in my escape kit, because it had a Union Jack on it.

"I did not ask their names so that there would be no possibility of betraying them after all their help. I made my way south during the day, by-passing a number of villages with the help of a fine map my helpers had torn from a phone book. At 10 p.m. I made a big mistake and ended up in the middle of the town of Corbie, which was a garrison town for the Germans. I decided the best thing to do was to carry on walking. During the journey through the town the local pubs were closing and the scene was the same as in England, servicemen and girlfriends walking arm in arm. The only difference being that the men wore German uniforms. The older women of the town were talking over their garden fences, just like home. I am sure my overalls and beret did not fool some of them; by the look in their eyes and their smiles, they knew who I was.

"On the outskirts of the town my heart rose even higher in my throat when two German Army Service Police stopped me and started asking questions. I managed to bring my only knowledge of French to use, 'Pardon.' They repeated the question and I thought they wanted directions, so pointing the same way that they were walking, I said 'A oui.' They said thank you in German and continued on their way, and I made my way in the opposite direction, not daring to run in case I caused anyone to suspect who I was.

"My left hip was stiffening up a bit, so I decided to find somewhere to sleep. I found a good shelter in some trees and settled down to sleep. After about ten minutes, air raid sirens sounded and some Ju-88s took off from a nearby airfield. I stayed in my hideout until dawn, then started walking again. My left hip was getting stiffer the further I walked. I was close to the little village of St. Saviour, where I hoped to cross the river Somme and was in a small copse, from which I could see a small anti-aircraft gun platform. While trying to make up my mind whether to carry on or rest my hip, two German soldiers from the A/A platform must have seen me in the copse. As they approached I hid the overalls and other gear I had been given. I thought that as they both had rifles and fixed bayonets it was wise not to argue. I was taken to their H.Q. in the village. The officer in charge shared his soup with me, but he only had one egg, so I was unlucky. A member of their secret police (a branch of the Gestapo) arrived to interrogate me. After about half an hour of questions from him and name, rank and number from me, he declared that I was a soldier and therefore a prisoner of war.

"I was taken to Amiens Prison — the one bombed by de Havilland Mosquito bombers in February 1944 to release French Underground members. I stayed there for five days and was then moved to a P.O.W. camp in Germany. While waiting for transport, a party arrived from another Amiens prison, and to my surprise, Jack Friday, our bomb-aimer, was one of them." (Evidently Jack did not remember seeing Roy until they met at the railway station.) "I found out from an American airman that Jack had been unconscious for three to four days. We were taken by bus to Brussels, where P.O.W.s were collected and sorted out. All Royal Air Force and Commonwealth aircrews were taken to the Dulagluft Interrogation Centre near Frankfurt. The journey from Brussels to Dulagluft took two days, and the night of June 23/24 we spent in an air raid shelter in Cologne hoping that the R.A.F. was having a stand down and going into town for a few beers! After about a week in Dulagluft, a party of about 400 aircrew were marched from Dulagluft transit camp to Wetzlau railway station to embark on our journey to Stalagluft 7 at Bankau, near Breslau on the Polish border. First-class travel was in cattle railway cars (10 chevals, 40 hommes).

"Stalagluft 7 was a new camp. So new, in fact, it was not ready for occupation. We were housed in small sheds which held six men — a good job it was summertime. After a few weeks the main camp was ready and we moved in and started to organize it as a permanently run camp. Things continued to run satisfactorily, with excitement every so often, and with instructions that once in a P.O.W. camp attempts to escape after D-day were only to be tried after very careful consideration by the escape committee. It was considered safer to be inside the camps than wandering around the countryside so far from the front lines. However tunnels were started and after a while sand was deposited where the guards could see it. This caused pandemonium to break out and the camp was turned upside down, keeping a large number of guards (goons) from other duties and giving us something to do to break the monotony.

"On January 17, 1945, all hell broke loose. At 10:00 hrs it was announced that the camp had to evacuate, as the Russians were coming — the Russians were coming! Panic subsided, as we were staying for two or three days. On January 18 at 20:30 hrs, the main camp was marched out northwest. Jack Friday went with this party and we parted company until our eventual return to England. I stayed to assist with the stretcher cases of the hospital party. With the patients on lorries, the rest of the hospital party had to march to Krelisburg, about 7 to 8 kilometres. This was a civilian P.O.W. camp, housing civilians and merchant seamen. Our party was to move on again to Stalag 344 at Lamsdorf. Two motor trucks arrived, a covered one for stretcher cases and an open one for about 40 others.

"At Stalag 344 we were put in the R.A.F. compound as this was basically an Army camp. There was very marked activity by the Russians all around the camp. We got reports all the time from the camp radio. We heard that Breslau was all but surrounded, and Breslau was our only way out to the west. On February 21 the main camp marched out to what the Germans said was a safer camp. (Was any part of Germany safe now?) On March 3 a train loaded with all the R.A.F. in Lamsdorf left for an unknown destination. The German High Command had decreed that all R.A.F. P.O.W.s were to be sent to the southern redoubt of Bavaria to be used as hostages for bargaining purposes.

"We arrived at Stalag 7B at Memmingham, near the Swiss border. This camp had Poles, Serbs, Russian, French and American Army P.O.W.s. I spent my 21st birthday here. On March 19 we were on the move again, this time to Stalag 383, until April 18, when all the camp was marched off again but the hospital party remained behind. April 22 was the day of our liberation at Stalag 383. During the day the German Camp Commander surrendered to the Senior British Medical Officer, who was then the most senior officer in the camp. At 16:10 hrs two American jeeps arrived outside the camp. When they came in they could not believe that we had the German guards as our prisoners. We had to show them proof. The Yanks evacuated us to Frankfurt Air Base and put one Air Force man in charge of 23 ex-P.O.W.s, i.e. 24 to a plane party, and flew us out in Dakotas to Rheims, in France. Being from an R.C.A.F. squadron, I reported to the R.C.A.F. interrogation office. From Rheims the same 24 in a group were flown to Wing in Cambridgeshire, England in a Lancaster bomber. Home Sweet Home!

"I arrived back at my own home on V-E Day, May 8, 1945, having been a P.O.W. for about ten and half months. While Jack Friday was waiting in Bournemouth to be shipped back to Canada, he paid a visit to my home in Guildford, and unfortunately, as the pubs were closed, we had to reminisce over a ten-year-old bottle of elderberry wine. It was during this reunion that I found out that Jack had been liberated by the Russian Army in April, after many forced marches and temporary camps. Thus ended a very eventful part of our lives."

JACK FRIDAY

Jack's memories of those marches are full of sorrow and hardship. Many of the prisoners of war died due to starvation and exposure. They started off on one of these marches in a blizzard without any preparation, which was unusual for the Germans, as they were normally very thorough in everything they did, even in near defeat. Jack lost track of time, as it was all he could do to keep going, and with little food it was difficult. They were housed in barns or slept in the open at night. Many prisoners escaped in the confusion. How many survived or were again recaptured he does not know. They were finally put aboard a cattle car and travelled for five or six days without food, water or latrines, and more of his compatriots succumbed to this treatment. Finally he ended up at Stalag 3A. After liberation he returned to England in mid-May, and to Canada in June, where he was demobbed as a F/O. Even today Jack remembers his days in the R.C.A.F. with fondness and says he really enjoyed them, irrespective of his miserable experience as a P.O.W.

PAT BROPHY

Back at the crash site of KB726, just outside the village of Gaudiempre', when Pat regained his composure he found that he was not seriously hurt, except for the loss of a large patch of hair.

"After regaining my wits, I threw my parachute and harness into the fire of the aircraft for quick disposal, I then started to crawl away from the area as fast as possible into the darkness, as there were lights coming towards me. After moving a considerable distance through the field, which turned out to be a cow pasture, I started walking, with a definite perfume of the countryside clinging to me. I had a compass as part of my escape kit, which was enclosed in a service button. After walking for some time, I realized that I had travelled in a circle, even though I was following the compass direction. Then I realized that I was carrying my revolver in my belt at my waist and it was attracting the compass needle. After sticking it in the back of my belt, I carried on walking until I approached a village. I evidently walked right by a German Army post as I entered the village early in the morning.

"The first person I met was a young man delivering milk (the only person awake at that hour, 5 a.m.). I asked him if there were any Boche around. He pointed out where they were located. He then led me to his mother's house, that of the Cressons, where I met Madame Cresson. She could speak English, which was a great help. She explained that her two sons, Pierre and Paul, were members of the French Underground, Voix du Nord (V.D.N.)."

PIERRE CRESSON

The young man who had found Pat Brophy was Paul Cresson. Pierre, his brother, was awakened very early in the morning by a gardener who said his horses were in danger, as a big aircraft had gone boom near his fields and that there was an aviator in the village. The story told by Pierre may not be exactly correct, as he told it to the editor's husband, without an interpreter, with limited English, limited French, and by using cartoons and diagrams, but they communicated very well. It was in fact most entertaining to witness. Pierre was anxious to prove that they could do it without the help of an interpreter. His life before, during and after the war really deserves a book in itself, as it is a remarkable life. His part in the story's emphasis is to honour the thousands of people from many occupied countries who helped the Allied airmen evade capture, and the hundreds who lost their lives in so doing.

Pierre was born in April 1918 and became a soldier in 1936, in the Cavalier 9em Cuirassier. He was sent to the French-Spanish border during the Spanish Civil War to control the influx of refugees into France, 1937-38. He was later sent to the Italian border when Italy invaded Albania in April 1939, and then to the Franco-German front ahead of the Maginot line in 1940. There he was badly wounded by machine-gun bullets in four parts of his body. He recovered in hospital and made a number of trips between occupied France and Vichy. During the invasion of France he was wounded again by shrapnel from a bomb dropped by a Stuka dive-bomber Ju-87, which also damaged his hearing.

He became a leader in the French Resistance and was a specialist in helping Allied airmen evade capture. In 1943 he was taken prisoner by the Gestapo, held for eight days and transported from Arras to Belgium via Boulogne and Mons. He evidently outwitted the Gestapo, as he convinced them that he was Albert Catteau — a very common name in northern France and Belgium. He somehow obtained a document that he stamped with their clearance while somebody was out of the room, and he walked out a free man. He joined the local Belgian Resistance for 20 days before returning to his home in France, in Warlincourt near Gaudiempre'.

Though his specialty was looking after Allied airmen, he also did some sabotage. Once his group derailed a train, hoping it had gasoline aboard, but unfortunately it was empty. They then helped the Germans with the repairs, very slowly. He assisted 63 or 64 airmen and 6 Russian P.O.W.s to evade recapture between 1942-45. In 1942 the escape route was to Switzerland, in 1943 to Spain, and in 1944 via fishing boats from Boulogne to England. Their group was known as the Voix du Nord, 11th Secteur. With the invasion of Europe in 1944 it was safer to hold on to the airmen and wait for liberation, rather than pass them down the line.

When he first saw Pat Brophy on the evening of June 14, he did not think Pat was in great shape, as he assumed that he was suffering from concussion and shock after being thrown from the aircraft. The loss of some hair from his scalp gave him an unusual appearance. There was no time to inspect him carefully, as the Germans were roaring around the countryside looking for the airmen of the various aircraft that had been shot down that night. Pierre and his brother therefore hid Pat in the barn behind their mother's home. They buried Pat's uniform, dog tags and revolver in the barnyard at the back of Madame Cresson's house. They had to move Pat during the next couple of days from Pas en Artois to Warlincourt, where he would stay with Mr. Amadee Capron in a schoolhouse which had a bell tower, like a church. He then returned to Paul and Pierre's mother's place at Pas en Artois. During this time they realized that Pat was all right, and by the end of June they realized that they had quite a character on their hands. While Pat was with them he helped Pierre salvage a machine gun and some ammunition from the wreck of KB726, as well as the fire axe that Andy had used in his attempt to save Pat. Later also Pierre salvaged the tail wheel and used it on the farm's wheelbarrow for a number of years after the war. It was returned with other salvaged items, including a machine gun and revolvers, as souvenirs to the Canadian War Museum at the ceremony in 1981. The group was able to salvage this much from the crash site, as the Germans were too pre-occupied with the Normandy invasion. Normally they removed all aircraft wrecks very quickly for examination and intelligence information on the latest equipment used by the Allies.

Following a message on the B.B.C. radio Pierre gathered his scattered airmen together for a planned pickup by aircraft, but it was blocked by the Germans and had to be cancelled. The group always had to move the airmen whenever they thought that the Germans were coming on a search of that particular area, and also to ease the problem of one family having a number of extra mouths to feed without the benefit of ration cards.

They also sabotaged trucks going in and out of a German supply depot by putting miniature hedgehog metal devices on the roads to blow the tires. This was more a nuisance than a threat to the Germans and did not warrant the risk of the deadly reprisals that could be taken. Pierre lost a lot of his good friends, who were also senior leaders in the Resistance, to the Gestapo. One was executed only two days before the Russians liberated the area in Germany where he was held captive. Another friend was beheaded by the Gestapo because he refused to talk.

Pierre said that he was so accustomed to the bombers going over and bombs dropping that he did not hear the Mynarski aircraft crash. Over the years he said that 248 bombs had been dropped in his neighbourhood by both the Germans and the Allied air forces. After the war he built his house on top of an old bunker which was part of the old V-1 buzz bomb site, so his wine was very safe. The house was called the Son-Bloc, or Blauchaus.

PAT BROPHY

"While at Warlincourt I met Lt. Cliff Williams, an American P-38 pilot from Silsbee, Texas, and we were then together until liberation. We were moved from Pas en Artois to St. Leger with Mr. Petit, and then to Ecoust St. Mien with Mr. Mark Harley. He gave us ID cards and F.F.I. armbands, so we were legal! Mine said I was a student and a deaf mute. This masked my lack of French. It was while we were with Mark that we had a close call with the Germans. Cliff and I escaped detection by being hidden in a tomb-like building in the graveyard. We had to hide under the marble slab when four Germans brought in a dead German and laid him on the slab. We had to sleep with the dead German for two nights, with the aroma from a dead body.

"While I was with Mark Harley, I helped in the sabotage of a bridge, communication lines and power lines. Rather than cut them we would throw a line over them and pull them down or short them out. Mark knew which lines were important to the Germans, as he worked on the communications under their supervision, but was at the same time a member of the Resistance.

"Mark moved us to Billy Montigny, where we met Madame Heller on July 7. We stayed with her for four days and met up with other evaders, F/0 Danny Murray from Red Deer, Alberta, also an air gunner like myself, and a British air gunner, W/0 Maurice Bemrose from London, England. Madame Heller, for lack of space, had to move us to Saullaumines with Mr.and Mrs. Dernoncourt on July 11. They owned a general store-cum-house. There the four of us met up with three other airmen, two Aussies (F/0 John Cullity, an air gunner from Needlands, West Australia, and F/0 George Morrison, a navigator from Conley Vale, New South Wales) and another American fighter pilot (Lt. Bill Dubose, from Redwood, California). We had two French collaborators as neighbours on one side and German soldiers billeted on the other. The logistics and risk of hiding seven airmen must have been great. The problem of food was partially solved with potatoes and black market steaks. Every meal included a very large pile of potatoes. I came out of hiding many pounds heavier and well tanned. It was in Sallaumines that we were finally liberated by a British Army Tank Battalion on September 1, 1944.

"Then the celebrations began with champagne and ended with champagne. Much to my surprise, the two so-called female collaborators with the Germans from next door, walked in with a bottle of champagne for each of us — so they must have known that seven of us were there! But this gesture did not save the two females from having their heads shaved. This was a form of punishment done by the French to all females who collaborated with the Germans. We took part in the celebrations and parades at Sallaumines and Billy Montigny — 'Thank You's - Merci's' — during September 1 to 3. We met 10 other evaders, making 17 in all, that had been hidden in the area. This was a terrific feat, to hide so many from the watchful eyes of the Nazis and collaborators. Then it was on to Pas en Artois, Ste. Leger, Ecoust St. Mien, Arras, Amiens and Lens with more of the same and a mess dinner every night with the F.F.I. and the now Lt/Col Pierre Cresson, who turned up everywhere. He made me a Lt/Col also.

"On September 6/7 we were at Bethiane Aire enroute to Boulogne, but the threat of 50,000 Germans in our way changed our minds and we returned to Billy Montigny and said our final farewells. George Morrison and I then spent the day of September 9 together on our way to Vitry airfield for passage to the United Kingdom. We had to hang around the airfield area until the 13th, when we were airlifted by Dakotas to Reading, in England, and thence by train to London for debriefing and leave. It was then that I was able to tell the heroic story of how Andy had died trying to save me."

It was during this leave period that Pat and other returnees were to have all their souvenirs stolen while at a debriefing hotel in London. Unfortunately they were taken advantage of during the celebrations of getting back alive. It was also during this time of debriefing that Pat was asked for the D-ring from his parachute. When he explained that he had not used his parachute, the person did not really believe him and attempted to charge him the cost of two shillings and sixpence — petty but true. Later, when he returned to Canada, the Irvin parachute company sent him a gold Caterpillar pin again, assuming he had survived by bailing out. He returned the pin but kept the card, as he had not earned the award by using his parachute.

He met Jim Kelly in the Chandos Dive Bar, where he was greeted with "You're supposed to be dead, you old bastard." It was then that Pat learned of Jim's story about

Numb. 37754

5035

SECOND SUPPLEMENT

TO

The London Gazette

Of TUESDAY, the 8th of OCTOBER, 1946

Published by Authority

Registered as a newspaper

FRIDAY, 11 OCTOBER, 1946

Air Ministry, 11th October, 1946.

The KING has been graciously pleased to confer the VICTORIA CROSS on the under-mentioned officer in recognition of most conspicuous bravery: —

Pilot Officer Andrew Charles MYNARSKI (Can./J.87544) (deceased), Royal Canadian Air Force, No. 419 (R.C.A.F.) Squadron.

Pilot Officer Mynarski was the mid-upper gunner of a Lancaster aircraft, detailed to attack a target at Cambrai in France, on the night of 12th June, 1944. The aircraft was attacked from below and astern by an enemy fighter and ultimately came down in flames.

As an immediate result of the attack, both port engines failed. Fire broke out between the mid-upper turret and the rear turret, as well as in the port wing. The flames soon became fierce and the captain ordered the crew to abandon the aircraft.

Pilot Officer Mynarski left his turret and went towards the escape hatch. He then saw that the rear gunner was still in his turret and apparently unable to leave it. The turret was, in fact, immovable, since the hydraulic gear had been put out of action when the port engines failed, and the manual gear had been broken by the gunner in his attempts to escape.

Without hesitation, Pilot Officer Mynarski made his way through the flames in an endeavour to reach the rear turret and release the gunner. Whilst so doing, his parachute and his clothing, up to the waist, were set on fire. All his efforts to move the turret and free the gunner were in vain. Eventually the rear gunner clearly indicated to him that there was nothing more he could do and that he should try to save his own life. Pilot Officer Mynarski reluctantly went back through the flames to the escape hatch. There, as a last gesture to the trapped gunner, he turned towards him, stood to attention in his flaming clothing and saluted, before he jumped out of the aircraft. Pilot Officer Mynarski's descent was seen by French people on the ground. Both his parachute and clothing were on fire. He was found eventually by the French, but was so severely burnt that he died from his injuries.

The rear gunner had a miraculous escape when the aircraft crashed. He subsequently testified that, had Pilot Officer Mynarski not attempted to save his comrade's life, he could have left the aircraft in safety and would, doubtless, have escaped death.

Pilot Officer Mynarski must have been fully aware that in trying to free the rear gunner he was almost certain to lose his own life. Despite this, with outstanding courage and complete disregard for his own safety, he went to the rescue. Willingly accepting the danger, Pilot Officer Mynarski lost his life by a most conspicuous act of heroism which called for valour of the highest order.

LONDON

The London Gazette 8 October, 1946, announcing award of the Victoria Cross to Andrew Mynarski.

Andy's helmet and death. Pat was able to tell Jim what had happened to Andy and why he had died from burns to his body. When the story of his debriefing reached the higher brass, it was recommended that Andrew Charles Mynarski be posthumously awarded the Victoria Cross for his heroic attempt to save his crew mate at the cost of his own life. The award was approved, which was very unusual, as the Victoria Cross normally requires more than one eyewitness to the deed. The award was promulgated on 11 October 1946 in the London *Gazette*. It was the last award of the Victoria Cross made during WWII, due to the long delay of the true story. They were to find out later that Andy was buried with other airmen in a cemetery at Meharicourt.

Pierre Cresson was honoured by King Leopold of Belgium for his work with the Belgian Underground.

Pat returned to Canada in October on the liner *Isle de France* and took part in the preparation of the Tiger Force, until it was disbanded after cessation of hostilities in the Far East.

All the Canadian N.C.O.s were given commissions while they were away, backdated to June 1944. They often wonder if they had not been shot down, and Andy had not been awarded the Victoria Cross, whether they would have been commissioned.

Art believes he would have been reprimanded if he had returned from the raid, as the day before they had been low flying off the coast with other Lancasters and had interfered with some special anti-aircraft gun exercise taking place on a promontory, and were duly reported.

Footnotes:

1 Actual bomb tonnage was 13,417.
2 Other records and stories printed say the bombs had been dropped before the crash. This was not true, as the local French villagers were to see the Germans many days later drag the unexploded bombs away from the wreck with horses and detonate them in a nearby field. In fact Pat was not sure if the explosions he felt were bombs going off or just the aircraft fuel tanks exploding.
3 This was a V-1 or buzzbomb, unknown to Art at the time.
4 Could these planes have been nightfighters similar to the one that shot them down?
5 A French collaborator with the Germans, named after the original Norwegian collaborator.
6 These launching sites of the V-1s were to become coded as No Ball targets or ski-sites because of the appearance of the launching ramp. They were to receive much attention from Bomber Command as the attacks on England by the buzz bombs intensified.

Lancaster 10AR KB976 No.408 Squadron.

- N. Etheridge

KB892 and KB839 as 10MPs flying in formation with chin-radar. Both served with No.419 Squadron in England as VR.P and VR.D. They were flown back to Canada by Sqd/Ld J.W. Watt and Fl/Lt P.H. Hulk's crews in June 1945. KB839 was later retired to Greenwood and donated its engines to the CWH Lancaster project in 1987.

- CWHM

III

CANADIAN LANCASTERS AT PEACE

PRODUCTION AND SERVICE LIFE OF LANCASTER FM213

The CWHM Lancaster X FM213 was built in July 1945 as one of the last batch off the production line, before production stopped at FM229 in August 1945. FM213 was known as a rogue or jinxed aircraft on the assembly line, according to Ken Allen of Wardair, as there was always some snag preventing it from being accepted. When it finally left the assembly line, it was given a second test flight (August 31, 1945) by Don Rogers, Andy Gabura, Fred Lake and Tommy Thompson, after which it went into storage with many of its contemporaries. On June 21, 1946, it was taken on strength by the R.C.A.F., but conversion to 10MR/MP standards was not completed until 1951.

Starting in 1946, many Lancaster B.Xs were modified to nine different versions for post-war service. The R.C.A.F. designated the aircraft with Arabic numerals (10) with an alphabetical suffix indicating the peacetime duty for which it was modified. The versions are summarized below from K.M. Molson and H.A. Taylor's book of *Canadian Aircraft Since 1909*:

10AR - Specially modified for aerial reconnaissance. Similar to photographic reconnaissance. Three only, KB839, 882 and 976 were stationed at Rockcliffe with No.408 Squadron.

10BR - Bomber Reconnaissance. One 400 Imp. gal bomb-bay tank and depth charges. Four 10ARs were initially winterized and partly modified to standard 10BR and became 10BR(Intermin). A further nine B.X Lancasters were then converted to 10BR bomber reconnaissance. The first, FM221 was delivered to Trenton in June 1949.

10DC - Drone-carrying. Two only, KB848 and KB851. Two Ryan Firebee drones under each wing.

10MR/MP - Maritime Reconnaissance/Maritime Patrol. Radar and sonobuoy operators positions in the rear of the centre and rear section, nose and tail turrets only and rear observation windows. One bomb-bay 400 gal. tank, increasing the fuel to 2,554 gals and 15 bomb-carrier positions. They were fitted with de-icer boots, APU, AN/ARD-3 sonobuoy, Loran AN/APN-4, AN/APN Rebecca, SCR-718 high altimeter, AN/APN-1 low altimeter, H2S radar and a Pierce wire recorder. Over 70 Lancasters were modified to MR and later MP standards. The first MR prototype, KB903 cost $1,055,000 for 55 modifications both major and minor. It flew on December 29, 1950. This was the largest of the conversion programs, with 95 aircraft planned for conversion and possibly 118, but this was never authorized. Both de Havilland and A.V. Roe were involved in the program. The initial orders of 34 aircraft to de Havilland were contracted at $4,180,000. This was slightly more expensive per aircraft than the contract with A.V. Roe $163,000 vs $145,671, as de Havilland had to obtain kits and components from A.V. Roe and were on the learning curve of this type of aircraft. They achieved a conversion rate of approximately three aircraft per month.

10N - Navigation trainer. Five only were converted by Fairey Aviation Ltd. They were named FM206 "Northern Cross", FM208 "Polaris", FM211 "Zenith", KB826 "Orion" and KB986 unnamed. They carried two 400 gal. bomb-bay tanks and were fitted with de-icer boots, APU, C-2 compass, Loran and Rebecca.

10O - Avro Orenda engine test bed. Faired nose. The two outboard engines replaced by Orenda jet engines. One only, FM209.

Lancaster 10P MN207 No.408 Squadron flying over the fall colours. It was the last Canadian Lanc to be colour delivered to the R.A.F., in August 1944.

- *N. Etheridge*

Lancaster 10P FM209 modified as an Orenda jet engine flying-test bed. 　　　　 *- N.A.M.*

Lancaster FM215 modified as a 10P, on engine run-up at Malton, produced at the same time as FM213, note the 1947 roundel with the maple leaf in the centre. 　　　　 *- N.A.M.*

10P - Photographic Reconnaissance. This was the first of the post-war conversions of the standard Lancaster for photo-reconnaissance use in 1948. Nine were initially converted by Fairey Aviation Ltd. at a cost of $30,500 per aircraft for No.408 Squadron service, and in 1949 two more were converted with radar altimeters. They were FM120, FM122, FM199, FM207, FM212, FM214-218 and KB729. They did extensive aerial mapping of Canada and remained in service until 1962.

10S - Standard post-war bomber. Unmodified KB944, KB781, KB801, KB854.

10U - Standard bomber, unmodified.

Some of the early conversions were contracted with Fairey Aviation and later de Havilland Aircraft of Canada, located at Downsview, when A.V. Roe Canada Ltd. became overloaded with work associated with the CF-100 all-weather jet fighter and the development of the Orenda jet engines. This was to ensure two sources of supply and increase the delivery rate to the squadrons.

During these conversions an amusing telex was received by R.C.A.F. headquarters, which said that "the R.C.A.F. crew of FM208 found the aircraft could not be accepted as the three inches would not tether." It was later discovered that what the telex operator had tried to transmit was that "three engines would not feather." It turned out after another flight test by A.V. Roe which found nothing wrong, that the pilot was not following the proper procedure in cutting his mixture control.

After de Havilland Canada test pilot George Neal test-flew the FM213 aircraft on December 16, 1951, its first R.C.A.F. assignment was to No.405 Squadron based at Greenwood, Nova Scotia, where it was given squadron and unit code AG.J. It had a short career of 10.5 hours. flying, when it was heavily damaged at Trenton during its ferry flight en route to No.405 Squadron, where the undercarriage collapsed. The centre section was badly damaged and the aircraft was almost considered unsalvageable due to a very heavy landing under the hands of a sprog (inexperienced) ferry crew.

An eyewitness to the event was young L.A.C., E. Tech (A) W.L.(Bill) Sinclair, who was stationed at Trenton, during the winter of 1951, when the aircraft made its heavy landing. Sinclair was part of the crash tender crew. In his words, "On the final approach the throttles were cut (closed) when the aircraft was far too high off the deck (ground). To the best of my memory, it bounced, then ballooned into the air, and finally hit hard on the port undercarriage, which collapsed and caused large fuel leaks.

"Fortunately there were large snowbanks on each side of the runway and the aircraft skidded erratically, completing its trip into one of them. There was no resulting fire, and perhaps the snow kept the temperature down, soaked up the fuel and who knows, maybe snuffed out any fire.

"While the aircraft was still moving, the flight engineer had the aft escape hatch opened and was halfway out, just waiting for the aircraft to stop its merry ride. When the Lanc ended up in the snowbank, the flight engineer motored (ran) away at a high speed for some distance, then collapsed. I can't say I blame him at all.

"The pilot, I do clearly remember, when we arrived at the site, was standing up in the cockpit switching off everything in sight."

The other, more official and less colourful story of the incident records the event as:

No.50 Third Time Unlucky

Prior to being detailed to ferry a Lancaster aircraft FM213, the pilot had ten hours dual and one hour solo on the type. On final approach, upon completion of the ferry trip to Trenton, the pilot used full flap, despite the fact that the wind velocity at the time was 25 mph with strong gusts. The pilot was late in rounding out, and upon touching down,

One of the last conversions with the Avro workers. The hangar behind the aircraft is the one that burned down destroying the Orenda Engine's Lancaster test aircraft.   *- C. Sloat*

KB892 and KB973, as early versions of 10MPs flying information on the west coast from No.407 Squadron.   *- R.D. Page*

KB895, which served with No.434 Squadron as WL.O, was sold to a farmer in Alberta. Its centre section was used to salvage FM213 after its ground loop at Trenton. As KB895 was sinking in the mud it would have eventually crushed the two garages. - *C. Sloat*

Lancaster X FM208 just completed, later converted to 10N named Polaris. - *N.A.M.*

the aircraft bounced. The throttles were opened in an attempt to ease the aircraft back on the runway, but on touching down the second time the control column was held forward instead of fully back and the aircraft bounced again, even higher than the first time. After the third bounce, the *starboard* tire blew out and the starboard undercarriage collapsed. The aircraft groundlooped and ended up facing in the opposite direction.

A "B" category crash.

It was dismantled and returned to storage at de Havilland, where it languished until 1952 awaiting a replacement centre section which was finally found out west.

At the end of World War II, the Canadian government was anxious to dispose of all military wares, including its aircraft. A group of scrap merchants bought more than 40 Lancaster Xs from War Assets Corporation to be melted down into aluminum ingots for making pots and pans. Most of these aircraft were stored at the Penhold and Pearce airports in Alberta.

When the Korean War began, the R.C.A.F. became aware that they needed an aircraft of this type to fulfill their anti-submarine requirements. The Lancaster X was chosen and the hunt was started for engines and spare supplies to build up the fleet of aircraft modified for Maritime Reconnaissance/Maritime Patrol.

Found Bros. Aviation Ltd., Malton had recently purchased 44 Lancasters, including the aircraft stored at Penhold and Pearce, to fulfill a potential offshore engine requirement. This included 165 engines remaining on the airframes. It was inevitable then that the Canadian government, through their contractor, turned to the Found Brothers for the supply of the necessary spares. In all, over 70 Lancaster Xs were modified to meet this maritime condition, which required the removal of the mid-upper turret, removal of the guns from the nose and rear turrets, and the addition of rear observation windows. There were extensive internal modifications for sonar and radar stations, and the bomb bays were adapted for 400 gal. auxiliary fuel tanks to extend the patrol range.

After further consideration of the damaged centre section of FM213, the R.C.A.F. consulted with de Havilland about the feasibility of repairing the aircraft should a replacement centre section be found. Therefore, it was not surprising that de Havilland contracted with Found Brothers to supply a replacement centre section.

Found Brothers knew of a Lancaster which had been purchased from War Assets by a farmer near Penhold, Alberta. He intended to make it into a novel tool shed. This aircraft was Lancaster X KB895, which was built at the end of 1944 and ferried to England. It was taken on strength by No.434 Squadron in the spring of 1945. After V-E Day it was ferried back to Canada and eventually struck off strength on January 2, 1947. When the farmer purchased it, he built three ramps and pulled it up onto piles of logs approximately six feet high. There it sat for a number of years, as the farmer's interest in the project waned. He was now the proud owner of a derelict Lancaster bomber in his back yard — which must have been an eyesore to his wife. Due to the weight of the aircraft on the pile of logs, as time elapsed they were slowly sinking into the ground. Thus the wings of the aircraft were threatening to flatten his garage and existing toolshed, over which they extended. When Found Brothers approached the farmer to purchase KB895 for its centre section, the farmer was delighted and very co-operative, glad to be rid of such a problem. The aircraft was dismantled and the centre section was shipped to de Havilland on the largest flatcar in service in Canada at that time. Due to the foresight of the designer and manufacture for interchangeability, the centre section was mated with the salvageable remains of FM213 without trouble. Thus FM213 is really a hybrid of two aircraft FM213 and KB895 (FM213-KB895).

When the aircraft was finally completed and modified to 10 MP conditions, it was test flown by Bob Fowler in 1953. After major surgery and modifications FM213 had a long, trouble-free life and was one of the last Lancasters to be retired from the R.C.A.F.

During her career she was stationed with No.405 Squadron at Greenwood, as well as No.107 Rescue Unit at Torbay.

It is impossible to record all the crews who flew FM213 during her service life, but a few stories are recorded here. The names of some of her crews, are summarized at the end of this section.

Arriving at Greenwood in August 1953, FM213 was flown by Harry Savelle on August 21 for a one hour air test. Shortly after, on August 22/23, Lancaster KB999, with F/O Staners as captain, was reported missing north of Churchill, Manitoba. On August 23, No.405 Squadron Lancasters were deployed to take part in the search. Savelle was then captain of 213 and took nine hours to reach La Pas due to bad weather at Churchill, with a U/S artificial horizon. The next day they flew to Winnipeg to get it fixed and then back to Churchill to take part in the search. During the next five days they carried out search patterns, lasting 11.25, 6.50, 6, 9.50 and 9 hours. respectively. They were rewarded on the 29th when Staners and his crew were found alive beside a small lake northwest of Churchill. The crew of 213 were able to drop cigarettes and chocolate bars to them out of the flare chute. Savelle says that it would have been a nice twist of fate if FM213 had been the aircraft that spotted them, but a Dakota from the SAR unit at Winnipeg had the privilege. It was a happy day to find them all alive after the rash of fatal Lancaster crashes that had occurred in the early 50s. They flew back to Greenwood on September 1, taking 6.40 hours. The only other time Savelle flew FM213 was to Rockcliffe on October 19. He left it there and brought KB857 back to Greenwood the next day.

A New Zealander, Darcy Packwood, reported flying her as second pilot on December 6, 1953, in Operation Dust Devil, a flight of 10.15 hours duration, including 4 hours on instruments. This was evidently a fighter affiliation training exercise where the fighters attacked the Lancaster formation in dummy quarter attacks. They evidently scared the hell out of him, according to his account, as they came too close for comfort.

S. Kostenuk, the author of *R.C.A.F. Squadrons and Aircraft*, with J. Griffin, flew with FM213 in FM233 as a wireless operator, while they were with No.405 (MR) Squadron. FM213 was coded as VN.213 He was able to film FM213 from his aircraft while taking part in NATO exercise "Mariner", which took them from Greenwood to St. Eval, England, in 1953. Peter Mossman has dedicated his painting of the aircraft in memory of the late F/O Samuel Kostenuk.

FM213 spent most its life stationed with No.107 Rescue Unit at Torbay, three miles northwest of St. John's, Newfoundland. F/L Cy Dunbar is one the pilots who flew FM213 extensively, 448 hours out of a total of 2,514 hours on Lancasters. He is still flying today (Boeing 737s) with Canadian Airlines International (ex-Eastern Provincial Airways). He flew FM213 between July 30, 1957 and July 10, 1963. The other two Lancs stationed there at that time were FM104 (now at Toronto Lakeshore) and KB943 which was scrapped when it was retired. In his 114 trips in FM213, then designated as CX213, he and his crew performed many duties. His crew consisted of two pilots, navigator, radio officer and flight engineer. His memories of flying FM213 are summarized below from an article written by Chuck Sloat.

He described their assigned duties which included: searches for lost hunters, cars in snowdrifts, fishermen, fishing boats, intercepts on and escort of aircraft flying westbound over the North Atlantic and approaching Newfoundland with one or more engines shutdown, escort duties for the Royal flights passing through the squadron's area of responsibility, and DUCK-BUTT operations which were in support of aircraft on ferry flights from Canada to Europe.

It is worth describing some of these operations in more detail:

Cy Dunbar and crew. L. to R. Russ Morefield, co-pilot; Don Reynolds, radio operator; John Caron, navigator; Cy Dunbar, captain. At Torbay 1958. *- CWHM*

FM213 taking off from Prestwick. *- W.G. White*

DUCK-BUTT OPERATIONS

During the ferrying to Europe of such aircraft as the F-86 Sabres, CF-100 Canucks, T-33 Shooting Stars and Beech 18 Expeditors, the requirements were twofold: first to provide an airborne search and rescue facility, and second to provide a beacon (homing facility) on which the overflying aircraft could "home."

This meant the Lancaster would position itself at the mid-point of the intended flight path of the aircraft on the ferry path. There they would set up a race-track pattern at right angle to the intended flight path of the ferry aircraft. This was usually done at 8,000 - 10,000 feet. While doing this the radio officer would broadcast a continuous signal on a predetermined frequency and Morse code designator. Once the aircraft had overflown the position, they would follow to their predetermined base. Their positions could be on any one of the legs of the flights from Goose Bay; Sonderstrom, Greenland; USNAS at Keflavik, Iceland and then on to Prestwick, Scotland.

They also carried out "running DUCK-BUTTS," which meant they arrived "on station" prior to the mid-point position and continued flying towards Prestwick. The timing was such that the ferry aircraft would fly overhead as they passed the mid-point position. These ferry flights all had operational names like NIMBLE BAT, JUMP MOAT I,II,III,IV and First and Second SILVER DOZEN.

SEARCH AND RESCUE

For this they were equipped with Lindholme gear, which consisted of two survival kits and two life rafts which were all roped together. They carried five parachute flares for illuminating search areas and APS33 radar for search or navigation purposes.

SARAH was the designator for Search and Rescue Airborne Homing. When they received a distress signal they manoeuvred the aircraft so that they would receive a coded signal equally in their head set and fly to the source on a heading that gave increasing signal strength. Having flown over the signal source they would fly a pattern at 90 degrees to the first track, if they had not obtained a visual sighting, to obtain a fix on the source.

During service at Torbay, CX213 escorted the Royal family three times during their transatlantic crossings in 1957- 58. She was seen in such places as Iceland; Prestwick, Scotland; Azores and Bermuda.

INTERCEPTS

One of their requirements was to be on 24-hour standby to respond to calls for assistance in searches and intercepts. These usually involved military or civilian four-engine aircraft which had one or more engine problems. After leaving their ready or standby quarters attached to the hangar and having obtained their briefing, they would normally be airborne in 15 to 25 minutes. They would then fly towards a position about 50 to 75 miles ahead of the intended track of the aircraft they were trying to intercept.

Once in the area, they would fly a race-track pattern at right angles to the intended track of the aircraft, which they tried to intercept at about 6,000 to 10,000 feet. At 50 miles separation they would attempt UHF radio communications and advise the aircraft that they were firing flares to which the intercept aircraft was to respond. This made visual interception easier and once this was obtained they escorted the aircraft to the nearest suitable airport for landing and then returned to base.

BLOOD DROP

Another of their jobs in the winter was to drop blood to isolated communities such as the Grenfell Mission at St. Anthony, located on the northern peninsula of the island. This meant dropping the blood in a shockproof basket (3 ft. by 2.5 ft.) which was connected to a small parachute. This was loaded in the bomb bay from one of the bomb shackles. The drop was usually done from 100 feet and released by the pilot at the appropriate moment. With practice they were almost able to drop the basket into the arms of the reception committee.

Another duty was to local flying displays for Air Forces Day at Torbay. This usually consisted of a "short field" take-off, followed by a slow fly past with everything hanging out, gear and flaps down and bomb-bay doors open, then an infield turn with one engine shutdown and another with two engines on the same side shut down and the props feathered, followed by a high speed-pass and steep pull-up.

One crew inscribed their names on the inside of the aircraft and were duly recorded by Greg Hannah before restoration and painting of the inside. They were written in pencil in the front turret and consisted of F/L Hobdon, F/L Dunbar, F/O Aubin, F/L Bemister, W/O Mann, Sgt. Dunn, Cpl. Ouelette, LAC Murray, LAC Farwell - 9th August 1959 - Torbay to Keflavick for Operation "Second Silver Dozen." The men were acting as air sea rescue patrol between Torbay and Keflavick, for 12 T33s from Trenton on their transatlantic crossing to No.4 Wing in France.

On September 9, 1959, with F/L Dunbar at the controls, they took part in "Duckbutt" with a crew consisting of F/O Aubin, F/O Young, F/O Bemister, F/O Bates, Sgt. Dunn and F/O Keiler.[1] These names were again inscribed on the inside of the fuselage.

In 1959 the operating units pleaded with headquarters to have the Lancaster replaced, as they were concerned with the flight safety of the crews, or having to restrict the flying of the aircraft due to the age, lack of spares and difficulty of maintaining the high standard demanded by long over-water flights.

A view of the choir, choir boy unknown! circa 1958.
- CWHM

It was not until 10 October 1963 that a telex was received authorizing the unit to strike off FM213 and FM104. CX213 was finally retired from active duty on November 6, 1963, and flown to Trenton by F/O Love, F/O Harley, Sgt. Armstrong and LAC Cockerline. This was again recorded in the front turret,"Torbay-Trenton-Scrap 6 November 1963."

It was placed in storage at No.6 RD Storage Depot, Dunnville. It had 4392.3 hours. on the airframe when it was handed over. This was an amazing record for an aircraft that was built for war, where the life expectancy was often 100 hours or less.

It would probably have been sold for scrap metal except for the intervention of Bill Clancy of the Royal Canadian Legion (Branch No.109) of Goderich, Ontario.

SOME OF THE CREW OF FM213

Sgt. Armstrong
F/O Paul Aubin
F/O Richard Banigan
F/O Bates
F/O Bemister
Cpl. Bissonette
F/O Cliff Burkart
F/O Caron
LAC Cockerline
F/O Ivan Delong
F/L Cy Dunbar
Sgt. Dunn
F/L Eric Edwards
LAC Farwell
F/O Folkins
W/C Forbes
Bob Fowler
F/O Al Fox
Andy Gabura
F/O Rod Galloway
F/O Mike Garvey
F/L Gerding
Sgt. Hannington
F/O Harley
F/O Doug Hazelwood
F/O Herbert
F/L Hobton
F/O Hubon
W/C Hunt
W/C Jackson
F/O Keech
F/O Keiler
F/L Kerr
F/O Kimbal
Fred Lake
F/L George LeValliant

F/O Love F/O Ed Lowery
F/O Jack Mann F/L Smokey
McLennan
F/L McLeod
F/L Ken McMillan
F/L Ross Menzies
F/O Jim Mitchell
F/L Monty Montgomery
F/O Russ Morefield
LAC Murray
F/L Namby
Gorge Neal
F/O Ernie Neal
F/O L. Noel
F/O G.D. Owen
F/O Darcy Packwood
F/L Plunkett
F/O Vic Poole
F/L Raymond
S/L Rich
F/L Jack A. Richardson
F/L Rod Richardson
Don Rogers
F/O Harry Savelle
Sgt. Steavens
Tommy Thompson
F/O Toze
F/O Bob Veale
Sgt. J.L. Webber
F/O Harry Wellon
F/O Harry Wells
LAC Wheadon
F/L Wright
F/O Jim Young
F/O Zachurwk

RETIREMENT OF FM213

BILL CLANCY

In December 1963 Bill Clancy became alarmed at reports concerning the destruction of all surviving W.W.II. aircraft for aluminum salvage. Every day the television news showed reports of zero time but obsolete aircraft falling victim to giant shears. A few months later the R.C.A.F. honoured the retirement of the last Lancaster Xs in service. "The ominous implications goaded us into action" was how Bill Clancy expressed the beginning of the project that brought FM213 into caring civilian hands.

A personal letter to the Hon. Paul Hellyer, then Minister of National Defence, on behalf of the Goderich Chapter of the Royal Canadian Legion, resulted in almost immediate response. It was later learned that of 50 applicants this group was the successful recipient of one of the three remaining aircraft. The telex authorizing the sale of FM213 was dated July 1, 1964.

Following positive response, the Legion members formed a Lancaster Memorial Committee to legitimize Bill's decisive and most successful action. FM213 had been offered for disposal at the Canadian counterpart of the Arizona desert: R.C.A.F. Dunnville. Keith "Hoppy" Hopkinson of Sky Harbour fame flew the delegation to Dunnville to receive their prize at a price of $1,300. But one carburetor on the dusty ground told the story. She was in no condition for a ferry flight to Goderich. Disappointment was coupled with tragedy a week later when "Hoppy," the spirit of the developing project, was killed in an air crash at Sky Harbour. The next week was no better. When Bill Clancy phoned the "Chiefy" at Dunnville to enquire as to whether circumstances had changed, he was informed that unnamed persons had removed the engines, installing them in FM104 in order to ferry that aircraft to Toronto for display at the C.N.E. waterfront.

Bill called R.C.A.F. headquarters in Ottawa and contacted the Chief of the Air Staff, who replied, "Oh! They did, did they? We will be in touch." Within days the engines were transported back from Downsview to Dunnville, and on April 29, 1964, Wing Commander McDonnel advised Goderich that the R.C.A.F. would be pleased to provide a crew to deliver the now airworthy FM213 to Sky Harbour. Civilian contractors had spent over 400 hours upgrading the aircraft to ferry flight standards and she was now at R.C.A.F. Trenton for final work, test flights and ready, on 180 hours maintenance.

Sky Harbour had prepared for the arrival with a joint airshow. Group Captain Keith Greenway of R.C.A.F. Clinton co-ordinated the effort and provided the Honour Guard. The maintenance crew at Trenton were up early. Sure enough an engine would take two hours to start. Once in the air, however, Captain F/Lt Donald "Monty" Montgomery, D.F.C., reported that she flew like a dream. Montgomery had one passenger aboard, Sgt. Forest. The delivery route covered, in salute, several inactive war bases, including Mount Hope, also still active Centralia, Clinton and finally former #12 E.F.T.S. Sky Harbour at 13:59 hrs, one minute early. During the airshow, where four Centralia Chipmunks heralded the arrival of FM213, and immediately preceding the arrival of FM213, an Expeditor from R.C.A.F. Centralia hurried into the circuit to land and taxi up to the receiving area. It was delivering a Lancaster dinghy hatch cover that had blown off minutes before as the Lancaster did its Centralia passover. Shortly after, the rest of her landed without further incident, except that the pilot had to do a quick turn at the end of his landing run on the grass runway to avoid the light planes parked there.

It was received by Air-Vice Marshal J.A. Sully on behalf of the Legion, Town, Township and County. A formal ceremony took place with a colour party and a guard of honour. The logbook was presented on a special R.C.A.F. cushion by Monty to W/C C.H. Vinnicombe representing the R.C.A.F., who in turn presented it to A/V/M Sully (retired). He accepted them on behalf of the Goderich Legion 109.

FM213 in front of the colour party.   *- CWHM*

Fl/Lt Don Montgomery, D.F.C. receives the special R.C.A.F. cushion from W/O J.C. Reid, with FM213's logbooks on it for presentation.   *- London Free Press*

FM213 was stored at Sky Harbour for two years while a permanent display area was decided upon. Tours through the aircraft interior were popular at the time and virtually no vandalism occurred during this period. The biggest problem was that of birds in general, but especially starlings demanding a series of ingenious devices to fill up attractive entrance spots, including the exhaust ports.

Eventually sufficient funds ($5,000) became available to move the aircraft to its "final" resting place on land, dedicated by Colborne Township, adjacent to Sky Harbour. Dedication ceremonies were held on September 15, 1968, with both American and Canadian aircraft in attendance, and Major General Chester Hull, D.F.C. as guest speaker. General Hull had served with No.428 "Ghost" Squadron at No.6 R.C.A.F. Group Bomber Command.

"I made sure we mounted her at the jack points to ensure minimal structural damage and stress, so she could be brought down again should we ever have the resources to make her an airborne memorial," he explained, as once more FM213 had been saved by Bill Clancy.

During her years on the pedestals, the twin problems of normal deterioration and vandalism were starting to outdistance the committee's ability to restore and repair her, as the original committee, through retirement, death and moving had been reduced to three people.

At this point Bill Gregg and Murray Smith made contact with Bill Clancy and through fate and chance it proved to be a serendipitous event. Bill later told them that he had begun to despair of ever getting her back in the air, "when you two fellahs came along." With the arrival of this encouraging support, Bill continued to carry the ball until the final transfer to CWHM in 1977.

In 1975 Bill Gregg, with his wife Carol, had taken his three young sons to Goderich to visit a friend of Carol's for the weekend. This friend, Liz Mignotte, lived in an apartment in a beautiful old estate home between the Maitland River Valley and Lake Huron beach. This home was situated on a road which led right past Sky Harbour Airport where the Lancaster FM213 was well tethered on three pylons. After inspecting the grounds and the beach, both father and eldest son logically turned to the subject of the plane, how it got there and who owned it. Liz had fully anticipated the questions and explained that Bill Clancy, a local optometrist who had served in the Air Force and now belonged to the Legion looked after it. Bill then suggested to Liz that she enquire whether it could be made available to a museum capable of flying it.

BILL GREGG AND MURRAY SMITH

Bill Gregg's story of his meeting with Murray Smith is typical of the many introductions of members to CWHM Bill recalls, "Having one of Ernie Simmons' Yale aircraft in our backyard seemed quite logical to me at the time. After all we had a farm, a big yard and three small boys. One glimpse of that silver-painted Yale was enough to draw Murray Smith directly down our driveway."

Following retirement from the R.C.A.F. in the 1960s Murray had stayed as close as possible to his beloved aircraft by joining Air Canada as an aircraft maintenance engineer. He had recently joined the fledgling Canadian Warplane Heritage group in Hamilton and like all good members had joined the search.

"Through Murray's influence I was soon to join CWHM as did the Yale in our yard, along with another I had acquired following the dispersal in 1970 of Ernie Simmons tobacco fields air force in Courtland, Ontario.

"By the next year and our holiday weekend in Goderich, I had become a bona fide member of the CWHM search and rescue team. I reacted to the discovery of FM213 as Murray had to our Yale."

FM213 waiting to be finally placed on pylons.   *- J. McNulty*

The official party at the dedication ceremony after FM213 was up on her pylons. L. to R. Capt. M. Brooks, Brig. F. Clift, Capt. E. Mailloux, J. Maclaren, Dr. H. Chambers, A. Nicholson, C. Krauter, Dr. F. Hatch, Col. E.W. Ryan, Maj. Gen. A.C. Hull, Dr. G.B. Clancy, M. Gaunt, L. Grey.
                                                                                     - CWHM

When Murray and Bill arrived at Sky Harbour to meet Bill Clancy, his frustration showed immediately as he explained, "I sure don't want to part with it but if we don't get more support from the Legion, something's got to happen. They won't even approve $1,500 to paint her, in spite of the fact it's a terrific deal. The community seems to have lost interest and I've tried to maintain her with funds from weekend tours conducted by local air cadets. It's not enough. Time, weather and more recently vandalism are taking their toll."

Bill could sense Murray's concern as they climbed the ladder to the rear door. Once inside, apprehension soon gave way to excitement as Murray yelled back as he scrambled over the main spar, "She's O.K. She still smells right." And right she was. Even the Aldis lamp was still stowed in place. It would seem that discipline exhibited by Goderich air cadets had been far superior to most R.C.A.F. stations. Vandalism, though evident, was external and minimal.

Murray and Bill attended the next regular Thursday night work session at CWHM to talk to Dennis Bradley and the late, and sadly missed, Alan Ness, two of the original directors, and at the time, the two senior executives of the group.

"What would an airworthy Lancaster bomber do for your collection?" Bill asked. Bradley replied, "You're kidding? Boy, wouldn't that do it?"

Alan Ness's usual second sober thought was to support the idea, and this was sustained throughout subsequent negotiations. It even included one Harvard trip to Goderich to "show the flag." Bill says he will never forget their inspection from the air of the Maitland River Valley on the way home.

Murray Smith had already investigated the other Lancaster prospects in eastern Canada and had confirmed FM213 as his top priority. KB839 at C.F.B. Greenwood, Nova Scotia, was of particular sentimental interest to him. This aircraft had been virtually stripped out by souvenir hunters and was in a very sad state. Murray and Bill like to feel that their objections filed with the Base Commander were, in part, responsible for the subsequent static display restoration of "D" Daisy.

The other "KB" series Lancasters last in R.C.A.F. service had been like KB839, modified to an A.R. status, most identifiable by the lengthened nose section. It was known that KB976 had been purchased by the Strathallen Collection from Neil Menzies of St.Albert, Alberta and had been ferried to Scotland by a Caledonian Airlines crew. Murray still preferred an aircraft that had seen active service in Europe, so that left KB882. He found her at St. Jacques, New Brunswick, on the Quebec border, carefully mounted and well protected by fencing. All four propellers still pulled through, but Murray was disturbed to find an upper hatch missing, and the cockpit circuit breaker panel had been removed by chopping through the wiring. The town clerk informed Murray that a Lancaster group from Oshawa had given the aircraft a detailed inspection some time previously. The town did not want to part with the aircraft, but the clerk, true to his word, arranged to have the hatch opening weatherproofed. On most recent inspection, in September 1987, the aircraft was still in good condition.

So it was back to the lowly FM213 manufactured at the cessation of hostilities in 1945, but still a Canadian Mk B.X that had provided years of excellent service in search and rescue out of Torbay, Newfoundland.

Armed with no more than a verbal go-ahead from Bradley and Ness, Murray, Bill and Jim Mulholland arranged with Bill Clancy to meet with the Legion board of directors at Goderich. Jim had served on KB839 over Europe and joined his efforts with theirs on behalf of CWHM The reaction was positive, but within two months the board of directors changed quite significantly and they had to start all over again. At one point they were turned down, but with persistence a final decision was made by the Legion board within the year. FM213 was to be offered to CWHM for $10,000 in cash. The Legion wanted to decrease the mortgage on its new building with the proceeds from this aircraft, which had been donated jointly to it by the town, the township, the county and by the federal government.

According to Bill Gregg's recollection the CWHM board was willing to offer $5,000, but Bill, Murray and Bill Gregg were opposed in principle to paying cash. The impasse was eventually resolved, again mainly through Bill Clancy's efforts. He arranged to have himself appointed as Legion representative in further negotiations, and several foundations were contacted, including the Atkinson Foundation, which was approached by John Hindmarsh of Goderich, another friend and ally of the project. Bill Clancy learned that Air-Vice Marshal Sully, who had officiated at the 1964 FM213 arrival ceremonies at Goderich, had been honoured by his family through the establishment of The Sully Foundation. Bruce Sully, who had replaced his father as president of Dominion Road and Machinery, a major Goderich industry, agreed that it would be most significant to have the first bequest of the foundation designated to the purchase of FM213, and subsequent donation to CWHM

In his following comments Bill Clancy omits divulging that the ultimate, ironic twist was of his creation, as the $10,000 bequest went, not to become a principal payment of the Goderich Legion mortgage, but became principal for high school scholarships in the name of the Legion and A.V.M. Sully.

BRUCE SULLY

It was arranged that Bruce Sully, an aircraft enthusiast who also owned Business Aircraft Services in Goderich, would fly to Toronto for a dinner meeting with Dennis Bradley to get acquainted and formalize proceedings for the donation of FM213 from the Sully Foundation to CWHM. Bill Gregg suspects that Dennis will long remember his first encounter with Bruce Sully's rather expressive and colorful personality at the "airport strip" hotel.

That was it. All that remained was a second formal contact with CWHM brass at the airshow transfer ceremony at Goderich in 1977.

In the meantime Bill Gregg, Murray Smith and Bill Clancy completed their last significant contribution to the project by arranging the lowering of FM213 from the pylons and taking her back across the road to Sky Harbour.

Bill Clancy had indeed done a professional job of bolting the two forward pylons to the main spar and the third to the tail oleo. Virtually no structural damage had been incurred, and since all three mounts were at jack points, stress had been minimal. The job was further simplified by the excellent assistance of Wayne Juniper, Chief Engineer of Business Aviation Services.

In the absence of a large crane, it was decided to try to lower the undercarriage, service the oleos, block up the tires, inflate them and cut off the pylons. It worked. The hydraulic reservoir was still full of fluid so hand pumping opened up the bomb bay doors. Bill will never forget the sound back of the pump when Murray selected gear down. The gear dropped normally and ground locks were deployed from storage.

Wayne (Howdy Doody) Juniper supplied desiccated nitrogen for the oleos and obtained the services of a local welder to cut the pylons. In the middle of the operation, one of the local famous "blows" came in off Lake Huron, but fortunately everyone stayed on the job and down she came to safety.

Bill says he missed what was probably the best part of the operation. Bruce Sully's Champion Road Graders employees filled in the ditches, made a special draw bar, and towed Murray and FM213 across to Sky Harbour with a road grader. After all the years, the pneumatic brakes, always notorious for leaks, held the charge and functioned perfectly in a steering role. It was reported that Murray's glee could be heard through the open cockpit window over the sounds of the diesel grader as FM213 once more arrived on airport tarmac.

With the help of a number of CWHM volunteers, including Walter Schmidt, John Dunn and others, it was soon established that ferrying the aircraft was out of the question. The exhaust ports had been sealed, with good intentions, but this caused all engines to seize and they were subsequently deemed unusable. The airframe, however, showed only minimal corrosion and the long job of preparing the aircraft for airlift was passed on to other willing volunteers.

It is important that full acknowledgement is made of the indispensable role that Bill Clancy played and the kind assistance and hospitality of local friends of the project, such as Wayne Juniper and John Hindmarsh, who both provided money, expertise, equipment and even accommodations. The essential role of Bruce Sully is self-evident. FM213 was never dishonoured by being sold, as Bill Clancy stated so aptly, "to a feather merchant."

RECOVERY BY HELICOPTER

On July 1, 1977, the ownership of FM213 was formally handed over to CWHM in a simple ceremony when Bill Clancy handed over the logbooks to President Dennis Bradley. Bill Gregg also had found the Aldis lamp still in the aircraft, in a drawer and gave it to Ron Page for safekeeping until the CWHM Museum could look after it. It is now in the archives in the safekeeping of Curator Anna Bradford.

Now the logistic problems mounted — how to move it to Mount Hope before any more deterioration could take place. As the engines were not usable, and new ones were not readily available, except at a price CWHM could not afford, it left only two possibilities: take it apart in sub-sections and transport it by road or suitably stripped, airlift it by helicopter.

The project co-ordinator at that time was Eric Grove, a member who spent many hours trying to find a solution to this transportation nightmare. There were no Queen Mary trailers still around in Canada that could be used to transport the fuselage in sections (they had once been used to transport damaged sections from crash sites back to the factories for repair). As the aircraft would probably receive more damage in dismantling and transfer by this method, it was decided to contact the Armed Forces to see if they would do the airlift as a training exercise. They were evidently agreeable after some discussion and correspondence, as long as the aircraft weight was reduced to a bare minimum. Once this was decided, the long process of stripping the aircraft began.

First the four props had to be removed and shipped to Mount Hope, where they were hung on the dividing wall of Hangar No.4. These were taken off as the snow fell during the winter of 1977/78, and this was a cold and thankless task. Each sortie to Goderich required a great deal of organization among volunteer crews, accommodation, tools and equipment, and the transportation of the parts removed back to Mount Hope. The ailerons were removed and stored on the wall of No.4 Hangar with the fabric and trim tabs removed. What happened to the trim tabs is not known, but as the restoration story will tell, they caused a few problems to replace.

Next the engines were removed and transported to Hamilton airport one by one. As only one engine stand was available, temporary ones of wood had to be made to accommodate them.

To convince people that the engines were not usable, Ron Page and Greg Hannah removed one cylinder bank on two of the engines via pressurized oil in two cylinders. Engine cylinder liners and piston rings were rusted together.

Next the rudders and elevators and nonessential equipment inside were removed and

FM213 flying off the Newfoundland coast.   *- CWHM*

The handing over of the log
books of FM213 to Dennis
Bradley the President of
CWHM, 1977.
- CWHM

Removing the propellers and engines in terrible conditions, winter 1977/78.

- CWHM

The Chinook trying a
short-sling lift, which was
abortive, June 1979.

- CWHM

Eric Grove inspecting the insides of the aircraft, the view looking forward.   *- CWHM*

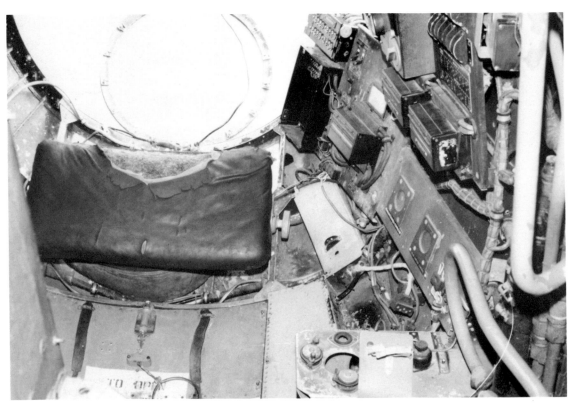

Condition of the bomb-aimer's position.   *- CWHM*

Condition of the aircraft before much equipment was removed for air lift, looking rearwards. *- CWHM*

The hardy crew removing the wings, spring 1979. *- CWHM*

Coming in to land at Mount Hope, after record breaking flight.   *- Hamilton Spectator*

stored at CWHM. The aircraft was covered with tarps to try to prevent any further damage by the weather and curious sightseers.

In the spring of 1979 a major effort was mounted to remove the outer wing sections. This was done with the assistance of some ground crews from the Armed Forces base at Trenton and the kind assistance of John Hindmarsh, who contributed $1,000 to defray some of the cost. This operation turned out to be far more difficult than expected, for the following reasons. The necessary removal of the rusted screws from the panels was time-consuming, and then the large bolts holding the wings together would not move, again close tolerance and corrosion. Finally, thick straps joining the spar were reluctantly cut and the wings lowered for transportation. These wings required a special government permit in order to transport them to Mount Hope.

After the aircraft was weighed and found to be in the range of a helicopter lift, it was made ready for the airlift. Through the kind offices of General A. McKenzie, permission was obtained for the use of a helicopter from No.450 Squadron to lift the Lancaster as a training exercise. In June the great day came. The Armed Forces Boeing Chinook CH-147 helicopter arrived to try its luck at lifting the old Lancaster. The crew of six included Major Ed Booth and Captain Lemieu. The aircraft was slung by three slings to the helicopter and the pilot wound up the engines to maximum power, but other than raising the tail the lift was aborted, as the crew said it was too heavy. The effect of the relatively short slings that were being used was unknown at that time. These slings caused the helicopter to be too close to the fuselage, which produced a negative lift from the twin-rotor downwash and gave the illusion of extra weight.

After reweighing the aircraft, the Armed Forces were convinced to try again but this time with longer, 58ft. slings. Finally, on November 5, 1979, FM213, with the same crew as before, became airborne again, but only with a struggle. It was not until the helicopter was able to get out of the ground effect that the crew became sure they could lift it and fly to Hamilton. There were moments of apprehension as she was moved forward in the air and started to swing under the helicopter, even though she had an air drogue attached to the tail for directional stability. The loadmaster of the helicopter was all set with his thumb on the button ready to drop the load if it presented a danger to the helicopter. Fortunately for everyone concerned she straightened up and flew right, all the way to Hamilton airport. This weight of lift and distance flown set a new world record for this type of helicopter. She was gently landed at Hamilton without mishap after a 1 hour 40 minute ride. That is more than can be said for one member, who took off in a light aircraft to follow and photograph the Lancaster and helicopter, but in the haze lost his way and never did see the aircraft airborne ("Which Way" McMaster).

Now FM213 was stored in the back of Hangar 4, awaiting restoration, like a mournful ugly duckling, sans wings, engines and rudders.

Footnotes:
[1] Cy Dunbar has now requalified to fly the Lancaster, October, 1988.

Forlornly tucked away in a corner awaiting restoration, Merlin engine in fore-
ground.   - CWHM

The original Lancaster, Firefly, Seafire and Lysander crew all dressed up in their Sunday best
for the Royal visit by Prince Philip, summer 1980. L. to R. Dave Hill, Wilf Riddle, Dougie
Atkinson, Jim Gibson, Ron Page, Bill Swift, Jim Miller, Greg Hannah.   - G. Hannah

IV

THE RESTORATION STORY
OF THE LANCASTER 10 MR/MP FM213

THE WAITING PERIOD - 1979-83

CWHM was now the proud owner of a Canadian-built four- engine Lancaster bomber, the biggest aircraft in the museum's collection by far, and the organization was overwhelmed by the prospect of restoring such a large and complicated aircraft. The logistics were myriad. As CWHM is a charitable foundation with limited funds and only voluntary members, the task of restoration seemed impossible. Though various jobs of cleaning and removing minor equipment were done, as well as the cataloguing and storing of the original parts, she was to languish in a forlorn state for a number of years.

In 1980 His Highness Prince Philip visited the Canadian Warplane Museum to review the collection and spoke to the members. At this time a single crew was trying to make progress on both the Lancaster and the Firefly simultaneously. It was one of the few times the crew were all in uniform together. Three of those original team members are still active on the Lancaster today, Greg Hannah, Wilf Riddle and Jim Gibson.

During the two days of the 1981 Hamilton Airshow, the Lancaster was put on display and $700 was collected from some of the 26,000 attendees. This gave all the volunteers enormous encouragement.

But it still required a magic moment before the project was to get off the ground. This miracle consisted of two components, the first was a grant from the federal government, and the second was the timely procurement of a unique and experienced aircraft engineer, Norm Etheridge.

On February 16, 1983, when Norm Etheridge was between jobs, as his previous employer had gone out of the corporate flying business, he was approached by Phil Nelson, the General Manager of Canadian Warplane Heritage Museum at that time. Phil asked him if he would like to take on the job of restoring the Lancaster in Hamilton, and he agreed to think about it. About a week later Norm had another call from Phil urging an answer, as he explained he had acquired the services of four people who were to be employed under a Government Need Grant that Anna Bradford, the curator, had obtained. This grant was worth $104,000. Phil explained that someone was needed to take charge and train the people to do the restoration work on the Lanc. In a moment of weakness Norm agreed to do the job, and that was his first mistake! He travelled to Hamilton the next day to talk to CWHM about the requirements and to see the aircraft. He was astounded to see the condition the plane was in, and realized with much trepidation that what was needed was not a restoration job, but rather a complete rebuilding.

He also learned that he would have no choice of the people he must train. He would have Tim Mols, Wes Reginsky and Caroline Sawyer who had been trained at Centennial College in Toronto in the one-year Aviation course, with Michael Rossadivata and Bill Rothdeusch. The grant conditions were, that the people had to be unemployed and on welfare.

CWHM was not new to Norm, as he had been involved with them when they had purchased their original Fairey Firefly, a naval fighter aircraft, and needed someone to inspect and certify the aircraft as airworthy. This aircraft had been the very first aircraft acquired by the foundation, back in 1972, and Norm's Navy experience had convinced the Department of Transport to give him authority to certify the aircraft.

NORMAN ETHERIDGE

As Norm was the key figure in the Lancaster restoration project, it is only appropriate to describe his background. He attended Stanley Technical School, Norwood, Surrey, 1941-43, and joined the Royal Navy as a Naval Artificer Apprentice in January 1943 at the age of 15.

He served at many Naval and Royal Air Force stations and on aircraft carriers including H.M.S. *Theseus, Vengeance* and *Illustrious*. He serviced many different types of aircraft, from Stringbag Fairey Swordfishes to early jets such as the Supermarine Attackers, de Havilland Vampires, Sea Hawks and Fairey Gannets. He immigrated to Canada after leaving the Navy in 1957.

On his arrival in Canada, he joined Field Kenting Aviation for a two-week period and stayed for 12 years, acting as engineer on their survey aircraft all over North and South America, including Greenland, servicing Boeing B-17, Lockheed Hudson, Douglas A26 Invaders and Lockheed P38 aircraft.

He became Chief Aircraft Engineer for Inco Ltd. on Grumman Gulfstream II and Jet Commander for ten years, worldwide, and then taught school at Seneca College in a two-year aircraft course. He finally rejoined Field Aviation as Chief Inspector in June 1984, the position he still holds today.

So now CWHM had some money to pay for full-time help on the aircraft and a very competent aircraft engineer who could direct and guide the project, and also be able to call upon the rest of the industry for help through "the old boy network." Little did Norm know that it was going to take another five years to complete this massive project, and that he would be giving up every Saturday and a great many of his other hours also during these long years. Anybody in his right mind would have said it was impossible, but with perseverance and the spirit of the members it became possible, in particular by the help and money that swelled up from the grassroots through the indomitable Lanc Support Club.

RESTORATION BEGINS

The work on the Lancaster started on March 24, 1983, but effectively with only four trainees. Working conditions were deplorable. The aircraft, without wings, was located against a hangar wall with very little overhead lighting. Luckily there was a window in the wall which afforded some light. It was mid-winter and the hangar was not heated, but when the sun shone it melted the snow on the roof — and the roof leaked so badly that it rained on the aircraft. In the floor of the hangar was a swamp or sump, into which was placed a sump pump, and this pumped the water from the hangar through a hole in the wall. In this the crew were lucky, as they could have been frozen, died of pneumonia or been electrocuted due to power cords — but they survived.

Their next problem was twofold, as Norm did not know this aircraft (although to him an aircraft is an aircraft, is an aircraft) and he did not know the capabilities of the people whom he had to teach. Therefore, he decided that he would approach the task as a series of small projects instead of looking at the aircraft as one big project and becoming overwhelmed by it.

CWHM is made up of volunteers, and a few of these members had been associated with the aircraft since the time that it was handed over at Goderich. They had been responsible for the dismantling of the aircraft to get it to Hamilton and had removed parts from the aircraft when it was at CWHM. There had been very little if any direction given to the volunteers at the start of the restoration. Now there was an engineer who had overall responsibility and knew exactly what he was doing.

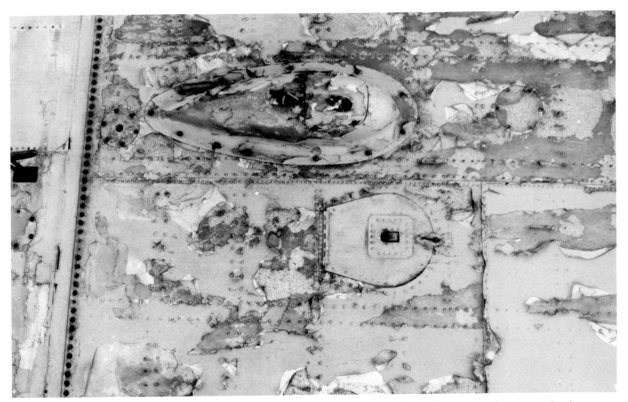

Example of the condition of the wing centre section under surface, the restoration crew had to contend with.   *- CWHM*

The original apprentices with Norm Etheridge.   *- K. Coolen*

During Norm's discussions with management, prior to starting the project, he had made it abundantly clear that the aircraft would be restored only one way, his way, which would be accepted by the Department of Transport and meet his engineering licence requirements. This was not intended to be a show of arrogance, but to have guidelines laid down so that as the project went along there would be no conflict in procedures or the approach to the myriad of problems which would undoubtedly arise. It has worked extremely well, with only a couple of heated discussions.

At the outset of the project, the apprentices made their work week from Tuesday to Saturday to ensure that the permanent staff and the majority of volunteers were working on the same day, each Saturday.

As a general rule Norm made a point of never telling any one of the volunteers that he/she could not work on the aircraft. However he did try to find out if they had any expertise in aircraft maintenance. Usually it was a negative answer, and so it became a situation where he could direct them to where they were able to help in a positive way. Very often the reality of working, cleaning or just performing basic tasks was not quite the image that the volunteers had in mind, and at times enthusiasm quickly waned.

FUSELAGE

Even though some of the larger and more problematic steps are described in detail, a lot of the jobs went on in parallel, depending on the amount and skill of the manpower available, particularly on Saturdays.

One of these jobs was the stripping of all the outside layers of paint on the fuselage and the same on the inside. This took many months of effort. It was a continuous job and thankless for some. But when it was done and the inside was chromated after corrosion prevention, the results were noticeably worthwhile. Many of the jobs described affected the fuselage as well as the individual components. For example, wiring, hydraulics, flying controls and instruments interacted with the fuselage, and the same goes for the engines, their structure and controls.

One large modification to the fuselage was the removal of the post-war radar dome behind the bomb bays, as the original aircraft KB726 VR.A was not fitted with H2S (Home Sweet Home or How Two See), the original blind bombing radar that was fitted on later aircraft. The large hole had to be skinned over and this was done in the later years of the restoration. Also the two observation windows at the back of the aircraft near the tail had to be removed and covered over. New aerials had to be fitted for the modern radio equipment. One of the most challenging jobs was the replacement of the greenhouse, or canopy, of the cockpit (see The Wooden Story) and the replacement of the astrodome and bomb-aimer's window in the nose.

THE UNDERCARRIAGE BEAM

With the aircraft on jacks and the inboard engine mountings removed, the undercarriage beams were exposed for better inspection. The undercarriage beam supports the top pickup for the landing gears at its lower end, and the top and bottom connections to the engine mount structures on the centre and top lugs. During inspection by one of the engineering apprentices, it was noted that there was a fine line across the left-hand outer member just above the lower lug — a crack. Nobody could come up with a satisfactory reason as to how it got there, or how long it had been there, but there it was, and again the project was in trouble.

Different suggestions were made. Find another aircraft and remove that same part and install it in our aircraft! There is a Lanc up north on a gunnery range — get that one and fit it on. Norm had to protest, because if one was found, what would be the chances of

Fuselage stripped and cleaned with aircraft on jacks.   - CWHM

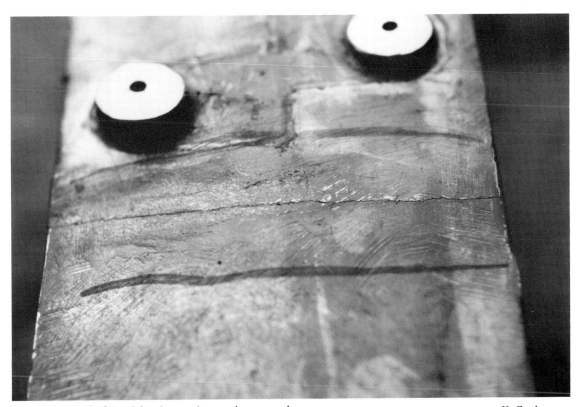

The crack found in the undercarriage casting.   - K. Coolen

Bomb bay roof showing the engine control cable and linkages under restoration, May, 1984.
- R.D. Page

The wooden panels for the electrical junction boxes and flight engineer's instruments.
- C. Sloat

The woodwork of the fairing
for the rear turret.
- *C. Sloat.*

Raising the wing for mating, February 1985.

- *C. Sloat*

all the holes fitting exactly to suit all the positions necessary on this aircraft? Also the cost would be phenomenal.

So the left-hand outer beam was removed and sent to Air Canada in Montreal to see if they could come up with a repair scheme which would allow the project to continue using the same beam, thus solving the problem. However their decision was negative. Rolley Roberge came to offer assistance. He reported that in Montreal there was a foundry that had been used in bygone days to manufacture these same beams. This raised spirits again and the old beam was sent to R. Mitchell Inc. to see what could be done. It was decided that they could remove the old unit, fill in all the holes and, using that as a pattern, cast a new beam. A price was negotiated, in which CWHM would pay only a nominal fee. Everything was under way again, and in August 1984 the unit was cast and sent back to Air Canada.

Once again, however, things were not so straightforward, because the Ministry of Transport, in their role as watchdog of the aircraft industry, asked that CWHM get a certificate of compliance to ensure that the material in the beam was as good, or better, than the original. How could they know what material was used 30 years ago? Luckily there was a machine that could produce a spectra-analysis of the material. A little spot of the material was put into this machine and out came a tape of all the elements in the test piece. There were 15 different elements besides aluminum in the test piece, with 11% concentration of magnesium in it. The new beam was then tested and found to have 14 elements in it besides aluminum, but this time with a high concentration of silicon. The strength of the new piece was 43,255 lbs. per square inch. Fifteen different X-rays were supplied to show the integrity of the beam, and with the certificate of compliance in hand the project was off and running again.

Once the beam was cast, it was in the Air Canada machine shop, that holes were drilled in the new casting, but left a few thousandths of an inch small. Rolley Roberge came to Hamilton with the beam and the holes lined up without any problem, and when he reamed the holes the bolts fitted perfectly — another hurdle successfully cleared. Further machining work had to be done in situ by Greg Hannah to mount the various engine control brackets, and they were done with great precision.

THE HYDRAULIC SYSTEM

When CWHM had the agreement with Air Canada to help with the work, all of the hydraulic components were sent to them. Air Canada managed to carry out work on several units and returned them to CWHM, but it was discovered that many hydraulic seals not of the current style were needed. On the museum's behalf Air Canada investigated means of having new ones made. They informed CWHM of the cost, which was quite high. CWHM tried to get certain other groups who at the time were involved with rebuilding, or who had intended to rebuild a Lancaster, to become involved and share the cost.

This idea fell flat and all the hydraulic units were returned to CWHM. This presented one more problem. It was then realized that it would have to be done by the crew. In this light, Dowty Canada was approached and problems discussed with Barry Fletcher, Production Support Manager. He was extremely sympathetic but explained that what CWHM needed was beyond his area of responsibility. A new approach was needed.

Drawing on Norm's experience, it was decided that it is harder to go up the ladder of responsibility to obtain decisions than it is to start at the top. So the Managing Director of Dowty in England, Sir Robert Hunt, was approached by Norm Etheridge. He discussed in his letter his previous experience with a Hawker Sea Hawk while serving with the Royal Naval Fleet Air Arm. During that time there was a "Dowty representative." It was his job to keep all company systems in first-class condition, which he did very well. Sir Robert was reminded of this, also that the Lancaster hydraulic system was a Dowty system, which it was hoped would have the same support as in previous times. No direct reply was given, but after a period of three weeks a call was received from Barry Fletcher in Ajax. He suggested that Norm must have some influence, as an edict had come from England that Dowty Canada should support the Lancaster cause. Arrangements were made to meet at CWHM and Barry took all the components back to Whitby, plus as many spare units as CWHM had, the requirements being that the units must be overhauled.

The units were all disassembled and inspected according to the current Dowty standards, both nondestructive testing and visual. Once again the problem of seals arose. Barry Fletcher approached the company in England and then there was a long wait. Mr. Tony Thatcher, who by this time was the new Managing Director of Dowty England, was then contacted and told of the previous correspondence with Sir Robert Hunt. A quick reply indicated that the seals were no longer current and tooling would have to be made by them in England to produce the seals. Dowty Canada then came to the rescue and assembled and tested the units.

BOMB DOORS

The bomb doors had to have holes cut into the inside of the door panels for inspection and no corrosion was revealed. However there were a few areas of damage that were found requiring that skins be removed and general repairs made.

When the doors were moved, there was an awful creaking from the bearings, and so the doors were removed. It was found that there were 16 bearings in each door, divided between seven pickup points. Most were floating bearings on a shaft, but the centre bearing pickup was the master which locates the doors; the floating bearing allowed for expansion. All of the bearings were badly corroded and some were actually broken. The hinge bolts were also badly corroded. All of these bearings and hinge bolts had to be renewed.

The bearing support plates inside the bomb bay were also very badly corroded and needed removing. Some had to be remade and all had to be cadmium plated and reinstalled.

The door seal was very badly damaged and none of the crew had any idea what could be done about this. However, one day a visitor by the name of Floyd Hendricks from Epton Industries came by. He was very interested and thought that perhaps he and Epton Industries could help. If a little section of the seal could be sent to him, he said he would see what could be done. A short while afterwards a message came to say that it was possible to make the seal and how much would CWHM need? A quick calculation showed that about 35 feet would look after the doors, but, thinking that the Battle of Britain Memorial Flight (B.B.M.F.) might be able to use some, the length was doubled to 70 feet. Everything went well and the seal arrived and fitted perfectly. Another example of corporate help. Ironically, on a visit to B.B.M.F., Chief Engineer Norm Etheridge found that their bomb doors had a different type of seal. Epton Industries also supplied the project with other rubber seals for undercarriage doors.

After the bomb doors were completed they were incorrectly painted and had to stripped again. Barbara Hoover, a remarkably dedicated and good-natured worker, spent many months on this job, right down to the last speck of paint around each rivet.

THE WOODEN STORY OF FM213 Chuck Sloat

In the spring of 1983 Norm Etheridge approached Chuck Sloat a master cabinetmaker, to enlist his expertise in solving problems with the wooden items that needed replacing on

The Lancaster's massive bomb
bay 34 feet, before restoration.
- *K. Oakes*

Below:
    Bomb bay clean and shiny,
    after many months of
    meticulous cleaning by
    Barbara Hoover.
            - *R.D. Page*

the Lancaster. Chuck had been a part of the Cessna Crane restoration crew for a number of years, replacing and manufacturing many of the wooden parts of the Crane aircraft. His first reaction to the request for his services on the Lancaster was one of disbelief, as he thought (as did many others) that it was an all-metal aircraft.

It may surprise the readers of this book to learn of the amount of wood used in the construction of the Avro Lancaster. Even the veterans who flew the aircraft and serviced it were amazed at the number of wooden components when they toured the restoration project.

THE TAIL TURRET FAIRING

The first job was to replace the tail turret slipstream deflector. This deflector prevents buffeting of the tail turret by the slipstream from the fuselage. There was not much left of it after so many years of exposure to the elements. It is fabric covered over 1/16-inch plywood, with wedge-shaped stiffeners beneath and a large rear former, on which are mounted the rear navigation lights.

The wedges were shaped from Sitka spruce and the two-piece rear former cut out of ½-inch Finnish 12-ply sheeting. These were glued together with M.O.T.-approved epoxy cement and secured to the airframe using brass screws. Holes were drilled in both sides of the former to accommodate the nav light mounting at a later date. When the skin, made of 2-ply plywood 1/32-inch thick, was cut to fit, it was given two coats of spar varnish, with tape over the areas where the wedges would be glued. The skin was then glued to the wedge formers and secured by brass brads.

It took four months of Saturdays to build it and the gluing could only be done when the temperature was above 40 degrees F. When the temperature was only 50-60 degrees, it took up to a week to cure.

Upon completion, the outer surface of the skin was coated with dope-compatible sealer. Eventually it was covered with fabric, then the edges were taped and the entire unit was doped.

ELECTRICAL PANEL

The next job was an odd-shaped 10-foot-long electrical mounting board on the starboard side of the cockpit. All wiring to all points of the aircraft traverse this board, much of it to the flight engineer's panel, which is secured to the fuselage frame and is located just above the board. This mounting board is in five sections, and once the wiring is complete, it is covered by five corresponding metal panels. This was another glue job that was held up because of cold temperatures in the hangar and took almost five months before completion.

WING TIPS

Another unusual wooden component was the two-foot bow between the nav and formation lights in each wing tip. What was left of the original port section was enough to use as a pattern for the two required. Although they were a mirror image of each other, it was somewhat of a challenge, as each had to be shaped to fit the curvature of the wing tip, and also each had to be curved to conform with the airfoil shape of the wing tip. They were made out of solid maple and a large number of screws were required to secure the skin to each bow. This required pre-drilling of the wood before final installation.

OUTBOARD STARBOARD AND PORT ENGINE
REAR NACELLE FAIRINGS STARBOARD

Few people realized that the outboard engine rear nacelles fairing frameworks were constructed out of wood. As shown in the photograph, the structure is six feet long and three feet deep. Many members likened it to a bathtub or canoe but Chuck thought it more resembled a surrealistic sentry box when standing on its forward edge. The original fairing had been constructed in jigs by craftsman employed in furniture and piano factories and had used 1/8-inch plywood reinforced at the edge attachment points with solid wood pieces. To make the job simpler and stronger 5/8-inch mahogany plywood was used.

Chuck had a major problem making the fairing so that the former's position would match the holes in the skin. After a number of tries a solution was found. Using the skin as a jig, the component was slowly moved, starting at the rear and working forward, former by former, with the able help of Wilf Riddle. Much to their surprise it worked and when it was mated up to the engine nacelle it fitted almost perfectly, with only minor adjustments. This one component took eight months to complete (winter 1985/86).

PORT FAIRING

The port fairing was remade after the canopy work and, with the lessons learned on the starboard, was a lot easier. The addition of Bill White's extra hands also made a great difference. The component still took two months to complete.

CANOPY

The canopy was in very poor condition and was made out of wood, metal and perspex. The rear half of the canopy frame work was wood, the front half was formed out of one-inch-diameter stainless steel tubing. The original wood structure was rotten and had collapsed, therefore the original shape was not available to copy, and there were no drawings or jigs, so Chuck had to use ingenuity again. He made the three progressively smaller bows by laminating 1/8-inch Sitka spruce strips, glued with epoxy and clamped around each of the jigs he had built. A week later they were removed from the jigs and planed to the appropriate thickness and then assembled with the stringers. It was at this time he received the help and assistance of a new member, Bill White, who was also a carpenter/cabinetmaker. Together they completed the framework and painted it a flat black. After mating it to the front steel section and mounting both on the fuselage over the cockpit opening, it was impossible to tell which part was wood. In late 1986 the perspex was installed again with the helping hand of Fleet Industries in training the staff to form and fit the material, which is very brittle and difficult to handle well.

ESCAPE HATCHES

There are a number of escape hatches on the aircraft which have wooden frames either covered in perspex (cockpit) or, like the bomb-aimer position, wood framed and metal skinned, similar to the rear door and the mid-upper gunner's hatch just behind the canopy. Bill White did most of the work on the various hatches.

TRIM TABS

The story of the trim tabs and how they were fabricated by Roy Pacey is described in the aileron section.

Assembly of fairing former to its skin. - *C. Sloat*

Starboard outer engine fairing formers and
stringer frame work.   - *C. Sloat*

The rear cockpit canopy framework in early
construction.   - *C. Sloat*

The nearly completed perspex of the cockpit
canopy.   - *C. Sloat*

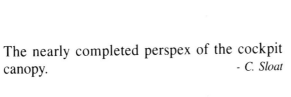

During early restoration, 1984 - Norm Etheridge inspecting the work that Ron Wylie is doing on the outer wing.
- *N. Etheridge*

Wing tanks, wiring and instrument tubing in place or slide on the wing outer section.
- *A.R. Topham*

MISCELLANEOUS

There are a number of other smaller pieces of wood in the aircraft, including leading edge-shaped plugs at the outer ends of the stabilizers.

It was an eye-opener for Chuck and many other members to realize that the Lancaster was not, indeed, an all-metal aircraft!

(The presence of an escape hatch behind the canopy was unknown to wireless operator Jim Kelly and pilot Art de Breyne until they read the draft of this section 44 years. later. Roy Vigars, the flight engineer, remembered, but he had experienced one blow off on take-off in another Lanc!)

THE OUTER WING SECTIONS

The wing tips were removed early in the move from Goderich, and the outer wing panels were moved from place to place at Mount Hope without any work being carried out on them until early 1984. In general terms they were a mess. As with the rest of the aircraft, it was decided to treat it as a whole series of smaller jobs without looking at the outer wing panel as a whole, and each wing panel as a separate entity — but where to start!

WING BOLTS AND SHACKLES

One of the first jobs that had to be done was the removal the remaining bolts still stuck in the starboard spars and the replacement of the cut links or shackles. During the removal of the wings at Goderich, it was necessary to cut two of the spar shackles on the starboard side as four of the bolts were impossible to remove. Some of these bolts were stuck in the centre section spars and some in the outer section. The ones in the wings were relatively easy to work on, but the ones in the centre section were difficult because of the height of the aircraft. Two of the bolts were very stubborn. Both mechanical and hydraulic methods were tried, but to no avail Then a small hole was drilled in the centre of the bolt and slowly increased in diameter to 0.5 inches. This was filled with dry ice and the same methods of applying pressure were tried again. But the bolts still would not move. At this point Air Canada sent Rolley Roberge to Hamilton from the Dorval Maintenance Base at Montreal to see if he could be of assistance with such a stubborn problem. (This was August 16, 1983, and was CWHM's first contact with this remarkable man, who was to be a major player in the solutions to many problems the project ran into over the next five years.)

Rolley spent a couple of days trying the various methods and increasing the hole in the bolts to a larger diameter. But again without success. After Rolley's return to Montreal, the laborious process of increasing the hole diameter was continued. One of the bolts was drilled out with increasing drill sizes until it was a thin shell. With careful heating of the spar stub the remainder of the bolt was driven out. The bolt heads of the last bolt were cut off carefully to minimize the length of drilling. When the hole reached one inch diameter, a hacksaw was used to slit the bolt along its length. At this point the bolt came free.

Now the job was to clean up the holes in the main and rear spars on the outer wings and the centre section. Due to the corrosion over the years of these tight tolerance bolts, all the holes in the spars had to be reamed very carefully and the diameter measured accurately. The serviceable bolts had to be nondestructive tested, rechromed and nickel plated to bring them up to the size of the clean holes. Again Rolley Roberge came to Hamilton airport, December 5 to 8, 1983, to do the reaming and measurements. Air Canada took on the job of making the new bolts and refurbishing the old ones. American threads were used on the new ones allowing standard aircraft nuts to be used. The steel in the bolts had to be analyzed and the strength matched with today's product. Also the shackles that were cut on removal of the wings at Goderich had to be manufactured as mirror images of those on the other side. This difficult operation was again performed through the kind offices of Rolley Roberge of Air Canada, Dorval. The last job in this area was the NDT of the main and rear spar stubs, which were done in situ by an Air Canada Supplies technician using an eddy current technique. This was done on December 23, 1983.

TRAILING EDGES AND FLAPS

The next job attempted as a crew was removal of the inboard trailing edges on both sides of the aircraft. The crew had to instantly learn basic lessons regarding the dismantling of an aircraft. It was necessary to realize the importance of the marking and tagging of every part as it was removed, for each one would later need to be replaced on the aircraft. One problem to be solved was that the trailing edges needed to be attached with hundreds of British B.S.F.(British Standard Fine) Simmonds type-nuts to studs attached to the wing spars. It was known that British nuts and bolts could be exchanged with American hardware, but to replace nuts with British B.S.F.-type lock-nuts would be very difficult, as they are used very seldom now, even in England.

Inspection of the trailing edges brought out a problem that would be found throughout the aircraft and which is prevalent in modern, as well as old aircraft. This is corrosion, and all kinds of corrosion were found. Normal surface corrosion and the more dangerous inter-crystalline corrosion, as well as the most common corrosion, due to bird nests and droppings, which cause a chemical reaction to the aluminum alloys. All these types of corrosion were found. Now the young crew members had to learn to identify the types of corrosion, the correct way to treat surface corrosion and how to cut out and replace material damaged by inter-crystalline corrosion. These initial lessons would pay dividends as the work progressed and the crew were left more and more to their own devices, and with less supervision to allow them to gain more confidence in their own ability.

Having such a diverse crew brought some problems that were new to the original crew. A female aircraft mechanic was one of them. As with all new graduates, the student mechanics were over-confident and it was somewhat difficult to explain to them that at school they had worked on aircraft that would never fly again, whereas now they were working on a real aircraft that would truly fly again. This time NO mistakes could be allowed, as lives would depend on their work.

It took much longer for the volunteers to understand, and as with most volunteers, many of them did not appear on a regular basis. There were however some folks who came out in true colours, and they needed direction into areas where they could work without getting into trouble. This required extreme caution in order not to offend anyone. One regular volunteer loved to drill out rivets and there were many to be drilled. There is a technique to doing this, and though Norm showed him many times how to do it correctly, it didn't make any difference, and consequently when he drilled out a 1/8-inch rivet, it always meant that a larger hole had to be repaired. He apparently liked to drive the drill through the skin. Eventually, and with care, he was directed to projects like cleaning or corrosion treatments, and his drills were somehow spirited away.

As already mentioned, the wing trailing edges were to be removed first, and that job in itself was quite difficult, as it had been attached with B.S.F. nuts to special studs at about three-inch intervals at the top and bottom rear spars. To enable access to these nuts, large areas of skin at the lower side had to be removed either by extracting rusted screws in some areas or pop rivets in others. People like Wilf Riddle still walk around with a slight list after crouching so long under the wings that were on movable trolleys about *three* feet high. Eventually the wings were ready for inspection.

120

The amount of work to be done on the units was extensive. The flap control tubes and also the aileron control rods and cables that run through the trailing edges had to be removed. It was decided, with so much to do and very little space or tooling available, that it would be better to send them to Air Canada for rework. The usual scourge of aluminum corrosion was evident and had to be treated, but cracks and other damage had to be repaired. Many feet of gang channel anchor nuts had to be changed because over the years the locking devices in the nuts had deteriorated, and they also were of B.S.F. or B.A. threads. These were all changed to North American style. An extra-long truck was required for the transportation of the trailing edges because of their length and height when standing on the spars.

The job was completed very satisfactorily, and it was returned later that year. However one small but amusing piece of information came to light, as along the trailing edge areas there were several holes in each wing section. A report came back from Air Canada that the 0.5 calibre bullet holes had been repaired. Now who were CWHM to disillusion them? But the real truth was much less romantic. During its life on the pedestal in Goderich the flaps had drooped, and to prevent vandalism and attempt to keep out the birds, the flaps had been pushed back to the housed position and large bolts and wire had been pushed through them to hold them up. The crew, themselves, repaired the other "bullet" holes in the flaps.

The interior of the wing was another challenge. Fuel tanks #2 and #3 had to be removed, and to gain access to them it was necessary to extract hundreds of rusted screws to remove wing panel skins. The tanks are held in place in cradles and these were secured by steel bands. All the flexible fuel hoses were rotted through and these had to be removed carefully to retain identifiable lengths. The tanks were then easily removed by detaching turnbuckle clamps. It was also surprising to find that some of the steel bands had corroded enough that they had to be replaced, and therefore the steel pins also had to be checked for corrosion. The fuel bays were remarkably clean, and it was easy to treat and re-apply zinc chromate paint.

Between the two tank cavities was a harder area to address. This was where the outboard engine sub-frame attaches. But it was still necessary to inspect and re-apply corrosive protector. Outboard of the #3 tank it was necessary to remove some small skin panels to be able to get into the wing for inspection and application of corrosion protection. While all the panels were open, another problem had to be attended to. During removal of the wing tips and trailing edges, quite a few of the special studs had broken, and of course new replacement studs were not available. New ones had to be made, and these were made with American-style threads and cadmium plated for protection. The position of these studs had to be identified to ensure that the correct style of nut would be used when installation occurred at a much later date. Whichever section was being inspected and treated, the condition of the spars was of prime importance. All repairs of a minor nature would be made in accordance with the normal repair manuals.

The leading edge sections of the wing are in two definite areas, firstly outboard of the engine position and secondly between the outboard engine and the wing joint.

It was decided very early in the restoration to remove all the wing anti-icing systems, and so all of the lines and valves inside the wing leading edges were removed and disposed of. However, it left a problem of hundreds of rivnuts along the wing skins that used to house the rubber de-icer boots. Some of these had been ripped out before the aircraft arrived at Mount Hope, and this process had left large holes. Each one had to be repaired individually, but quite a few were fixed by just installing soft countersunk rivets. Other repairs had to be of the patch variety. Inboard of the engines again meant panels being removed to allow access. In here many pipes, hoses and cables were installed to transmit information and services from the outboard engines. These were clamped to

The large hydraulic jack that operates the flaps.   - *A.R. Topham*

The restored flaps, with their repaired bullet holes?   - *A.R. Topham*

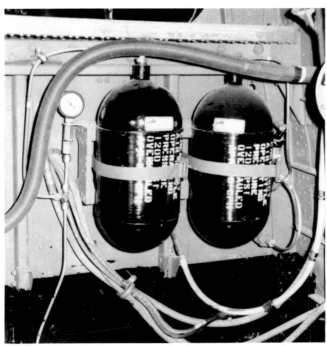
Emergency air bottles for the hydraulics, which were used on the second flight, when the hydraulics failed.
- A.R. Topham

The progress on the cockpit area by June 1987.
- A.R. Topham

brackets inside the wing, and the whole package was removed as one and installed on a bench. It was decided, because of inaccessibility after reinstallation, that every hose, tube and wire would be replaced. It was comparatively easy to do this on the bench, but in the case of the small tubes it wasn't possible to identify the service until it was replaced into the wing. The electrical wires were much easier and they all had new identification numbers installed as per the wiring diagrams. Before all this material could be replaced, considerable cleaning, corrosion removal and reprotection had to be carried out because the exhaust gases from the outboard engines had made their way into the leading edges during years of use in Air Rescue Service.

RUDDERS AND ELEVATORS

Among the very important items that needed careful inspection and repair were the control appendages. During March 1984 the tailplane was removed, inspected, repaired and reinstalled. During late 1983 and early 1984 the rudders and fins were inspected and found to require extensive repairs to the rudder spars, which had to be approved by D.O.T. New spars were installed on the rudders, which were then painted inside and out, and after balancing were hung on the aircraft during December 1984.

All the work on the wings, trailing edges and flaps came together when they were hung on the aircraft with D.O.T. inspection during April-May 1985. With the placement of the engine mounts on the wings and partially completed front turret and canopy, and the addition of the wingtips, the ugly duckling started to look like an aircraft again. All it needed was engines. These would be mounted in the succeeding years. It was displayed in this condition at the 1985 Hamilton Airshow and produced a focal point for the Lanc Support Club, invoking a great deal of interest with the resultant supporting contributions. Its large wingspan (102 ft.) provided excellent shade for the many spectators.

AILERONS AND AILERON TABS

During the period of disassembly for delivery to Hamilton, the ailerons were removed, stripped of all fabric, and the frames hung on a wall. But what happened to the aileron trim tabs? There are two on each aileron, one a balance tab and one a regular tab. Also, what happened to the control rods? The crew were in a bad situation because little was now known of the method of their construction. The description in the manual states, "It is made up of a spruce framework completely covered by three ply, and attached by a piano type hinge."

Chuck Sloat, a member of CWHM, was on vacation in Calgary, and as taking photographs of aircraft and Lancs in particular, was the norm for Chuck, he took a photograph of the Lancaster on display. In the photo the aileron trim tabs were shown to be hanging on their control rods in a completely dilapidated state. The situation was discussed with Calgary and an agreement was reached that, if they would ship what remained of their trim tabs, sets of solid trim tabs would in turn be made to put on their aircraft for show purposes.

A box was received which contained what were pieces of rotten wood. However one tab had the length and shape of the spar and a couple of small ribs, but impressions of the spar provided the number of ribs needed and the angles of the ribs to the spar. It even showed the size of the gussets used. The other tab was similarly in pieces, but also had about a foot of the plywood covering left. That gave the requirements of covering thickness and even a few brass nails to show how the plywood was attached to the ribs and spars.

Here was all the information needed. There was Sitka spruce left over from the canopy frame manufacture, and thin Finnish aircraft plywood was purchased.

Raising the wing for mating, February 1985.

- A.R. Topham

With the information and materials, Ray Pacey was asked to make two sets of tabs, one of which was to be a mirror image of the other. When they were made, and of course protected with varnish, they had piano hinges fitted to them and were covered with fabric, just like the book described. Thanks to the Calgary group's co-operation, both parties were well satisfied.

Both ailerons needed minor metal repairs and, of course, new bearings to prepare them for covering. The members of the permanent staff Tim Mols, and Wes Raginsky, knew little of fabric work, but with the help of Cam Harrod they soon learned to do a first-class job. The material used was synthetic Lincoln cloth, which requires a different method of application than the old-fashioned cotton fabric. It wasn't long before the job was under way. One difficulty encountered was that the fabric was secured by metal sealing strips, each one fitting only at its specific location, and there were 60 individual strips on each aileron. Each of these had to be identified for position and numbered before the covering was installed and they lost sight of the rivet holes. A tedious job but time well spent.

The coverings were completed and balancing carried out. When the ailerons were hung on the wings, the trim tabs were fitted and the wings were now essentially complete.

RESTORATION OF THE FRAZER-NASH GUN TURRETS by Jim Buckel

The Lancaster was usually fitted with three hydraulically-operated gun turrets: one in the nose,and the others in the mid-upper and tail positions. Early Lancs also had a ventral (belly) turret, but this was later replaced by H2S ground-mapping radar. There were many variations of armament on Lancaster aircraft, but the three Frazer-Nash turrets were the most common wartime installation. The Mynarski Memorial Lancaster will be equipped with three turrets, although it will be some time before the mid-upper turret will be finished.

The major problem in restoring the turrets was in being able to work with the British nuts and bolts. The Canadian-built Lancasters utilized American bolt sizes and threads, but the gun turrets were made in Britain and used the British sizes and threads of the time. These were also used in the Merlin engines. The British no longer use these sizes, which created the difficult task of finding wrenches and sockets that fit the British bolts. This problem was easily solved by borrowing wrenches from the people working on the engines.

The special British wrenches were needed mainly for taking the turrets apart, which involved considerable time and patience. The hydraulic parts were the first to be removed, as they would not be reinstalled due to a Ministry of Transport decision that the turrets would not be allowed to move while the Lanc is in flight. The reason is that the movement of the turrets disturbs the airflow over the aircraft. After all the parts were removed from the frame of the nose turret, it was paint-stripped, cleaned and repainted. In special cases parts were repaired or replaced. Then assembly started. During assembly British-tapped holes were retapped to take American bolts, and clearance holes were drilled to take slightly larger American bolts. One problem during assembly was that of the British-threaded studs which could not be changed, so the British nuts were used again.

While work on the nose turret was progressing, the perspex was being cleaned and polished. In good condition except for dirt and a few scratches, the perspex had not yellowed or cracked. It was polished with very fine emery cloth. When assembly of the turret was finished, the framing which supports the perspex was bolted to the turret. The reassembled turret was checked and then installed in the Lanc.

Attention was then turned to the partially completed Frazer-Nash tail turret. It had been started, but the person working on it had left to work on another aircraft. Since

The ugly duckling sees the light of day with her restored fuselage, wings and tail and starts to look like an aircraft again, May 1985.
                                                                    - C. Sloat

The original condition of the rear turret when FM213 was still on its pylons.
                                    - CWHM

Front turret complete except for guns.
                                    - A.R. Topham

nobody had worked on the tail turret for some time, a lot of the parts had been scattered around the hangar, requiring a lot of time and frustration to find them all. Most of the parts were small, as the main structure had already been restored, so progress appeared slow. A few parts had to be made, such as a floor, a spent casings chute, and a fairing at the bottom of the perspex which covers the bolts that fasten the turret to the airframe. The old perspex had cracked and yellowed during its exposure to the elements, and as a result all of the perspex in the tail turret needed to be replaced with new material. As well as preventing the turrets from rotating, the elevation of the guns had to be fixed. Some of the parts which were designed to slide when the guns elevate were missing, so new ones had to be made. It was decided to change the parts slightly and bolt them in position to prevent the guns from moving.

While the perspex was being shaped for the tail turret in Fort Erie, work was started on the mid-upper turret. The first task was to build a stand for mounting the turret while it was being worked on. The armoured "skirt" was then removed and will not be replaced because it blocks passage along the fuselage. The skirt protects the gunner's legs and prevents him from kicking anyone (especially the belly gunner in early Lancs). Next was the very important gun travel interrupter mechanism, which prevents the gunner from shooting off the tail, wings and canopy. The operating levers, which follow a track on the top of the large fairing which surrounds the turret, had broken off and eventually replacements will have to be made. The operating shaft was still intact, but it had to be removed to allow access to the gun cradles. Considerable time was spent trying to remove it with the least amount of damage to the shaft. Once it was removed, the gun cradles were removed. The tail turret returned from Fort Erie and attention was turned to its completion. Much work is needed to complete the mid-upper turret, especially the frame for the perspex, which is twisted and cracked, and all the perspex needs to be replaced.

When work commenced on the tail turret again, serious consideration was given to the problem of finding guns for the Lanc. Eight Browning 0.303″ machine guns were needed: two each in the nose and mid-upper, and four in the tail turret. When the B-25 Mitchell was restored, Heinz Hormann made the Browning 0.50″ machine guns for it and he volunteered his time to make the eight guns for the Lanc. A real Browning 0.303″ was found and used as a pattern to make the eight dummy guns. Once the guns were made they were assembled and test fitted. Fitting perfectly, they were removed for painting. The guns were installed in the nose and tail turrets while work continued on the tail turret to complete it for the first flight of the Lanc.

ENGINES, PROPELLERS AND FIRE SUPPRESSION SYSTEM Gil J. Hunt

When all the engines had been brought to Mount Hope, it was realized that all FM213 engines were frozen. This was quickly recognized when two of the banks of cylinders had to be pressurized with oil to remove them, as the piston rings had rusted to the steel liners of the cylinder walls. Thus, to get the aircraft airborne again, it was necessary to get four zero-time overhauled Packard Merlin 224s. The hunt for Packard Merlins began even before the major restoration started in 1983. A number were acquired from various sources. The most productive was the donation of two 224s still in their protective transport cans, in excellent condition but time expired. These came with the powerful Orenda Iroquois jet engine, complete with its afterburner, which was developed for the Avro Arrow program and appears to be the engine used in the B-47 flight test, for it still had all its flight-test instrumentation on it. Also in this package were two J-75 jet engines which powered the first five Arrow aircraft, before the program was cancelled in 1959.

CWHM had four old York engines which had been salvaged and donated from a

The Lancaster slowly emerges like a butterfly, at the June 1986 airshow, with one engine and prop installed.   - R.D. Page

Jim Buckel admiring his handiwork of the nearly completed rear turret.   - CWHM

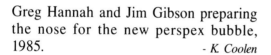

The basket case in which the Frazer Nash
FN50 mid-upper turret was received. - *CWHM*

Greg Hannah and Jim Gibson preparing
the nose for the new perspex bubble,
1985.
                                    - *K. Coolen*

The new front turret and nose cone.   - *K. Oakes*

crash site in the Canadian Arctic, and a number of others were gathering dust in the old fire-hall storage area.

Early in the protracted period prior to Norm Etheridge coming on the scene, Phil Nelson had recruited Gil Hunt to join the organization as a member. Gil was with Orenda Engines as Chief of Vendor Quality Assurance, having considerable experience in overhaul of Rolls Royce engines, and he knew a number of people in the aviation community. It is important to give Phil Nelson a great deal of credit in the early days, and up to the time of his leaving CWHM, for his support and help in getting things done for the Lancaster. He and Gil Hunt had many discussions concerning the technical problems associated with its eventual flight and meetings with Air Canada personnel. They also discussed the possibility of flying the aircraft in conjunction with the 40th anniversary of the T.C.A. flight of the Lancastrians.

Thus, with Jim Gibson, who also had Rolls Royce and de Havilland engine experience, Doug Atkinson, an ex-R.A.F. flight engineer, and Greg Hannah, a very experienced machinist, a capable engine team was formed.

The initial response to enquiries re overhaul of Merlins from Air Canada or Rolls Royce U.K. and Montreal was not encouraging, as none of those companies had the capability at this time to overhaul such ancient artifacts.

There had been sporadic attempts to get Lancaster KB889 at Oshawa Airport airworthy. However it was learned via the grapevine that Doug Arnold, a wealthy British antique aircraft collector, was negotiating to purchase it. It was believed that the engines were low time and had been rotated at intervals over the years. It was agreed with Doug Arnold in writing that CWHM could have the engines in exchange for their good offices in assisting Mr. Arnold to obtain the necessary export permit for the aircraft. He did not need the engines, as he was going to fit Merlin Mk 500s, which he had obtained from Spain, rather than the Packard Merlins, when he restored the Lancaster in England.

Permission to remove the engines as agreed had been slow in coming from England, so Gil Hunt took a trip to Oshawa and discovered that the aircraft was being rapidly dismantled and crated on Mr. Arnold's instructions. CWHM was put in a quandary, because if they let the aircraft go with the engines, they would have little jurisdiction over them once they were out of the country.

The only course was to inform the Canadian government and elicit the good offices of the Canadian Aeronautical Preservation Association to have the export permit withdrawn until the engine problem was resolved. The outcome of all this was that Doug Arnold was fined $4,000 for attempting to illegally export the ex-R.C.A.F. Lancaster KB889 from Canada, as he had failed to honour the agreement made with CWHM and C.A.P.A. This agreement stated that the aircraft could be exported if its four Merlin engines were turned over to CWHM, but because Mr. Arnold had decided to take the engines to England first, his export permit was withdrawn until the problem could be resolved between all parties. This was done with a full legal document and the aircraft was released when the engines arrived at Mount Hope.

When the engines were received, it was discovered that their condition and running time was not as good as had been thought. As the Department of Transport required CWHM to have the engines completely overhauled by a certified shop, the search began for a good overhaul shop that could take on the project with minimum cost. Most of the major engine shops in the United States are located on the West Coast and would make for prohibitive transportation costs.

Fortunately CWHM came in contact with JRS Enterprises located in Minneapolis, Minnesota, owned and operated by J.R. Sandberg. Sandberg was interested in the project and agreed to help by overhauling four engines and a spare in return for the use of all the engines CWHM had collected, plus a certain amount of money to cover costs. This was a

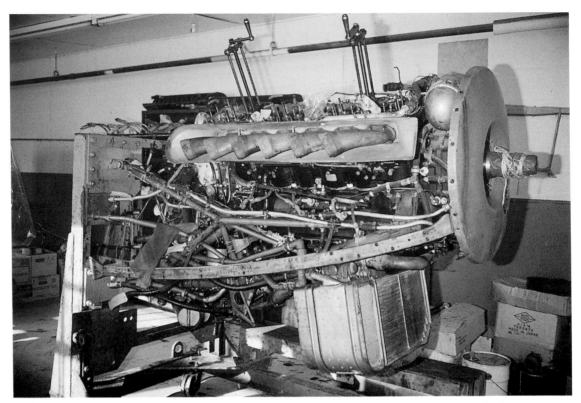

Original engine of FM213 with bank pullers on it, to remove the frozen cylinders.
- R.S. Hoover, CWHM

Lancaster KB889 at Oshawa being dis-assembled for shipment to U.K. for Doug Arnold. CWHM received the four Merlins from this aircraft. *- CWHM*

very generous offer and was immediately accepted. Now the bird had the promise of four rubber bands that would really work.

After the initial batch of engines were shipped to JRS in 1983, attention was turned to other items associated with the engine installation. The first item was the engine mounts or bearers, which had to be stripped down, X-rayed and crack tested at the Air Canada facility at Malton. They would then be repainted and built-up ready for the engines and installation on the aircraft. Other items were oil tanks, oil and coolant radiators, and associated valves which had to be cleaned, tested and overhauled at an approved facility.

There was also a multitude of accessories and engine instruments, consisting of electric starters, generators, air compressors, fuel pumps, vacuum pumps, hydraulic pumps and various actuators. These all had to be overhauled, tested and approved for service, again by certified facilities. Fortunately most of this work was donated by the various companies as their interest in the Lancaster project. This was a major help in keeping the expenditures flow down, as with such a large project funds were extremely limited.

All this occurred during the period 1984 to early 1986. The question everybody kept asking was when would the first engine arrive? The first engine test run of SNO 345052 occurred on April 14, 1986. Thus the big question was answered one day in early May 1986, when a blue engine container arrived from JRS. There was much jubilation as the bolts were removed, the lid was lifted, and there to everybody's delight was a gleaming black-painted Rolls Royce Packard Merlin 224 in all its glory. Many photographs were taken of the event and the people involved. It was decided that every effort should be made to have the engine mounted on the aircraft for the Hamilton Airshow in June.

It then became a logistics race to get the engine to Air Canada, mounted and fitted with its ancillaries and back to Mount Hope on the aircraft. With the help of Air Canada and the dedicated work of Gil Hunt, Jim Gibson, Wes Raginski, John Cummins and Tim Mols, the seemingly impossible was accomplished. The learning curve of handling and fitting a Merlin engine after so many years (35-40) was an experience that both old and new engineers alike enjoyed. The engine was offered up to the No.3 position (inner-starboard) and a propeller was temporarily installed to make it look more complete for the airshow.

From 1986 to the present, the people actively engaged as engine crew have increased in number and, under the supervision of Jim Gibson and Gil Hunt, now include Harry Huffman, John Cummins, Norm Carson, Al Dunphy, Tim Mols and Wes Raginski. Electricians include Karl Coolen, Fred Lowe, and Don Pendergast, assisted by Wilf Riddle. Machinists are Greg Hannah and Bill Striowski, while cowlings have been looked after by Carl Haycock and his crew, and many others who stripped paint and cleaned parts, a much valued and tedious part of the restoration process which took more than 2½ years.

After the airshow, where the aircraft was a popular item on display and encouraged new supporters to enrol and make contributions to the Lancaster project, the propeller was removed and the large job of fitting coolant and oil lines, throttle, mixture and pitch control system cables and chains, sprockets, etc., began. The initial trials of fitting the cowlings could then commence. The second engine SNO V344519, was test run on January 19, 1987, and the test was witnessed by Jim Gibson, who got through a snowstorm to be there.

As JRS was expending 800 man-hours per engine with two people working on them, the tempo of engine deliveries would be maintained. The No.2 engine was delivered in late February. It was prepared for installation at Mount Hope by Tim Mols, Wes Raginski and volunteers, rather than at Air Canada's facilities, to ease the transportation logistics and allow the engineers to qualify for their future M.O.T. approval. The No.2 engine was

First overhauled Packard Merlin 224 engine arrives at Mount Hope, April 1987. Some of the volunteers who were involved with Lancasters. L. to R. Roy Freckleton, navigator; Bill Randall, pilot; George Sobering, pilot; Don Montgomery, last pilot to fly FM213; Richard Banigan and Russ Morefield, who flew FM213 at Torbay; Stu Brickenden, pilot; Karl Coolen, electrician.
- K. Coolen.

First engine fully equipped being hung on the aircraft.
- A.R. Topham

First engine mounted on aircraft with propeller and spinner.　　　　- *K. Oakes*

Second engine on aircraft, port-inner.　　　　- *K. Oakes*

Nearly finished hinged leading edge for the position between the fuselage and the inner engines.

- K. Oakes

FM213 with two engines mounted and canopy perspex not complete, June 1987.

- CWHM

installed on the aircraft in the No.2 position, port-inner, during April. Again for the airshow in June, the two engines were rigged with propellers and spinners, and the other two engine mounts were hung temporarily with some cowling in place.

In the spring JRS indicated that there was a shortage of serviceable major engine parts, such as cylinder banks and heads, out of all the engines CWHM had sent them. The problem was where to find some more serviceable Packard Merlins quickly. Fortunately Terry Bannerman came to the rescue by making CWHM's plight known to Canadian Armed Forces base Greenwood, which had a Lancaster KB839 (it saw service with No.419 Squadron at Middleton St.George from January to June, 1945) on display as a "Gate Guardian." An agreement was struck with the base commander that CWHM could have all the parts they had removed from the aircraft and the engines as long as CWHM provided a means of hanging the props and exhaust stacks from false engine mounts, so the aircraft would still look complete.

On May 16 a crew consisting of Tim Mols, Wes Raginski and Jim Gibson left for Greenwood to remove the engines and install exhaust stacks and props on dummy engine shafts. They returned ten days later after a very successful trip, thanks to the co-operation of Canadian Forces base personnel. The four engines on wooden stands fabricated by Bill White and the numerous large boxes full of Lancaster parts and equipment arrived later, courtesy of the Armed Forces. After inspection by Sandberg the engines were shipped to Minneapolis.

So the total number of Merlin engines collected and shipped were 22:

4 original engines off FM213 - frozen
3 York engines brought in from a crash site in the Arctic
4 Greenwood Merlins taken off aircraft KB839 on display at base
2 Packard Merlins in cans from Moncton, which came with Orenda Iroquois and two J-75s jet from the Avro Arrow program
2 Merlins stored in firehall
1 Merlin painted for demonstration on a stand
1 tank engine - Oshawa
1 converted for marine use - Oshawa
4 from Oshawa Lanc KB889 from Doug Arnold

The third engine, SNO V346178, was test run on August 11 and was witnessed by Jim Gibson. By September the third engine arrived at Mount Hope and was placed on its mount and installed in No.4 position, starboard outer. By the end of the year it was possible to believe that Lancaster FM213 would once again have four rubber bands to turn its propellers.

Art de Breyne, the pilot of the original Lancaster KB726, arranged for all the exhaust stacks (48) to be repaired or remade where the damage and corrosion was too extensive to be repaired. This was done at the company which he previously owned EZFLOW, a stainless steel pipe component facility.

A major milestone was achieved in the Lancaster restoration project when the fourth engine arrived on February 5. The engine was placed on its mount in March and hung in No.1 position, port outer. Now the myriad of detailed installation of equipment and controls could be done for all engines, and the excitement of a possible first flight in 1988 was starting to mount.

PROPELLERS

The propellers were shipped to Western Propeller (Atlantic) Ltd. for overhaul and inspection. They were in relatively good condition and were returned at no cost without

Rear of No.3 Firewall showing the complexity of equipment that had to be restored and fitted, March 1987.
- *A.R. Topham*

Port-outer engine nacelle, with engine mount and radiator, April 1987. - *K. Oakes*

Three engines on and perspex covered, port outer engine mount and cowlings fitted. - *R.D. Page*

The nearly completed aircraft with all engines on, in time for the June Airshow, 1988.
- *N. Etheridge*

any major problem, and painted with their decals. This was a very generous donation as this company also balanced the spinners.

THE FIRE DETECTION AND SUPPRESSION SYSTEM

The aircraft as CWHM received it had most of the old aircraft systems in it, but all of the fire bottles were missing and all of the fire-detection heads were badly corroded.

In 1985 Norm Etheridge was told by Jim Thompson of C.F.H.Industries in Montreal that his company would like to assist in the project. However he was leaving to join another company and René Gagnon would be taking his position. There were several discussions and René wrote to Graviner on behalf of CWHM to see if they had any original equipment that could be made available to install on this aircraft. Unfortunately they did not, so the requirements had to be rethought. Graviner and G.L. suggested that a modern type of fire extinguisher bottle could be used, a Graviner P.No.89A. The problem, of course, was that there were no bottles that could be used, and eight of them were needed.

The problem was solved rather ironically. The Canadian Warplanes Heritage Museum was due to have its annual airshow on Saturday, June 21, 1986, and one of the participants was to be a Royal Air Force Handley Page Victor aircraft. This aircraft arrived on Wednesday, June 18, but unfortunately it was severely damaged on landing at Hamilton airport. The aircraft was broken up after the accident and the fire bottles that had all been activated on impact had been thrown aside. There were seven bottles that were suitable for the requirements. They were sent to C.F.H. for overhaul and the eighth bottle was also supplied by them. The old type of bottles were bromide-filled, but the new bottles were filled with Halon 1200.

Because of the difference in the style of the firing head, the bottle would no longer fit into the support brackets. Again it meant that changes were necessary. René Gagnon supplied a bracket that fitted the new style bottle, and it was comparatively easy to make new support ends, similar to the pattern, to fit on all the original mounts.

The overhaul of a fire bottle was very expensive. The cost of the firing bracket alone was $350. Of course C.F.H. could not absorb the whole cost of the overhaul of the units, but René Gagnon was very generous in his donation. Once the bottles were mounted, the aircraft wiring was not connected to the firing cartridges until assurances were made that the wiring had been checked and rechecked. During regular maintenance each bottle was disconnected just to be on the safe side.

A new fire-detection system was installed, consisting of helium-filled detector tubes which if exposed to an increase in pressure from heat would activate the fire bottle cartridge and which had a fail-safe switch if they sprang a leak. Systron Donner of California supplied the detector system through C.F.H., which is now called CASP (Aerospace) Inc.

UNDERCARRIAGE

This part of the aircraft gave more trouble than any other portion of the project.

In the early days of the restoration all the landing gear was removed and sent to Air Canada for overhaul, on the assumption that the aircraft would be using Lancaster tires and brakes. But only the drag link mechanism could be overhauled and certified for service. When the oleo legs were disassembled and reassembled, it was discovered that the oleo seals were no good, due to internal leakage, and Air Canada had no solution to the problem.

About that time the condition of the original tires gave major concern, as they were not fit for service. They were built with rayon cords and Dunlop was approached to discuss the problem. CWHM was told that a tire with rayon cords would only have a life expectancy of ten years. We were 20 years over the limit and there were no more Lancaster tires available nor were there moulds still available, as production had ceased many decades ago.

While a new source of supply was being investigated, temporary oleo legs acquired from another source were installed to allow the normal movement of the aircraft, with the original Lancaster brakes and tires.

The only tires that would be available to fit the aircraft were the Avro Lincoln bomber type, which meant that Lincoln oleo legs, brakes and wheel assemblies would be needed. This same assembly was fitted to the Avro Shackleton, which was a development of the Lincoln for maritime reconnaissance.

Fortunately the R.A.F. was extending the life of the Shackletons in service while they resolved the replacement of their AWAC aircraft. Thus they had ordered a new production batch of tires for the Shackletons from Dunlop Division in Birmingham, England. CWHM was able to obtain six sets of brand-new tires from this source and they were shipped over by air in March 1988.

Now that the tire problem was solved, the search started for a suitable set of Lincoln oleos, brake and wheel assemblies. Doug Arnold, who had obtained the Oshawa Lancaster, had a set in England that CWHM could purchase.

Before purchasing these it was necessary to inspect them, and this required Norm to go to England. Unfortunately it was not possible to do a 100% inspection, as the assemblies were all covered in a red-coloured protective coating. However they looked reasonable, and with the proper overhaul procedure seemed usable.

After settling accounts with Doug Arnold in U.S. currency Norm was able to enlist the help of his cousins Pauline and Jim Simpson, who were also Lanc Support Club members. They arranged and paid for the transportation of the assemblies from Bitterswell to Brize Norton, an R.A.F. station. Terry Bannerman, the general co-ordinator and trouble-shooter for the project, made arrangements with the Canadian Armed Forces to pick up the gear with the normal Hercules aircraft at Trenton, which flies the transatlantic route to Germany via England. The last leg of the journey was by truck from Trenton.

On receipt of the oleos and wheel assemblies, it was back to Air Canada, who were asked to try again. Rolley Roberge was sent from Montreal to inspect them and reported back to his base in Dorval, where it was decided to go ahead. The parts were cleaned of their protective gunk. However, Air Canada would not go ahead and start the overhaul until they had new seals in hand, as they did not want the parts lying around awaiting delivery of seals. So a frantic search started worldwide to find a source. Even Dowty, the original landing gear manufacturer, could not help CWHM. But a local seal manufacturer, Thompson Gordon, came to the rescue and made a set of seals suitable for the job. The company was also a member of the Lanc Support Club. With the oleo leg and wheel assemblies were a set of tires, which appeared to be in good condition. Attempts were made to have these inspected and certified as spares. Air Canada was not able to inspect them, but Air Treads of Kingston thought they could. Unfortunately the tires were far too big for their machines. It was at this time that Dunlop and the R.A.F. came to the rescue with a new production batch.

Meanwhile, the Lanc project group found that one of the brake housings was badly corroded and had a broken flange, the others were marginal but acceptable. There were four in all, two for each wheel. So it was back to CWHM's friend and supporter Robert Mitchell in Montreal, who had cast the undercarriage support beam. A wooden mould of the housing was made and successful castings completed, much to their credit of a "One Off" item.

The brake pads were badly worn and the shoes had to be replaced with new ones,

141

The final Lincoln undercarriage and wheel assembly.

- R.D. Page

Greg Hannah, with Don Schofield, filing the new Lincoln
brake housing casting for brake shoe assembly.   *- R.D. Page*

which were provided by a CWHM member from a company specializing in brakes. Of the four brake drums, one was u/s and the others had normal service heat cracks which were acceptable. A replacement for the unserviceable one was required, and the worldwide network turned up some in South Africa. After many phone calls, significant money transfer and suitable air shipment, the drums arrived. But they were Lancaster type, not Lincoln, which are a number of inches in diameter bigger. After recovering from this setback, the Lanc project had an unexpected boost from England. Mr. Church and Dick Richardson, who were also restoring a Lancaster (ex-Strathallen) which had been badly damaged by the collapse of their hangar agreed to give us two Lincoln brake drums — a very kind offer.

So with new inner tubes and brake shoe bladders from B.B.M.F., and with the bronze separators which were manufactured locally by George Sobering, the Lancaster now had a new set of legs to walk on. In the meantime, so as not to hold up the project, the initial engine run-ups were done on the original Lancaster tires and assemblies.

Norm Etheridge receiving a cheque on behalf of the Lanc Support Club, from R.C.A.F. A No.447 Wing, surrounded by a good group of the hardworking volunteers.   - *N. Etheridge*

Engines, canopy and u/c masked and aircraft primed.   *- G. Hill*

Beginnings of camouflage.   *- G. Hill*

V

THE RUSH TO THE FIRST FLIGHT

During late winter and early spring 1988 it was decided that the Mynarski Memorial Lancaster should have a firm date set for its inaugural flight and introduction to the public at large. This became possible when the fourth engine arrived in February. September 24 was the chosen day and all the energies of the organization's various groups were concentrated on achieving this objective. At that time there was a myriad of jobs to complete and the schedule at times did not seem possible. The list of work to be performed looked insurmountable. In early spring the list of some of the major items looked like this:

Starters and generators still awaiting delivery from overhaul.
Flying controls require minor modification.
Hydraulic pumps still being overhauled.
Glycol and hydraulic fluids to be delivered.
Aircraft to be weighed empty after painting.
Cowlings still require a lot of detailed work to repair fasteners and cracks.
Assemble Lancaster tire, wheel and brake assembly for engine run-up.
Make new brake housing for Lincoln wheel assembly.
Lincoln brake pad assemblies still being manufactured.
Hydraulic system still needs final assembly and additional parts still to be delivered.
Hydraulic fill and bleed of system after completion of system to be done.
Hydraulic and undercarriage retraction tests, with A/C on jacks.
Engine coolant systems need to be filled with glycol and pressure tested.
Fire detection system still to be delivered and installed, wiring to be put in place.
Minor installation work on fire bottles.
Electrical wiring systems still not 100% complete and need ringing out to check
  circuits.
Lincoln oleo legs still held up by delivery of seals.
Oil and fuel loading and testing after A/C is weighed.
Fuel gauges to be calibrated.
Spark plugs to be delivered and installed in all engines (96).
Radios to be obtained and installed.

These were the obvious items. There were many smaller jobs and also pieces of equipment to be obtained, too numerous to mention. The task before the restoration team was enormous but possible if the various items still outstanding were delivered. As it turned out the Lincoln undercarriage was to be the real cliff-hanger.

PAINTING OF AIRCRAFT

It was originally planned to have the aircraft painted in time for the Hamilton Airshow in June, but this was not possible, as the cleaning and preparation could not be done in time. One of the bigger tasks was the removal of all external chromate paint, which was not compatible with the new Imron Aviation polyurethane enamel paint donated by Dupont Canada Ltd., which required a special primer.

It took four weeks of stripping (90 gals. of stripper), sanding, prepping, and a final six days masking and painting. Glen Sabatine of Haldimand Auto Parts, Caledonia donated

Squadron markings and roundels being masked and painted VR.A.   - *G. Hill*

Filling her tanks for the first time and there were no leaks, a great compliment to the crew.
                                                                                 - *N. Etheridge*

A view from above showing escape hatches and camouflage painting.   *- N. Etheridge*

The cockpit and instruments after restoration, 1988.   *- R.D. Page*

his technical and logistical support and the actual painting was completed by Keith Jewells and associates of Jewells Auto Body, Caledonia. It took 351 litres of paint, 2,286 metres of masking paper, 48 rolls of 2″ masking tape, 48 rolls of ¾″ masking tape. Actual painting time took 43 hours to cover the Lancaster's 5,600 sq.ft. The job had to be done in stages; clean and wash, acid clean with Du Pont's CORLAR wash primer, then prime with Du Pont's high solid polyurethane primer, mask and paint battle black the bottom surfaces, mask and paint the camouflage top surfaces, then mask and paint the roundels and letters. Only then could the aircraft be weighed. The paint added 500 lbs. to the aircraft, much less than a conventional aircraft paint job.

FIRST ENGINE RUN-UP

After the aircraft was painted and weighed in at 32,500 lbs. empty, the major push was on for first engine run-up after 24 years of silence. This was originally planned for August 9 but was cancelled because of threats of thunderstorms much to the disappointment of many of the crew who had taken the day off to be there.

First it had to stop at the fuel pumps to take on 600 litres of gasoline, for the first time in 24 years. Everybody waited with bated breath to see if there were any leaks from the connections made during rebuilding. There were none. This was a good indication of the standard of work that had been maintained during its restoration.

Then, on Wednesday, August 10, with John R. Sandberg in the cockpit and the other engineers aboard at 11:15 hrs the No.4 engine was gently turned over, and with the usual blue oil smoke, it sprang to life, but only for five minutes, as it had developed a fuel leak at the carburetor. At 11:20 hrs No.1 was started. It only ran for two minutes, because of a fuel leak at the nozzle to the supercharger. No.4 was then restarted after the leak was corrected and ran for fifteen minutes. No.3 was tried but only ran for two minutes because of a blown hydraulic line, as the relief valve had been set at 1,300 psi rather than 850 psi. After a lunchtime break, and with the hydraulic pumps disconnected, all engines ran together at 15:30 hrs for nearly half an hour, and they all purred like good Merlins, with temperatures and pressures all in the green. The sound of all the mighty Merlins running at one time put to rest the doubts of the skeptics who said it could not be done.

The day that the engines ran for the first time coincided with the visit of Pierre Cresson. He had a reunion with Pat Brophy and was interviewed by the media, reliving the old days back in France in 1944.

On succeeding run-ups one of the coolant radiators sprang a leak. This required replacement by one of those obtained from the Greenwood Lancaster. All the various run-ups to adjust and correct the various snags and adjust numerous engine controls took time and ate away at the days before the first test flight and the inaugural flight.

LINCOLN U/C CHANGE-OVER

After the engines were run on August 10, the priority switched to the change-over to the Lincoln oleo legs, wheel, tires and brake assemblies. One was relatively easy to assemble, but the other required hand-fitting of the brake shoe assemblies to the newly cast and machined brake housing. After many hours of laborious filing and fitting, it was assembled and put on its axle, and the old lady had new legs. This was completed on August 20. The retraction test indicated a leak in one of the retraction actuators and that had to be sent away to A.C. for correction. The test also indicated that the oleos had to be adjusted so that the retraction sequence would operate smoothly. While the aircraft was on jacks for the tests, the engine test could not be done, further interfering with the schedule.

On September 6 M.O.T. did their inspection and found only 49 snags, nearly all of which were minor in nature. This was a great credit to the engineers and crew who completed this mammoth restoration job on such a large and complicated aircraft.

Flight engineer's panels after restoration, 1988.   - *N. Etheridge*

Part of the flight engineer's panels before restoration, circa 1977.   - *CWHM*

First engine run-up August 10, 1988, all engines ran together for the first time in 24 years at 15:30 hrs.   - *R.D. Page*

RADIOS

The procurement of radios for the Lanc was a major problem for the restoration team, as they had to be modern ones, suitable for relatively long-distance navigation, and they had to meet the requirements of M.O.T., as the Lanc would be flying to many places in Canada and U.S.A. Today's radios are a far cry from the relatively crude communication devices of the wartime Lancasters. Fortunately CWHM was able to obtain a brand-new set through the kind offices of Bill Deluce, President and Chief Executive Officer of Air Ontario Inc., ex-Austin Airways, in co-operation with Kitchener Aero Avionics, King Radio and Northern Airborne.

They supplied a King Golden Crown III Series Avionics package worth $60,000. This is the same type installed on the modern de Havilland Dash 8 type aircraft and consists of two nav comms, one HSI pictorial nav indicator, one A.D.F., transponder, D.M.E. with marker, encoding altimeter and gyro-compass system. A Loran navigating system will be fitted later. This air navigation and communication avionics package required five different types of aerials to be fitted to the fuselage. It was all remotely installed ahead of the cockpit in the bomb-aimer's area, on the old camera-mounting frame of the original aircraft. Fortunately it only requires one display and control panel in the cockpit, thanks to today's miniaturization, as that is all the space available!

The system design, installation and certification of the avionics package, with its special wiring, control and power cables, were donated in association with Barry Alwood of Kitchener Aero Avionics.

Austin Airways had previously donated the museum's first Avro Anson V, C-FHQZ in 1975, when it was retiring its old fleet. This Anson and its sister, C-FHOT, donated by INCO, are the only ones of their kind flying in the world.

The radios were installed during August just in time for the first flight.

King Golden Crown III radios installed on old camera mount in bomb aimer's position.
- R.D. Page

Radio control panels mounted above the feathering switches.   - *N. Etheridge*

The H.S.I. Instrument mounted to the left of the blind flying panel.   - *N. Etheridge*

FIRST FLIGHT

Originally the first flight was planned for Saturday 10th, but because of a magneto drop of 300 rpm on one engine, only high-speed taxi tests with the tail in the air were attempted. A spark plug change cured this magneto drop, delaying the first flight until Sunday, resulting in the disappointment of a large number of supporters who had attended specially for this event.

The first flight, under her own power, after FM213's 24-year retirement took place on Sunday, September 11, 1988, at 13:25 hrs. This again, had been delayed by an excessive mag drop on No.4 engine. As the old girl lifted off the runway very gracefully, the crowd of volunteers gave a triumphant shout of joy and applause. There were a great many tearful eyes in the crowd, as the day for which so many had been working so hard for so long had arrived. The flight lasted one hour, during which time various handling, flying characteristics and system tests were done. The slow rate for the wheels to lock down suggested air in the hydraulics so the air test was terminated. The first flight was concluded with a flawless landing at 14:25 hrs with Sqd/Ldr Tony Banfield, the former Commanding Officer of the RAF's Battle of Britain Memorial Flight, at the controls; Bob Hill, as second dickie; and Norm Etheridge, Tim Mols as flight engineers.

Tony who had been Commanding Officer of the RAF's Battle of Britain Memorial Flight for the last three years, had flown their Lancaster *The City of Lincoln* for many hours and was also a qualified test pilot. He had come over to test fly our Lanc C-GVRA, between jobs. As was usual with such complicated machinery, Sod's Law prevailed, and limited him to only two flights, before he had to rush back to England a week late, to take up his new position with Trent Air Services at Cranfield.

The crew after first flight on September 11, 1988. L. to R. Sqd/Ld Tony Banfield, former CO of BBMF, captain; engineers, Tim Mols, Norm Etheridge; Bob Hill, co-pilot.   — *N. Etheridge*

High speed taxi trials September 10, 1988, when she got her tail off the ground.   *- R. Pratt*

Taxiing in after successful taxi trials, with some of CWHM aircraft on her port and civil
aircraft on her starboard.   *- R. Pratt*

Nose-up to the fuel station to replenish her tanks to be ready for first flight.   *- R. Pratt*

Airborne for the first time in 24 years under her own power, September 11, 1988.   *- R. Pratt*

The second flight was made on Wednesday, September 14. On this flight trouble arose when a ¼″ line to the undercarriage retraction actuators fractured while in flight and coincided with a progressive electrical system failure due to a faulty contact in one of the regulators. This fracture produced loss of hydraulic fluid from the system, which allowed air into the system and caused both hydraulic pumps to seize and fail their quill drive shafts. The emergency system for lowering the undercarriage worked perfectly and Tony was able to land without incident. Another minor problem was that the U/C warning horn sounded when the aircraft was in cruise power with the U/C fully retracted. The flight lasted 1.35 hours, landing at 19:25 hrs, just as the sun was setting. Therefore Tony was not able to check-out any CWHM pilot as planned, before he had to return to England to take up his new job after retiring from the Royal Air Force.

With the inaugural flight on the 24th quickly approaching, there was tremendous pressure on the crew and organization to find replacement pumps and to install them on the aircraft. The National Aviation Museum came to the rescue, as the only hydraulic pumps still available in Canada that would fit the Merlins were those on the Lancaster at Ottawa. These were quickly obtained and installed on the engines. While the hydraulic pumps were being replaced, all lines to the undercarriage, flaps and bomb doors similar to the one that had failed were replaced with new tubing. The hydraulic system was refilled and bled. It is very difficult and laborious to bleed all the air out of a large system after such an event.

All the snags that had occurred were corrected and the aircraft was able to fly three times on September 23, one day before the inaugural flight. These flights lasted 30 minutes, 35 minutes, and 1.10 hours respectively. The crew on the first flight that day were Stu Brickenden, captain; Bob Hill, co-pilot; and Norm Etheridge and Gil Hunt, flight engineers. Greg replaced Norm on the second flight, and Gil was replaced by Don Schofield on the last flight. The aircraft was finally ready for its introduction to the public. When Stu took over the controls it was the first time in 25 years he had flown as captain of a Lancaster. Stu Brickenden from Brampton is a corporate pilot with Innotech and was in the R.C.A.F. from 1943-72, when he flew Lancasters with Search and Rescue. He has now accumulated over 18,000 flying hours on 40 types of aircraft. Bob Hill, who had been flying with Tony Banfield, had unfortunately not been able to obtain the required number of hours on the Lancaster to qualify as first pilot on a new type. Bob was also in the R.C.A.F. during 1960-66 and is a pilot with Air Canada, filling the role of Manager, Flight Standards and DC-8 Freighters. He has over 11,000 flying hours on many types, including CF-100 Canuck, CF-101 Voodoo, as well as DC-9, DC-8 and L-1011 aircraft.

INAUGURAL BALL

The original Mynarski crew, consisting of Art de Breyne from St. Lambert, Jim Kelly from Willowdale, Roy Vigars from England, Bob Bodie from Vancouver, Pat Brophy from St. Catharines, and Mrs. Stephanie Holowaty, Andrew Mynarski's sister from Winnipeg, started to arrive on the Wednesday before the inaugural flight to sign the marvellous painting by the renowned artist Robert Taylor. (see pg. 51) It depicts the original KB726 returning to Colerne, near Bristol, after their first mission on the early morning of D-day, June 6, 1944. This painting was commissioned by Mike Johnson of the Wings Gallery, Oakville. The crew signed 1,250 prints Thursday and Friday, and on Friday saw the CWHM's Lancaster fly for the first time. These prints had already been signed by the three Bomber Command Victoria Cross holders, William Reid, Norman Cyril Jackson and Roderick Alistair Brook Learoyd. Jack Friday came in earlier to do some signing but was unable to be at the ceremonies, as he had agreed to attend the wedding of his son on that Saturday, long before the date of the Lancaster's first flight was known.

Private Selection

CANADIAN WARPLANE HERITAGE MUSEUM

To Commemorate

THE FIRST FLIGHT
OF THE MYNARSKI LANCASTER

September 1988   Hamilton, Ontario

Product of Canada / Produit du Canada   Andrés Wines Ltd., Winona, Canada

Andres Wine label
commemorating
the first flight.
- Andres Wine

The old and new aircrew of No.419 Squadron at the Lancaster gala ball. L. to R. Jim Kelly, 1944; Vincent, 1988; Pat Brophy, 1944 holding the original fire axe of KB726; Ken Branston, 1944; Major Bart Wickham, 1988; Stephanie Holowaty, holding a portrait of her late brother Andrew Mynarski; Art de Breyne, 1944; Lt. Col. M.J. Bertram, CO No.419 Squadron, 1988 holding a plaque of Andrew's medals and portrait; Roy Vigars, 1944; Bob Bodie, 1944; Steve Charboneau, 1988.   *- H. Swierenga*

The evening before the flight was spent celebrating, with a ball at the Chandelier Place, Stoney Creek, with over 600 guests in attendance. It was a colourful, full scale black tie and mess dress affair, with a special Lancaster wine donated by Andres served with the dinner. The tables were decorated with flowers, R.C.A.F. flags and samples of the French *Lancaster* cosmetic.[1]

The program included a traditional dance card and a message from Prince Charles, the Royal Patron of CWHM.

The head table included the Lieutenant-Governor of Ontario, the Honourable Lincoln M. Alexander, Minister of State, Transport; The Right Honourable Mrs. Shirley Martin, Ontario Minister of Culture and Communications; The Honourable Lily Oddie Munro, Regional Municipality of Hamilton-Wentworth; Chairman Williams Sears, City of Hamilton; Alderman R. Wheeler; Art de Breyne, Pilot of the Mynarski Lancaster; Dennis Bradley, President of Canadian Warplane Heritage Museum; Lieutenant-Colonel M.J. Bertram, Commanding Officer No.419 Squadron; Brigadier General J. O'Blenis, C.D. & Bar, Deputy Commander Fighter Group CAF, the guest speaker; Major William W. Randall, C.D., Chairman of the Lanc Support Club; Reverend Charles Beaton; and William T. McBride, who acted as Master of Ceremonies. One of the special guests was Andrew Mynarski's sister, Mrs. Stephanie Holowaty, wearing Andrew's Victoria Cross.

The colour party duties were performed by the Air cadets of No.779 Black Knight squadron. In his speech during the ceremonies, Art de Breyne reminded the guests that though they were gathered together to honour a special man and his aircraft, they should not forget those heroes who are not remembered today. He illustrated his point by describing the graveyard where Andrew Mynarski was buried: there is a gravestone close to him marking the spot of P/O C. Weaver, an American pilot in the R.C.A.F., who had earned his D.F.C., D.F.M. & Bar by the time he died at the young age of 19, on January 28, 1944. These decorations were the equivalent of earning three D.F.C.s. His brother, died later with the American Forces at Iwo Jima.

INAUGURAL FLIGHT

Saturday, September 24, 1988, turned out to be a picture-perfect day for late September. The gates were opened at 09:00 hrs and the crowds started to pour in. The original Mynarski crew, accompanied by their wives and families, and Stephanie Holowaty, Andrew Mynarski's sister, and her daughter were involved with numerous interviews for the news media, including one with Elwy Yost of TVO, in the morning. Ken Branston, the original mid-upper gunner of the crew, also joined them.

The ceremonies started at 14:00 hrs and opened with an address by the President of Canadian Warplane Heritage Museum, Dennis Bradley, who introduced the guests on the dais. There was a "typical" Lancaster crew of old Bomber Command dressed in original R.C.A.F. uniforms. The crew included Larry Melling, pilot D.F.C. (61 ops), from Burlington; Fred Coleman, navigator (23 ops), from Hamilton; Roy Freckleton, bomb-aimer (33 ops), from Dundas; William Grenville, flight engineer (33 ops), from Hamilton; Robert Hide, wireless operator (10 ops), from Ancaster; Fred Passmore, air gunner (34 ops), from Dundas; and Wilf Larsen, air gunner (27 ops), from Medicine Hat. They were accompanied by the day's crew for the inaugural flight; Pilot Stu Brickenden, Co-pilot Bob Hill, Flight Engineer Norm Etheridge and George Sobering, D.F.C. Other platform guests were Major-General Brian Smith, Chief of Fighter Command, CFB North Bay, and Reverend Chuck Beaton of the Olivet United Church, Mount Hope, who had dedicated the aircraft four years ago. In his address Maj. Gen. Smith received a loud response to his remarks that Canada's Air Force units "are in the blue again." The Commanding Officer of No.419 Squadron, L/Col Murray J. Bertram, presented the pilots of the Lancaster with

The famous trio in flight, the Lancaster escorted by the CWHM's Hawker Hurricane and Cliff Robertson's Vickers Supermarine Spitfire.

- Hamilton Spectator

Dennis Bradley presenting the fire axe to Stu Brickenden, after receiving it from Lt/Col Murray J. Bertram, the commanding officer of No.419 Squadron; to be flown in the aircraft during the inaugural flight. - *C. Sloat*

Crews of today and yesterday. L. to R. Stu Brickenden, Bob Hill, George Sobering, Norm Etheridge, Wilf Larsen, Fred Passmore, Robert Hide, William Grenville, Roy Freckleton, Fred Coleman, Larry Melling.
- Hamilton Spectator

Major General Brian Smith, Chief of Fighter Command addressing the assembled guests.

- Hamilton Spectator

Rolley Roberge of Air Canada, Montreal, Bob Hill and Stu Hall, general foreman, Air Canada machine shops at Dorval. *- Hamilton Spectator*

A skydiver of the Hamilton Sport Parachuting Club opening the airshow. *- Hamilton spectator*

Art de Breyne back in the pilot's seat after 44 years. *- R.D. Page*

the original fire axe of KB726, to be flown on board at the ceremonial flight. It was later returned to No.419 Squadron for safekeeping.

The airshow started at 14:20 hrs with Bill McBride and Stu Holloway as commentators, and was opened by a colorful drop of eight members of the Hamilton Sport Parachute Club, jumping from the DC-3. One of the parachutists was Eileen Vaughan, who also took part in the opening ceremonies of the Olympics, Seoul, Korea. Her parachute had the five colours of the Olympic rings. Following this was a fly-by of aircraft belonging to CWHM's collection, starting with the elementary trainers (de Havilland Tiger Moth, Boeing Stearman, de Havilland Canada Chipmunk, Fleet Fairchild Cornell, Fairchild Argus, and the Fleet 21). These were followed by the advanced trainers (three North American Harvards, North American Texan and the Beechcraft Mentor). Then the transport aircraft (Cessna Crane, Beech 18 and the famous DC-3 painted as a Dakota). These were followed by the fighters (two North American Mustangs, Chance Vought Corsair, North American T-28 Trojan) and the larger aircraft represented by the North American Mitchell B-25 bomber and the Grumman Avenger. After these the CWHM's Hawker Hurricane and Cliff Robertson's Supermarine Spitfire took off in formation, an impressive aerobatic display was performed by the Spitfire, with the classical Victory roll. The modern jet-fighter F-5 from No.419 Squadron Cold Lake then put on an impressive aerobatic display dedicated to the solo pilot Captain Wes McKay of the Snowbird Aerobatic team, who had died the night before in a car accident.

Then the great moment finally came, and the Lancaster VR.A took off with Stu Brickenden and Bob Hill as pilots and Norm Etheridge, George Sobering as crew. It roared down the runway and took off dramatically at 15:30 hrs, carrying aloft the original fire axe that Andrew Mynarski used in trying to help Pat Brophy escape. After a number of solo passes, the Lancaster, Spitfire and Hurricane joined up together in formation as a salute to the R.A.F. and R.C.A.F. of yester years, making a wonderful sight not seen before by the vast majority of the 20,000 people in attendance. Lancaster FM213, now KB726 VR.A landed after a half-hour flight, giving her a total flying time of 4,397.8 hours on the airframe.

A Chinook helicopter from No.450 Heavy Lift Squadron was on display, representing the aircraft which had originally airlifted the Lancaster from Goderich to Mount Hope so many years ago. Also in attendance were two Sea King helicopters on static display.

It is impossible to list the many people who have given so much help and encouragement to the project and who came to share that wonderful occasion It was a great compliment to everyone concerned to see people like W/O Barry Sears (engineer), and his charming wife, from the Battle of Britain Memorial Flight. W/O Sears had assisted the project so generously and had travelled from the U.K. to share the ceremonies.

The day provided lasting memories for the more than 20,000 people in attendance. This day's events had taken many years of devoted work to achieve.

Footnotes:
---
[1] *Lancaster* cosmetics was founded in 1945, by George Wurz, and Eugene Frezzati. After release from a prisoner of war camp, they started a cosmetic factory in Monaco, and named it *Lancaster*, in honour of the bomber they so admired.

Portrait of P/O Andrew Charles Mynarski V.C. by Paul Goranson. *- Canadian War Museum*

VI

EPILOGUE OF THE MYNARSKI CREW

ANDREW CHARLES MYNARSKI was awarded the Victoria Cross posthumously on Friday, October 11, 1946. The medal was presented to his mother, Mrs. Stanley Mynarski, by the Lieutenant-Governor of Manitoba, the Right Honourable J.A. McWilliams on December 12, 1946.

It would appear that Art de Breyne started the process by recommending an award for Andrew and enquiring about the location of his grave at the end of 1945. The R.C.A.F. Casualty Officer had a long and difficult job in locating Andrew's grave. It was not until December 14th, 1946 that he received word that Andrew Charles Mynarski V.C. was buried in Grave No.46, in the Plot for British Airmen, in the cemetery at Meharicourt, Somme, France.

Since then there have been a number of dedications in his memory. These include the Mynarski Park housing development at Penhold, Alberta. Mrs. Anne Mynarski, his mother, was in attendance at the dedication.

A high school in Winnipeg was named after him in November 1955, when all of the crew attended except for Roy Vigars from England. This was the first time since the war that the crew had met together as a group.

Three lakes in northern Manitoba located at latitude 40 degrees 10 minutes, and longitude 99 degrees 12 minutes, were also named after Andrew.

In 1956 Andrew's mother attended the 100th anniversary of the awarding of the first Victoria Cross in England. It was a grand occasion.

A number of the crew got together in June 1958 at the R.C.A.F. Association Allied Air Forces Reunion in Edmonton.

In 1959 the Mynarski Trophy was presented for the best organization of recreation activities of married quarters. This trophy is now presented to the Air Sea Rescue Units. In 1985 it was presented to 103 Rescue Unit, CFB Gander, as an emblem of excellence in Search & Rescue (SAR) activities during the previous year. Major K. Gathercole and W/O F. Pilgrom accepted the award on behalf of the unit.

In 1965, at the 10th anniversary of the naming of Andrew Mynarski High School, the complete crew attended the function. This was the first time since the war that they had all been together and it was an emotional event for all of them.

A significant reunion and ceremony took place in 1981 in France and is best described by Art

ART DE BREYNE

"On June 13, 1981, five members of our crew arrived in Amiens to be greeted by a group of Resistance members known as 'Les Passeurs du Nord' who had passed airmen down the line. It was also the day of their reunion.

"At a ceremony in the village of Gaudiempre', where our plane had crashed, 1,500 people gathered to pay homage to Andrew Charles Mynarski, V.C., our mid-upper gunner, and Les Passeurs du Nord who had died trying to protect the Allied airmen. It was an impressive ceremony during which a bronze plaque from the crew was unveiled."

PROVINCE OF MANITOBA

"Lives of great men all remind us
We can make our lives sublime,
And, departing, leave behind us
Footprints on the sands of time."

🍁

Henry Wadsworth Longfellow

Mynarski Lakes

is named after

P/O Andrew C. Mynarski, V.C.

LATITUDE 56° 10'
LONGITUDE 99° 12'
ADOPTED ON MAY 5th, 1949

 CANADIAN PERMANENT COMMITTEE ON GEOGRAPHICAL NAMES

JW Grondall
Manitoba Representative

MINISTER
Department of Natural Resources

PRAIRIE CROCUS

Mynarski lake scroll.

- Art de Breyne

The plaque was inscribed with the following words composed by Art de Breyne:

EN CETTE COMMUE, LE 13 JUNE, 1944
S'EST ABATTU UN LANCASTER DE LA
"ROYAL CANADIAN AIR FORCE"
IMMATRICULE' "VR.A KB726"
CETTE PLAQUE DEDIEE A LA
MEMOIRE DE L'OFFICIER-PILOTE
ANDREW CHARLES MYNARSKI, V.C.,
FUT DEVOILEE LE 13 JUIN, 1981
PAR SES SIX COMPAGNONS D'EQUIPAGE
EN HOMMAGE ET RECONNAISSANCE AUX
PASSEURS DU NORD AFFILES A LA
"ROYAL AIR FORCES ESCAPING SOCIETY".
RASSEMBLES ICI CE JOUR, ET A TOUS
LES CITOYENS FRANCAIS QUI ONT PORTE
SECOURS AUX AVIATEURS DES FORCES
ALLIES TOMBES SUR LE SOL DE FRANCE.

Which translates to:

IN THIS VILLAGE, ON 13 JUNE 1944
A LANCASTER OF THE
ROYAL CANADIAN AIR FORCE
MARKED "VR.A KB726" CRASHED.
THIS PLAQUE, DEDICATED TO THE MEMORY OF
PILOT OFFICER ANDREW CHARLES MYNARSKI, V.C.,
WAS UNVEILED ON 13 JUNE 1981
BY HIS FELLOW CREW MEMBERS
IN HOMAGE TO AND IN RECOGNITION OF
THE "PASSEURS DU NORD" AFFILIATED WITH
THE "ROYAL AIR FORCE ESCAPING SOCIETY"
ASSEMBLED HERE ON THIS DAY, AND
ALL FRENCH CITIZENS WHO HAVE HELPED
THOSE ALLIED AIRMEN FORCED DOWN
ON THIS SOIL OF FRANCE.

"It was attended by Colonel Pattie, who represented the Canadian Armed Forces in Europe; the Naval Attache to the Canadian Ambassador to France; the Prefect du Pas de Calais, and the Gendarmerie Departementale formed a guard of honour. Some parts of the Lancaster VR.A recovered from the crash were turned over to us to be forwarded to the Canadian War Museum in Ottawa. Pat Brophy, who crashed with the plane and sustained only minor injuries, unfortunately could not attend. The ceremony took place a hundred metres from the centre of the village, on the spot where the wreck came to rest, scattering bombs in all directions.

The crew also visited Andrew's grave at Meharicourt and paid their respects to their fallen comrade. The line of airmen's graves includes the one of P/O Weaver, D.F.C., D.F.M & Bar, which Art referred to in his inaugural ball speech.

"In retrospect, after so many years, I have come to look upon my visit to France as a pleasant holiday I would not have wanted to miss. I saw France at the grass roots, came in contact with the best of its citizens and formed everlasting friendships. When no imminent danger threatened, living was very pleasant, the countryside was beautiful and then it was the best season of the year. This congenial quality of life I owe to the women who cooked for me, washed my clothes and showed me a lot of affection. Mrs. Bonneton who is now 89 and lives alone in the same house, was a real mother to me.

The crew in a lighter moment at the unveiling of the plaque at Gaudiempré on June 13, 1981. L. to R. Roy, Stephanie, Jack, Art, Bob and Jim.   - Art de Breyne

Art de Breyne addressing the assembled crowd with his crew and Pierre Bauset, the President of the Royal Air Force Escaping Society Canadian branch.   - Art de Breyne

The crew paying their respects at the grave of Andrew Mynarski and others at the cemetery at Meharicourt, Somme, France.   *- Art de Breyne*

Andrew Charles
Mynarski V.C.,
gravestone.
- Art de Breyne

Mr. & Mrs. Bonneton and Jeannette de Breyne at Tracy le Val, 1971.

- Art de Breyne

Two helpers of Art's, Raymond & Georgette lé Toquart with Jeanette, St. Lambert, 1987.

- Art de Breyne

Marquis Max de Broissia and Marquess Isabelle de Broissia, who hid Art de Breyne not far from his chateau and obtained his forged I.D. Card.

- Art de Breyne

Pierre Cresson, June 1981, who with his brother Paul looked after Pat Brophy after the crash of KB726.

- Art de Breyne

The cairn erected by "Le Souvenir Francais" at the roadside in Gaudiempré, 100 feet from where KB726 came to rest, in memory of Andrew Mynarski who sacrificed his life trying to save his fellow crew member.

- Art de Breyne

"We have had the pleasure of visits, on two or more occasions of the Bonnetons, the Lemaires, Gaston Barachet, and Max and Isabelle de Broissia, who attended the 1984 meeting. We have also had the pleasure of receiving Mrs. Jeanne Serant and daughter, who hid Jim Kelly and Bob Bodie while German troops were billeted in her house. Pierre Cresson, Pat Brophy's helper, has visited Canada on many occasions and is known to a number of our members. The fact that four members of our crew evaded successfully is a tribute to our helpers."

A cairn was erected by the roadside in Gaudiempré in May, 1983 about 100 feet from where KB726 VR.A came to rest. It was erected by 'Le Souvenir Francais' (French Remembrance Association) as a permanent reminder that KB726 came to rest there with special mention of Andrew Mynarski, who died trying to rescue his fellow crewmate.

In 1984 Art presented his story to the Royal Air Force Escaping Society at the Air Force reunion in Winnipeg.

Art recounts, "Two helpers of mine who did not visit Canada until 1987, Raymond and Georgette Letoquart, spent two weeks with us in September, visited Toronto, Niagara, Ottawa, Montreal and Quebec, and attended our annual Air Force reunion meeting in Kingston."

DEDICATION OF THE MYNARSKI MEMORIAL LANCASTER

In June 1984 a ceremony took place at Mount Hope in the No.4 hangar of Canadian Warplane Heritage Museum and the Lancaster FM213 was dedicated to the memory of Andrew Charles Mynarski, V.C., as the Mynarski Memorial Lancaster. A number of the crew were in attendance and the Reverend Charles Beaton dedicated the aircraft in memory of P/O Andrew Charles Mynarski, giving it the name "The Mynarski Memorial Lancaster." There was a full colour party and parade with a band, and many veterans from the Legions and R.C.A.F. associations took part.

In 1985, at the reunion of No.419, 420 and 428 squadrons, a ceremony was held at Middleton St. George airfield in England from which the three Canadian squadrons had operated. A memorial cairn was unveiled on this occasion. The airfield is now used as the Municipal Teesside Airport. A "Lancaster" room was also dedicated at the St. George Hotel which was the officers' mess of the old Air Force station. A presentation of a portrait of Andrew Mynarski was made to his sister Stephanie Holowaty by Shelia Barnett, the liason officer for the St.George Hotel, Teesside Airport. A painting of the original Lancaster KB726 by Robert B. Curry was also presented to be hung in the Lancaster room. Jim Kelly, Jack Friday and Roy Vigars attended. The local Oak Tree pub had a yellow ribbon tied around it for the celebrations.

FM213 has attracted many of the wartime and peacetime Lancaster crews to CWHM at Hamilton airport, as reunions and airshows have been staged there, and on one occasion recently two former wartime aircrew members met after 44 years. They were Art de Breyne and Bob Furneaux[1], who had not seen each other since the time of their liberation in 1944.

Some of the crew were in attendance at Hamilton airport in November 1987 when Art donated $5,000 to the Lanc Support Club matching the amount contributed by others who donated more than $50 per member. He attended again in April 1988 when the Listowel and Durham Legion members visited the Lancaster and various reunions took place.

Pierre Cresson visited Canada in August 1988 and met with Pat Brophy beside the restored Lancaster FM213, now painted in the colours of the original KB726 VR.A, during the first engine run-ups.

Art de Breyne with some of his crew, receiving a print of a Dam Buster Lancaster from George Sobering after presenting a cheque for $5,000 to the Lanc Support Club. L. to R. Ken Branston, the original mid-upper gunner; Jim Kelly, wireless operator; Pat Brophy, rear gunner; Art de Breyne, pilot; George Sobering, D.F.C., Pilot; Karl Coolen, Al Dunphy.
                                                                                                    - K. Coolen

The crew of the early days - L. to R. Don Montgomery, D.F.C., who last flew the Lancaster to Goderich; Tommy Thompson, Avro flight engineer; Don Rogers, Avro Chief test pilot; Fred Laker, Avro wireless operator.
                                                                                                    - J. Clarke

FM104 10MR C.N.E. Toronto, Waterfront.

FM136 10MR Calgary Centennial Planetarium, at McCall Field, Calgary, Alberta registered as CF-NJQ.

FM159 10MR Nanton, Alberta.

FM212 10P Jackson Park Sunken Gardens, Windsor, Ontario.

FM213 10MR Canadian Warplane Heritage Museum, Hamilton Airport, Mount Hope, Ontario, Flying Condition.

KB839 10AR Canadian Forces Base, Greenwood, Nova Scotia.

KB882 10AR St. Jacques Airport, Edmunston, New Brunswick.

KB944 10S National Aeronautical Collection, Rockcliffe, Ottawa, Ontario.

Lancaster KB882 on display at Edmunston, New Brunswick.   *- CWHM*

WHERE ARE THEY TODAY

The bond that was forged in the early days of 1943 has survived the passage of time and the crew still get together whenever they can and reminisce and joke about how they were able to survive together — then and now. It is amazing that they are all still alive today and all are happily married.

ART de BREYNE became a successful businessman, first in air-conditioning and then running a company manufacturing stainless steel piping components. He has twice retired and is still living in St. Lambert with his wife Jeannette and their son Andy. His daughter Louise is married and living in Ottawa.

BOB BODIE graduated as a Mechanical Engineer from U.B.C. After working in various power stations, he took an appointment with the City of Vancouver as a Smoke and Environmental inspector. He is now retired and living with his wife Rose. At 75 years of age he is still enjoying camping, canoeing and fishing. They have four children and five grandchildren.

JIM KELLY demobbed as F/O, joined Air Canada and became their Manager-Accounting Systems Development. He is now retired but still actively consulting for IATA on audits. He lives in Willowdale with his wife Lee. They have two children and three grandchildren.

ROY VIGARS rejoined the railway after being demobbed in 1947 as a W/O. He became an engineer with British Railways and later manager of a train section before retiring. He still lives in Guildford, England, with his wife Ellen. They have two sons and three grandsons.

JACK FRIDAY demobbed as a F/O joined Air Canada as a passenger agent at Thunder Bay. Now retired he is still living happily in Thunder Bay with his wife Shirley, and has five children and two grandchildren.

PAT BROPHY re-enlisted in the R.C.A.F. after a short period in civi-street and became a radar controller and instructor. Now, retired, he has recently moved to St. Catharines with his wife Sylvia. They have three children, two grandchildren and a great-grandson. His son Patrick is carrying on the family tradition as a member of the R.C.A.F., now serving in Germany as a radar controller on AWAC aircraft.

KEN BRANSTON the original MUG, mid-upper gunner, is retired and living with his wife Pat in King City. They have two daughters and two grandchildren.

Footnotes:

[1] Bob Furneaux, survived the raid on Cambrai, but was shot down while filling in as a mid-under gunner with No.425 "Alouette" Squadron, in a Halifax III, on June 15, 1944, when they attacked Boulogne in daylight. He evaded, and was looked after by the French Underground, and received similar treatment to Art. Bob and Art met after liberation, while waiting to be flown to England.

The portrait of Lancaster KB726 painted by Robert B. Curry which is also hanging in the Lancaster room of the St. George Hotel.   - *J. Challoner*

A modern portrait of KB726 over Ontario Place, Toronto by Thompson.
                                                                    - *J. Challoner*

TRIBUTE TO A LANC

In one brief moment on a summer's day,
You brought back memories of yesterday.
When you knew glory in those wartime skies,
But seemed outmoded in our children's eyes.
"It won the war," I said to them with pride,
Its contributions cannot be denied.
Her crew were brave and dedicated men,
She flies as well as ever she did then.
Dear Lancaster, you great illustrious plane,
How wonderful to see you fly again!

Author unknown

Banfield, Tony, " First Flight of The Canadian Lancaster," *Flypast*, December 1988.

Brickenden, J., "Heroes Were Made Of This," *Canadian Star Weekly*, Toronto, October 9/15, 1965.

Brophy, Fl/Lt G.P., and MacDonald, D. "The Thirteenth Mission," *Readers' Digest*, December 1965.

Crawford, R.E., "Production Methods at Victory Aircraft," *Canadian Aviation*, Toronto, Ontario, August 1943.

Garbett, M., and Roffe, M., *"Avro Lancaster in Unit Service,"* Arco-Aircam Aviation Series, Arco Publishing Co.Inc. New York, 1970.

Griffin, J., *"Canadian Military Aircraft: Serial Numbers and Photographs,"* Government press.

Gunston, Bill, *"World Encyclopedia of Aero Engines,"* P. Stephens Ltd., Thorsen Publishing Group, Northamptonshire, England, 1986.

Heathcote, Sq/L A.P., "Beware The Moose," Part IV, *The Roundel*, Vol.11, No.3, April 1959.

Heathcote, A.P., *"Moose Squadron - The War Years,"* Directorate of History, 1975, Unpublished.

Hunter, W.A., "Specific Details on the Manufacture of Britain's Giant Bomber, The Famous Avro Lancaster", *Commercial Aviation*, Vol.4, September 1942.

Hunter, W.A, "V for VICTORY - Canadian-Built LANCASTERS", *Commercial Aviation*, Vol.5, July 1943.

Hunter, W.A., "A.V. Roe Co. Ltd., England, and Victory Aircraft Ltd., Canada in joint production of Lancasters for war and peace." *Commercial Aviation*, Vol.6, April 1944.

Kostenuk, S., and Griffin, J., *"RCAF Squadrons and Aircraft,"* Samuel Stevens Hakkert & Co., Toronto, 1977.

Lewis, P., *"The British Bomber Since 1914,"* Putman, London, 1967.

MacDonald, D. "The 14th Mission," Special Feature, *Readers Digest* June 1982.

MacDonald, D., & Brophy G.P. "Andrew Charles Mynarski, V.C.," *Canadian Aviation Historical Society Journal*, Special Anniversary Edition, June 1984.

Molson, K.M. and Taylor, H.A., *"Canadian Aircraft Since 1909,"* Canada's Wings, Sittsville, Ontario, 1982.

Moyes, P., *"Bomber Squadrons of the R.A.F. and Their Aircraft,"* Macdonald & Co. Ltd., London, W.1., Great Britain, 1964.

Robertson, Bruce, *"Lancaster - The Story of a Famous Bomber,"* Harleyford Publication, Hertfordshire, England, 1974.

Saward, Dudley, *"Bomber Harris,"* Buchan & Enright, Pub., London, 1984.

Sloat, Chuck, "Maple Leaf Lancs, A Pilot Memories of C.W.H. Lancaster X FM213," *Aeroplane Monthly*, August 1988.

Turner, C.F., "The Ruhr Express," *Airforce*, Vol.V, No.3, September 1982.

A.A. or A/A - Anti-aircraft guns
AAEE - Aircraft & Armament Experimental Establishment
AC - Air Command
A/C - Aircraft
A.C.R.C. - Air Crew Reception Centre
A.D.F. - Airborne Direction Finder
A.F.C. - Air Force Cross
A.F.T.S. - Advance Flying Training School
A.G. - Air Gunner
A.O.S. - Air Observer School
AR - Aerial Reconnaissance
A.V.M. or A/V/M - Air Vice-Marshal
AWAC - Airborne Warning and Control
B & G - Bombing & Gunnery
BBMF - Battle of Britain Memorial Flight
BR - Bomber Reconnaissance
B.S.F. - British Standard Fine
C.A.F. - Canadian Armed Forces
C.B.E. - Commander of the British Empire
CFB - Canadian Forces Base
C.F.H. - Canadian Fire Hose
C.G.M. - Conspicuous Gallantry Medal
C.G.T.A.S. - Canadian Government Transatlantic Air Service
CI - Converted Instructional
C.I.E. - Commander of the Indian Empire
C/N - Construction Number
C.N.E. - Canadian National Exhibition
CNS - Central Navigation School
CO - Commanding officer
Corkscrew - a flying evasion manoeuvre
Cpl - Corporal
CU - Conversion Unit
CWHM - Canadian Warplane Heritage Museum
DC - Drone Carrying
D.C.O. - Duty Carried Out
D-Day - The Day the Invasion of Europe started
D.F.C. - Distinguished Flying Cross
D.F.M. - Distinguished Flying Medal
DIA - Damaged In Action
DISB - Disbanded
Dit Dah - Morse code - dot dash
D.M.E. - Distance Measuring Encoder
D.S.O. - Distinguished Service Order
EANS - Empire Air Navigation School
E.F.T.S. - Elementary Flying Training School

E.S.T.T. - Engineer School of Technical Training
F.F.I. - Free French of the Interior (communistic)
Flak - Anti-aircraft fire
Fl/Lt or F/L - Flight Lieutenant
Flt/Sgt - Flight Sergeant
F.N. - Fraser Nash
F/O - Flying Officer
F.R.Ae.S. - Fellow of the Royal Aeronautical Society
F.R.S.A. - Fellow of the Royal Society Arts
F/Sgt - Flight Sergeant
FTU - Flying Training Unit or Fighter Training Unit
FW - Focke Wolfe
G - Gravity
Gardening - Planting mines in enemy waters
G.C.B. - Grand Cross of the Bath
Gone For A Burton - Not to return from an operation
Harry Clampers - Thick fog or zero visibility
H.C.U.- Heavy Conversion Unit
High Cock A Lor'em - A R.A.F. mess party game
HP - Handley Page
hp - Horse power
H.S.I. - Horizontal Situation Indicator
H2S - Blind bombing radar
I card - Identification card
ID - Identification
INCO - International Nickel Company
I.T.W. - Initial Training Wing
Ju. - Junkers
K.C.B. - Knight Commander of the Bath
KIA - Killed In Action
Kite - aircraft
L.A.C. - Leading Air Craftsman
Lanc - Lancaster bomber
L.L.D. - Doctor of Law
Mail - Propaganda leaflets
M.C. - Military Cross
Me - Messerschmitt
m/g - machine gun
MIA - Missing In Action
M.S.G. - Middleton St. George
Mk - Mark
M.O. - Medical Officer
MOTU or (M)OTU - Maritime Operational Training Unit
MP - Maritime Patrol
mph - miles per hour
MR - Maritime Reconnaissance
MSc. - Master of Science
MU - Maintenance Unit
N - Navigation Trainer
N.A.M. - National Aviation Museum
NAAFI - National Army Air Force Institute - supplied tea and rock hard cakes for the
    forces

N.C.O. - Non-Commissioned Officer
NDT - Non Destructive Testing
N.F.B. - National Film Board
Nickels - Propaganda leaflets or pamphlets
Nr - near
N.S.C.C - National Steel Car Corporation
O - Avro Orenda Engine's test vehicle
O.B.E. - Order of the British Empire
On - On operations
Ops - Operational raids
O.T.U. - Operational Training Unit
P.O.W. - Prisoner of War
P/O - Pilot Officer
P.R. - Public Relations
P.R.U. - Photographic Reconnaissance Unit
R.A.F. - Royal Air Force
R.C.A.F - Royal Canadian Air Force
RU - Rescue Unit
S - Standard
SAR - Search and Rescue
S.F.T.S. - Service Flying Training School
Sgt. - Sergeant
SOS - Struck Off Strength or charge
Spoof - Diversionary attack using electronic countermeasures
Squad - Squadron
Sqd/Ld or S/L - Squadron Leader
S&R - Search & Rescue
S.S. - Schutzstafflen, Elite Guard of Nazi Militia
T - Training
Tarmac Duty - Square bashing or marching drill
T.C.A. - Trans Canada Airways
tit - bomb release switch or button
Tommy - British soldier WWI
TOS - Taken On Strength
U/C - Undercarriage
U.K. - United Kingdom
U.S.A. - United States of America
U/S - Unserviceable
USS - United States Ship
V.A.L. - Victory Aircraft Limited
V.C. - Victoria Cross
V-E Day - Victory in Europe Day
VR.A - No.419 Squadron & Aircraft Identification letters
V-1 Buzz bomb - Germany pilotless bomb powered by pulsating jet engine
WAC - Western Air Command
W/O - Warrant Officer
W.O./A.G. - Wireless Operator Air Gunner
W/C - Wing Commander
WWI - World War I
WWII - World War II

APPENDIX I

DONATING COMPANIES

The following companies were most generous to the restoration project, which doubtless would not have reached completion without their magnificent contributions.

NO.125 (CHELTENHAM) SQUADRON, A.T.C. U.K.
Ice Guards for Intakes

AIR CANADA
Special Processes & Machine Work

AIR ONTARIO
Avionics

ANDRES WINE LTD.
Wines for Special Functions

ANDY RUSSELL CO. LTD.
Special Instruments & Motor Overhaul

AVIATION SUPPLIES INC.
Spare Parts & Supplies

AVITRON LTD.
Overhaul Starters & Generators

BARTLETT BRAKE & CLUTCH
Brake Shoes

BAEUMBLER QUALITY SHEET METAL LTD.
Specialized Metal Forming

BATTLE OF BRITAIN MEMORIAL FLIGHT
Spare Lancaster Parts

CANADIAN ARMED FORCES
Transportations & Spare Lancaster Parts

CARL AIRCRAFT COMPONENTS MFG. LTD.
Specialized Machine Work & Cable Manufacture

CASP AEROSPACE INC.(Formerly CFH INDUSTRIES LTD.)
Fire Warning & Suppression Systems

CHUBB LOCKS
Hand Fire Extinguishers

CITY OF EDMUNSTON, NEW BRUNSWICK
Lancaster Spare Parts

DOWTY CANADA LTD.
Hydraulic Components Overhaul & Manufacture

DOWTY ENGLAND LTD.
Hydraulic Seals

DRUMMOND MCCALL
Copper Plate

DU PONT OF CANADA LTD.
Paint

DUNLOP ENGLAND
Tires

DZUS FASTENER EUROPE LTD.
Dzus Special Fasteners

EPTON INDUSTRIES INC.
Rubber Seals Products

FIELD AVIATION CO. LTD.
General Aviation & Engineering

FLEET INDUSTRIES (DIVISION OF FLEET
    AEROSPACE CORPORATION)
Perspex Forming

GOLDEN ARC PUBLISHING
Support for Special Events

HAWKER SIDDELEY CANADA LTD. (ORENDA DIVISION)
Nondestructive Testing

HALDIMAND AUTO PARTS
Painting Support

HOOKER CUSTOM HARNESSES
Seat Belts

INTERFAST INC. (INTERNATIONAL FASTENERS)
Wiring & Hardware

JEWELLS AUTO BODY
Painting of Aircraft

J.H.MCKINNON LTD.
Instruments Overhaul

JRS ENTERPRISES INC.
Engines Overhaul

KITCHENER AERO AVIONICS
Radio Installations

LEAVENS AVIATION INC.
Components Overhaul & Parts Supply

LABLANC INSTRUMENTS
Instrument Overhaul & Manufacture

NAVAIR LTD.
Avionics & Radio Overhaul

NORTHERN AIRBORNE
Audio Panel

ROBERT MITCHELL INC.
Specialized Metal Castings

SLATER STEELS CORPORATION
Steel Products

STANDARD AERO
Pumps & Component Overhaul

STANDARD TUBE
Steel Pipe Supply

TECHNISONIC INDUSTRIES LTD.
ELT Supply (Emergency Locating Transmitter)

TEMRO DIVISION, BUDD CANADA LTD.
Overhaul of Radiators & Valves

THOMPSON-GORDON
Hydraulic Seal Manufacture

THE TRIDON COMPANIES
Special Clamps

W.G. COX AVIATION SUPPLIES LTD.
Accessories & Components

WESTERN PROPELLER (ATLANTIC) LTD.
Propellor Overhaul & NDT

WRIGHT INSTRUMENTS LTD.
Instrument Overhaul & Repair

The Martin 250/CE electric turret installed April 1989, just before publication. This is further forward than the turret that was on the Mynarski Lanc.

LANCASTER MARK X REGISTER
SQUADRON AND SERVICE

SERIAL NO.	SQUAD LETTER	TOS R.A.F.	TOS R.C.A.F.	R.A.F. SQUAD SERVICE	CONVERSION R.C.A.F.	SOS	NOTES
FM100		APR 1945		20,32,22 MUs		JAN 1947 SCRAPPED	
FM101		APR 1945	29-08-45	32 MU	A 515 CI 09-08-46	25-03-48 DISPOSED	
FM102	AF	JUN 1945	07-09-45	32 MU	10MR 404 SQUAD 1951	16-07-52 CRASHED	QUEBEC CITY 22-07-52
FM103		JAN 1945	29-08-45	32 MU		16-01-47 DISPOSED	RECEIVED FROM 6 GROUP
FM104	CX104	MAR 1945	13-08-45	428 SQUAD	10MR 107 TORBAY 1962	10-09-64 SOLD	TORONTO RCAFA MEMORIAL
FM105		APR 1945	11-08-45	20 MU		27-01-48 DISPOSED	
FM106		APR 1945		32 MU		11-08-45 CRASHED	
FM107		APR 1945		HELD IN VARIOUS MUs		JUNE 1947 SCRAPPED	
FM108		APR 1945		HELD IN VARIOUS MUs		JUNE 1947 SCRAPPED	
FM109		APR 1945		32,20 MUs		MAY 1947 SOS	
FM110	LQ-R	MAY 1945	25-07-45	405 SQUAD	10MR	23-01-55 SCRAPPED	
FM111		APR 1945	22-08-45	32 MU		15-04-48 SCRAPPED	FROM MUTAL AID
FM112		APR 1945		20 MU		MAY 1947 SOS	
FM113		APR 1945		20 MU		MAY 1947 SOS	
FM114		APR 1945		20 MU		MAY 1947 SOS	
FM115	LQ-Z	MAY 1945	28-06-45	405 SQUAD	10MR 404 SQUAD	06-11-53 CRASHED	09-10-53, GREENWOOD
FM116		MAY 1945		32 & 22 MUs		JUN 1947 SCRAPPED	
FM117		APR 1945		20 MU		MAY 1947 SOS	
FM118		APR 1945	07-09-45	32 MU, CANADIAN ARMY		22-03-48	ARMY FOR INSTRUCTION
FM119		APR 1945		32 & 20 MUs		MAY 1947 SOS	
FM120	EQ-M	APR 1945	28-06-45	408 SQUAD	10P 408 SQUAD MN120	28-09-62 SOS	OTTAWA
FM121		APR 1945		218 & 39 MUs		JUNE 1947 SCRAPPED	
FM122	LQ-L	MAY 1945	28-06-45	405 SQUAD	10P 408 SQUAD MN122	25-09-62 SOS	OTTAWA
FM123		APR 1945	22-08-45	32 MU		16-01-47 SCRAPPED	FROM MUTAL AID
FM124		MAY 1945	11-08-45	32 MU	A 552 CI 24-03-47	27-04-54 SCRAPPED	
FM125		MAY 1945		32 & 39 MUs		JUNE 1947 SCRAPPED	
FM126		MAY 1945	22-08-45	32 MU	551 B CI 19-03-47	05-03-54 DISPOSED	
FM127		MAY 1945	22-08-45	32 MU		16-01-47 SCRAPPED	FROM MUTAL AID
FM128		MAY 1945	11-08-45	32 MU	10MR 404 SQUAD	08-05-56 SCRAPPED	
FM129		MAY 1945		218 & 39 MUs		JULY 1947 SCRAPPED	
FM130	EQ-M	MAY 1945	28-06-45	DISHFORTH, 408 SQUAD		22-01-47 SCRAPPED	FROM MUTAL AID
FM131		MAY 1945		218 & 20 MUs		MAY 1947 SOS	
FM132		JUN 1945		218 & 39 MUs		JUNE 1947 SCRAPPED	
FM133		JUN 1945		5 & 20 MUs		AUG 1947 SOS	
FM134		JUN 1945		5 & 20 MUs		AUG 1947 SOS	
FM135		MAY 1945		5,32 & 22 MUs		JUNE 1947 SCRAPPED	
FM136	RX136	MAY 1945	07-09-45	32 MU	10MR 407 SQUAD	10-04-61 MUSEUM	CALGARY, ALBERTA
FM137		MAY 1945		20,218,20 MUs		MAY 1947 SOS	
FM138		MAY 1945		HELD IN VARIOUS MUs		JUNE 1947 SCRAPPED	
FM139		MAY 1945		HELD IN VARIOUS MUs		JUNE 1947 SCRAPPED	
FM140		MAY 1945	04-09-45	5,218 MUs	10MP 404 SQUAD	28-09-55 SCRAPPED	AT GREENWOOD
FM141		MAY 1945		HELD IN VARIOUS MUs		JUNE 1947 SCRAPPED	
FM142		MAY 1945		HELD IN VARIOUS MUs		JUNE 1947 SCRAPPED	
FM143		MAY 1945		32 MU		MAY 1947 CRASHED	FLYING TO 20 MU
FM144		JUN 1945		HELD IN VARIOUS MUs		JUNE 1947 SCRAPPED	
FM145		JUN 1947		HELD IN VARIOUS MUs		JUNE 1947 SCRAPPED	
FM146		JUN 1945		HELD IN VARIOUS MUs		JUNE 1947 SCRAPPED	
FM147		JUN 1945		HELD IN VARIOUS MUs		JUNE 1947 SCRAPPED	
FM148	FC-D	JUN 1945	04-09-45	HELD IN VARIOUS MUs	10SR WINTER TRIALS	09-01-56 SCRAPPED	GREENWOOD
FM149						SOLD?	NO RECORD
FM150		MAY 1945		HELD IN VARIOUS MUs		JUNE 1947 SCRAPPED	
FM151		MAY 1945		HELD IN VARIOUS MUs		JUNE 1947 SCRAPPED	
FM152		JUN 1945		32 & 39 MUs		JUNE 1947 SCRAPPED	
FM153		JUN 1945	04-09-45	218 MU		19-01-48 SOS	FROM MUTAL AID
FM154		MAY 1945		32 & 39 MUs		JUNE 1947 SCRAPPED	
FM155		JUL 1945	07-09-45	32 MU		27-01-48 SOS	FROM MUTAL AID
FM156		JUN 1945		32 & 39 MUs		JUNE 1947 SCRAPPED	
FM157		JUN 1945		218 & 20 MUs		AUG 1947 SOS	
FM158		MAY 1945		32 & 29 MUs		JUNE 1947 SCRAPPED	
FM159	RX159	MAY 1945	07-09-45	32 MU	10MR 407 SQUAD,103RU	04-10-60 SOLD	GREENWOOD, NANTON,ALB.
FM160		JUN 1945		20,32,20 MUs		MAY 1947 SOS	
FM161		JUN 1945		20,32,20 MUs		MAY 1947 SOS	
FM162		JUN 1945		20 MU & OTHERS MUs		JUNE 1947 SCRAPPED	
FM163		JUN 1945		20 MU & OTHERS MUs		JUNE 1947 SCRAPPED	
FM164		JUN 1945		20,218,20 MUs		MAY 1947 SOS	
FM165		JUN 1945		39 MU		JUNE 1947 SCRAPPED	
FM166		JUN 1945		39 MU		JUNE 1947 SCRAPPED	
FM167		JUN 1945		39 MU		JUNE 1947 SCRAPPED	
FM168		JUN 1945		20 MU		MAY 1947 SCRAPPED	
FM169	ZK-J	JUN 1945		1668 CU & OTHER MUs		JUNE 1947 SCRAPPED	
FM170		JUN 1945		20,32,39,218,20 MUs		JUNE 1947 SCRAPPED	
FM171		JUN 1945		20,32,39,218,20 MUs		JUNE 1947 SCRAPPED	

FM172		JUN 1945	21-08-46	313 FTU	10MR 405 SQUAD	13-09-55 SCRAPPED	FROM MUTAL AID
FM173	AF-F	JUN 1945	21-08-46	313 FTU	10MR 405 SQUAD	13-09-55 SCRAPPED	
FM174		JUN 1945		HELD IN VARIOUS MUs		MAY 1947 SCRAPPED	
FM175		JUN 1945		HELD IN VARIOUS MUs		MAY 1947 SCRAPPED	
FM176		JUN 1945		HELD IN VARIOUS MUs		MAY 1947 SCRAPPED	
FM177		JUN 1945		HELD IN VARIOUS MUs		MAY 1947 SCRAPPED	
FM178		JUN 1945		HELD IN VARIOUS MUs		MAY 1947 SCRAPPED	
FM179		JUN 1945		HELD IN VARIOUS MUs		MAY 1947 SCRAPPED	
FM180		JUN 1945		HELD IN VARIOUS MUs		MAY 1947 SCRAPPED	
FM181		JUN 1945		HELD IN VARIOUS MUs		MAY 1947 SCRAPPED	
FM182		JUN 1945		HELD IN VARIOUS MUs		MAY 1947 SCRAPPED	
FM183		JUN 1945		HELD IN VARIOUS MUs		MAY 1947 SCRAPPED	
FM184				TCA	XPP CF-CMX TCA-105		
FM185				TCA	XPP CF-CMY TCA-106		TO G-AKDP
FM186				TCA	XPP CF-CMZ TCA-107		TO G-AKDR
FM187				TCA	XPP CF-CNA TCA-108		TO G-AKDS
FM188		JUN 1945		218,20 MUs		MAY 1947 SOS	
FM189		JUN 1945		218,20 MUs		MAY 1947 SOS	
FM190		JUN 1945		5 MU		03-08-45 CRASHED	LEAVING 5 MU
FM191		JUN 1945		HELD IN VARIOUS MUs		MAY 1947 SOS	HOUNSLOW
FM192		JUN 1945		HELD IN VARIOUS MUs		MAY 1947 SOS	HOUNSLOW
FM193		JUN 1945		HELD IN VARIOUS MUs		MAY 1947 SOS	HOUNSLOW
FM194		JUN 1945		HELD IN VARIOUS MUs		MAY 1947 SOS	HOUNSLOW
FM195		JUN 1945		HELD IN VARIOUS MUs		MAY 1947 SOS	HOUNSLOW
FM196		JUN 1945		HELD IN VARIOUS MUs		MAY 1947 SOS	HOUNSLOW
FM197		JUN 1945		HELD IN VARIOUS MUs		MAY 1947 SOS	HOUNSLOW
FM198		JUN 1945		HELD IN VARIOUS MUs		MAY 1947 SOS	HOUNSLOW
FM199	AF-K	JUL 1945	21-08-46	313 FTU	10P 408 SQUAD	02-06-60 SCRAPPED	
FM200		AUG 1945		20 MU		1947 SOLD AS SCRAP	
FM201		AUG 1945		RAE SEPT 1945		MAY 1950 SOLD	
FM202		AUG 1945		20 MU		MAY 1947 SCRAPPED	
FM203		AUG 1945		20 MU		MAY 1947 SCRAPPED	
FM204		AUG 1945		20 MU & EANS		MAY 1947 SOS	
FM205		AUG 1945		ORENDA			TEST BED FOR ORENDA 1951
FM206	CQ206	AUG 1945	21-08-46	20 MU	10N 'NORTHERN CROSS'	28-05-57 SOLD	CNS SUMMERSIDE
FM207	MN207	AUG 1945	21-08-46	LAST LANC X TO RAF	10P 408 SQUAD	28-09-62	USED FOR SPARES
FM208			21-08-46		10N 'POLARIS' CNS	28-05-57 SUMMERSIDE	BECAME CF-KHH
FM209			21-08-46	FLYING ENGINE TEST	10O ORENDA TEST BED	24-07-56 DESTROYED	BY FIRE, MALTON
FM210			21-08-46		10MR 407 SQUAD COMOX	23-01-55 SCRAPPED	SPARES AT GREENWOOD
FM211			21-06-46		10N 'ZENITH' CNS	08-05-56 SCRAPPED	VC-GSX, SUMMERSIDE
FM212			26-09-46		10P 408 SQUADS	09-10-64 SOLD	WINDSOR MEMORIAL
FM213	AG-J	CX213	21-08-46	405 SQUAD & 107 R.U.	10MR/MP RESTORED CWH	06-11-63 SO 30-06-64	GODERICH - CWH FLYING 11- 09-88
FM214			21-08-46		10P 413 & 408 SQUADS	23-03-50 CRASHED	
FM215			21-08-46		10P 413 & 408 SQUADS	28-09-62 SOS	
FM216	AP-D		21-08-46		10P 413 & 408 SQUADS	17-08-50 SOS	VC-APD
FM217			21-08-46		10P 413 & 408 SQUADS	02-06-60 CRASHED	
FM218	AP-U		21-08-46		10P 413 & 408 SQDS	05-03-52 CRASHED	VC-APU
FM219			21-08-46		10MP 407 SQUAD	17-05-65	DUNNVILLE
FM220	AF-M		21-08-46		10MR 404 & 405 SQUAD	23-06-55 SCRAPPED	AT GREENWOOD
FM221	DD-R		21-08-46		10BR PROTOTYPE	23-09-50 CRASHED	AT RESOLUTE BAY
FM222			21-08-46		10SR 103 RESCUE UNIT	04-04-56 SPARTAN AIR	SOLD, CF-IMF PHOTO SURVEY
FM223	N-223	AF-O	21-08-46		10MR 404 & 405 SQUAD	06-09-60 SCRAPPED	
FM224			21-08-46		10MR 405 & 407 SQUAD	17-05-65	DUNNVILLE
FM225			21-08-46		10MR 405 SQUAD	23-06-55 SCRAPPED	SPARES
FM226			21-08-46		10MR	29-09-55 SCRAPPED	SPARES, AT GREENWOOD
FM227			21-06-46		10MR 405 & 103 S&R	13-09-55 SCRAPPED	GREENWOOD
FM228			21-08-46		10MR 103 RESCUE UNIT	12-08-54 SCRAPPED	GREENWOOD
FM229	AG-R		21-08-46		10MR 405 SQUAD	13-09-55 SCRAPPED	AT GREENWOOD, LAST PROD MK X
KB700	LQ-Q	OCT 1943		405 & 419 SQUAD VR-Z	RUHR EXPRESS	02-01-45 BURNED AT	MID. ST.GEO, 1ST CANADIAN MK X
KB701		DEC 1943		419 SQUAD		16-05-44 CRASH BURNT	NEAR WOMBLETON 122hrs
KB702				TCA-CGTAS	XT CF-CMT TCA-101	1947-48-51	TRANS-ALTANTIC SERVICE
KB703				TCA-CGTAS	XT CF-CMU TCA-102	29-12-44 LOST AT SEA	ALANTIC
KB704	VR-Y	DEC 1943		419 SQUAD		11-05-44 CRASHED	
KB705	NA-F	JAN 1944		428 SQ,1664/66CU,20M	ROLLS ROYCE JAN 1944	MARCH 1946 SOS	INTERCHANGE TEST A/C
KB706	VR-A	DEC 1943		419 SQUAD		24/25 MAY 1944	MIA (AACHEN)
KB707	VR-W	MAY 1944		419 SQUAD		19-09-44 CRASHED	MIDDLETON ST GEORGE
KB708	VR-E	JAN 1944		419 SQUAD	ROLLS ROYCE 1944	25/26-08-44 CRASHED	OVERSHOT BOSCOMBE DOWN
KB709	NA-G	AUG 1944		428 SQUAD		29/30-08-44	MIA (STETTIN) 107 hrs
KB710	VR-W	MAR 1944		419 SQUAD		12/13-05-44	MIA (LOUVAIN) 107 hrs
KB711	VR-C	APR 1944		70MU & 419 SQUAD		01/02-05-44	MIA (ST.GHISLAIN) 92 hrs
KB712	VR-L	APR 1944		419 SQUAD		28-10-44	MIA (COLOGNE) 409 hrs
KB713	VR-X	APR 1944		419 SQUAD		12/13-05-44	MIA (LOUVAIN) 80 hrs
KB714	VR-Y	MAY 1944		419 SQUAD		13-06-44	MIA (CAMBRAI) 87 hrs
KB715	VR-T	MAY 1944		419 SQUAD		24-12-44 43 ops	MIA (LEHAUSEN AIRFIELD)
KB716	VR-D	APR 1944		419 SQUAD		07-05-44 CRASHED	MIDDLETON ST GEORGE
KB717	VR-E	APR 1944		419 SQUAD		22/23-05-44	MIA (DORTMUND) 94 hrs
KB718	VR-J	APR 1944		419 SQUAD		4/5-07-44	MIA (VILLENEUVE ST.GEORGES)
KB719	VR-T	APR 1944		419 SQUAD		24/25-07-44	MIA (STUTTGART) 225 hrs
KB720	VR-P	APR 1944		419 SQUAD & 1664 CU	1666 CU & 20MU 1944	MAY-1944 SOS	
KB721	VR-B	APR 1944	06-07-45	AAEE & 419 SQUAD	A 448 CI 29-08-45	25-11-48 SCRAPPED	54 ops
KB722	VR-A	APR 1944		419 SQUAD		5/6-01-45 CRASHED	Nr ST.QUENTIN, 63 ops
KB723	VR-U	APR 1944		419 SQUAD		4/5-07-44 181 hrs	MIA(VILLENEUVE ST.GEORGES)
KB724	VR-K	MAY 1944		419 SQUAD		28-08-44 CRASHED	MID.ST.GEO. 298 hrs
KB725	NA-L	MAY 1944		428 SQUAD		03-02-45 CRASHED	AT ELTON HALL

Serial	Code	Date	Date2	Squadron	Notes	Fate Date	Remarks
KB726	VR-A	APR 1944		419 SQUAD	Nr VARENNES	12/13-06-44 CRASHED	MIA(CAMBRAI) MYNARSKI V.C.46hr
KB727	VR-H	APR 1944		419 SQUAD		4/5-07-45 158 hrs	MIA(VILLENEUVE ST GEORGE)
KB728	VR-V	APR 1944		419 SQUAD		17-06-44	MIA 159 hrs
KB729					XPP CF-CMV TCA-103		TO G-AKDO
KB730					XPP CF-CMW TCA-104		TO AP-ACM
KB731	VR-S	APR 1944		419 SQUAD		13-06-44	MIA (CAMBRAI) 118 hrs
KB732	VR-X	MAY 1944	06-07-45	419 SQUAD TERMINATOR	OLDEST LANC MOST OPS	15-05-48 DISPOSED	NORTH CALGARY, 83 ops
KB733	VR-G	APR 1944	10-07-45	419 SQUAD	A 450 CI 29-08-45	18-05-48 SOS	
KB734	VR-F	MAY 1944		419 SQUAD		17-06-44 CRASHED	MIA,NEAR ZEIST 85 hrs
KB735	VR-O	MAY 1944		419 SQUAD		18/19-09-44 CRASHED	OVERSHOT EASTMOOR 314 hrs
KB736	VR-M	MAY 1944		419 SQUAD,1664 HCU		24-08-44 SOS	
KB737	NA-R	MAY 1944		428 SQUAD		25-10-44	MIA (ESSEN) 359 hrs
KB738	VR-D	MAY 1944		419 SQUAD		28-12-44	MIA (OPLADEN)
KB739	NA-W		16-06-45	428 SQUAD		12-03-48 SOS	WINTER TRIALS 1945/46
KB740	NA-V	JUL 1944		428 SQUAD		25-07-44	DIA
KB741	SE-Y	NOV 1944		431 & 434 SQUADS		14/15-02-45	MIA (CHEMNITZ)
KB742		JUN 1944		428 SQUAD		4-11-44 CRASHED	OVERSHOT,MID.ST.GEO. 314hrs
KB743	NA-I	JUN 1944		428 SQUAD		18/19-08-44	MIA (BREMEN) 159 hrs
KB744	NA-J	JUN 1944	06-07-45	428 SQUAD		13-05-47 DISPOSED	LETHBRIDGE
KB745	VR-V	JUN 1944		419 SQUAD		4-10-44 CRASHED	HIGH GROUND, HOPE 207hrs
KB746	VR-S	JUN 1944	06-07-45	419 SQUAD		16-01-47 SCRAPPED	PEARCE ALBERTA, 68 ops
KB747	NA-X	JUN 1944	06-07-45	428 SQUAD		19-01-48 SCRAPPED	
KB748	VR-O	SEP 1944	06-07-45	419 SQUAD	A 449 CI 29-08-45	18-05-48 SCRAPPED	59 ops
KB749	NA-A	JUN 1944		428 SQUAD		15-08-44	MIA (SOESTERBERG)145hrs
KB750	VR-N	JUN 1944		419 SQUAD		2/3-02-45	MIA (WIESBADEN)
KB751	NA-Q	JUL 1944		428 SQUAD		16/17-08-44	MIA (STETTIN)138hrs
KB752	VR-S	JUN 1944		419 SQUAD 'V'		08-04-45 CRASHED	ABANDONED IN AIR 51 ops
KB753	VR-L	JUN 1944		419 SQUAD 'B'		29-12-44	MIA (SCHOLVEN OIL REFINERY)
KB754	VR-C	JUN 1944		419 SQUAD		09-10-44	MIA (BOCHUM) 226hrs
KB755	VR-F	JUN 1944		419 SQUAD		7/8-08-44	MIA (CAEN) 122hrs
KB756	NA-Q	JUN 1944		428 SQUAD		05-08-44	MIA 62hrs
KB757	NA-C	JUL 1944	06-07-45	428 SQUAD		16-01-47 SCRAPPED	PEARCE ALBERTA
KB758	NA-Z	JUN 1944		428 SQUAD		12/13-08-44	MIA (BRUNSWICK)163hrs
KB759	NA-K	JUL 1944		428 SQUAD		28/29-07-44	MIA (HAMBURG) 85hrs
KB760	NA-P	JUL 1944	19-07-45	428 SQUAD		16-01-47 SCRAPPED	PEARCE ALBERTA
KB761	VR-H	JUL 1944		419 SQUAD		31-04-45	MIA (HAMBURG) 66ops
KB762	VR-J	JUL 1944				23-04-45 CRASHED	MID.ST.GEO. 73 ops
KB763	NA-S	JUL 1944		428 & 419 SQUADS		23-04-45 WRECKED	U/C COLLAPSED
KB764	NA-B	JUL 1944	09-01-46	428 SQUAD		01-02-46 DITCHED	OFF AZORES 04-06-45
KB765	VR-Q	JUL 1944		419 SQUAD		29-12-44 57 ops	MIA (SCHLOVEN OIL REFINERY)
KB766		JUN 1944		428 SQUAD		02/03-12-44 CRASHED	(BEAUVAIS TILLE)
KB767	VR-U	JUL 1944		419 SQUAD		01-11-44 DAMAGED	MANSTON 224 hrs
KB768		JUL 1944		428 SQUAD		05-12-44 COLLIDED	WITH 426 SQ A/C, RUGBY
KB769	VR-I	JUL 1944		419 SQUAD		14-01-45	MIA (MERSBERG REFINERY)
KB770	NA-D	JUL 1944		428 SQUAD		28/29-06-45	MIA
KB771		JUL 1944	06-07-45	428 SQUAD	No.2 AIR COMMAND	13-05-47 SCRAPPED	
KB772	VR-R	NOV 1944	13-07-45	419 SQUAD	EASTERN AIR COMMAND	13-05-47 SCRAPPED	64 ops
KB773	SE-A	AUG 1944	06-07-45	431 SQUAD		08-03-48 SCRAPPED	VULCAN
KB774	VR-P	AUG 1944	06-07-45	419 & 431 SQUAD SE-D		22-01-47 SCRAPPED	CLARESHOLM
KB775	VR-Y	AUG 1944		419 SQUAD		25-09-45	MIA (RUSSELSLHEIM)64 hrs
KB776	VR-F	AUG 1944		419 SQUAD		23-10-44	MIA 164 hrs
KB777	NA-V	AUG 1944		428 SQUAD		22-03-45 SHOT DOWN	BY JU88(HILDERSHEIM)
KB778	NA-Y	AUG 1944		428 SQUAD		5/6-03-45 CRASHED	FROM 2000 ft BARAQUE
KB779	VR-B	AUG 1944		419 SQUAD		06-12-44	MIA (OSNABRUCK)
KB780	NA-T	JUL 1944		428 SQUAD		14-10-44	MIA (DUISBERG) 168hrs
KB781	NA-U	AUG 1944	06-07-45	428 SQUAD	10S	13-01-56 SCRAPPED	ROCKCLIFFE
KB782	NA-H	AUG 1944		428 SQUAD		02-11-44	MIA 233 hrs
KB783		OCT 1944	06-07-45	AAEE & 419 SQUAD	A 451 CI 07-11-45	26-11-47 SCRAPPED	MARTIN TURRET TRIALS AAEE 1944
KB784	NA-K	AUG 1944		428 SQUAD		13/14-04-45	MIA (KIEL)
KB785	VR-Y	AUG 1944		419 SQUAD		24-11-44 CRASHED	NEAR BRADBURY RANGE
KB786	VR-P	AUG 1944		419 SQUAD		21-03-45 DITCHED	MIA RETURNING (HEIDE)
KB787	VR-M	SEP 1944		419 SQUAD		04-02-45 CRASHED	MIA Nr.ARDENNES(BONN)
KB788	VR-C	SEP 1944		419 & 431 SQUAD		01-13-44	DIA
KB789	WL-V	DEC 1944	06-07-45	434 SQUAD		08-03-48 SCRAPPED	VULCAN
KB790		MAR 1944		HELD IN VARIOUS MUs		MAY 1947 SCRAPPED	
KB791	NA-A	AUG 1944	06-07-45	428 SQUAD	No.2 AIR COMMAND	13-05-47 SCRAPPED	
KB792	NA-I	SEP 1944		428 SQUAD		2/3-02-45	MIA (WIESBADEN)
KB793	NA-E	SEP 1944		428 SQUAD		13-01-45 CRASHED	FIRE IN AIR, DURHAM
KB794		SEP 1944	06-07-45	428 SQUAD		16-01-47 DISPOSED	PEARCE
KB795	NA-Q	SEP 1944		428 SQUAD		07-04-45 CRASHED	LANDING MID.ST.GEO.
KB796	SE-R	SEP 1944	13-08-45	*419 & 431 SQUAD 'A'	DAMAGED 08-01-45	22-01-47 SCRAPPED	PENHOLD
KB797	VR-K	SEP 1944		419 SQUAD		07-04-45	MIA (DESSAU)
KB798	NA-G	SEP 1944		*419 & 428 SQUAD		28-12-44	MIA (OPLADEN)
KB799	VR-W	OCT 1944		419 SQUAD	THE MOOSE	14-01-45 100th LANC	MIA (MERSEBURG REFINERY)
KB800	VR-C	SEP 1944		419 SQUAD		14-10-44	MIA (DUISBERG)29 hrs
KB801	SE-S	NOV 1944	06-07-45	431 SQUAD	10S	08-05-56 SCRAPPED	AT CLARESHOLM
KB802	SE-V	NOV 1944	06-07-45	*419 & 431 SQUAD	No.2 AIR COMMAND	22-01-47 DISPOSED	
KB803	SE-N	NOV 1944		431 SQUAD		26-01-45 CRASHED	AT YAFFORTH
KB804	VR-E	NOV 1944		419 SQUAD		20-02-45	MIA (DORTMUND)
KB805		NOV 1944		5 MU & TFU		JUL-1947 SCRAPPED	USAAF REMOTE GUN CONTROL
KB806	SE-X	NOV 1944		431 SQUAD		15-01-45	MIA (LEUNA)
KB807	SE-B	NOV 1944	06-07-45	*419 & 431 SQUAD	No.2 AIR COMMAND	22-01-47 DISPOSED	
KB808	SE-U	NOV 1944		431 SQUAD		22-03-45	MIA DAYLIGHT RAID
KB809	SE-Q	NOV 1944		*419 & 431 SQUAD		21-02-45	MIA (DORTMUND)

Serial	Code	Date	Date 2	Squadron	Notes	Fate	Location
KB810	SE-H	NOV 1944	13-08-45	431 SQUAD		08-03-48 DISPOSED	AT VULCAN
KB811	SE-T	NOV 1944	06-07-45	*419 & 431 SQUAD		27-08-50 DISPOSED	AT CLARESHOLM
KB812	SE-F	JUN 1944	06-07-45	431 SQUAD		06-04-50 SOS	AT CLARESHOLM
KB813	SE-S	SEP 1944		431 SQUAD		25-10-44 CRASHED	INTO GROUND,TINGRITH
KB814	VR-N	NOV 1944		419 & 434 SQUAD WL-S		15/16-03-45	MIA SHOT DOWN BY FIGHTER(HAGEN)
KB815	SE-K	OCT 1944		*419 & 431 SQUAD		15/16-03-45	MIA
KB816	WL-G	DEC 1944		434 & 428 SQUAD		14-04-45 CRASHED	
KB817	SE-P	OCT 1944		*419 & 431 SQUAD		01-11-44	MIA 76 hrs
KB818	SE-G	OCT 1944		431 SQUAD		07-02-45 CRASHED	AT FORD
KB819	SE-J	NOV 1944	13-08-45	431 SQUAD		15-04-48 DISPOSED	AT CLARESHOLM
KB820	NA-M	NOV 1944	19-07-45	428 SQUAD CRASHED	03-12-44	06-04-50 DISPOSED	AT CLARESHOLM
KB821	SE-P	NOV 1944		431 SQUAD		06/07-01-45	MIA
KB822	SE-W	OCT 1944		431 SQUAD		25-04-45 COLLIDED	OVER SEA WITH KB831
KB823	VR-U	OCT 1944	06-07-45	419 SQUAD		27-01-48 DISPOSED	AT MEDICINE HAT
KB824	WL-E	DEC 1944	13-08-45	*419 & 434 SQUAD	DAMAGED 23/24-02-45	22-01-47 DISPOSED	AT PENHOLD
KB825	WL-A	DEC 1944	06-07-45	434 SQUAD		22-01-47 DISPOSED	AT CLARESHOLM
KB826	WL-K	DEC 1944	06-07-45	434 SQUAD	10N ORION CNS	28-05-57 SOS	SUMMERSIDE
KB827	SE-M	NOV 1944	13-08-45	431 SQUAD CRASHED	TWICE	22-01-47 SOS	AT CLARESHOLM
KB828		SEP 1944				25-09-44 CRASHED	IN TRANSIT
KB829	WL-C	DEC 1944	06-07-45	434 SQUAD		08-03-48 DISPOSED	AT VULCAN
KB830	WL-D	DEC 1944	06-07-45	*419 & 434 SQUAD		08-03-48 DISPOSED	AT VULCAN
KB831	SE-E	DEC 1944		*419 & 431 SQUAD		25-04-45 COLLIDED	OVER SEA WITH KB822
KB832	WL-F	DEC 1944		*419 & 434 SQUAD		22-03-45 COLLIDED	AND EXPLODEED, CROFT
KB833	WL-B	DEC 1944	06-07-45	*419 & 434 SQUAD		08-05-48 DISPOSED	AT VULCAN
KB834	WL-Y	DEC 1944		434 SQUAD		11-03-45	MIA DAY ATTACK (ESSEN)
KB835	WL-J	DEC 1944		434 SQUAD		15/16-03-45	MIA SHOT DOWN BY JU88, LANDEN
KB836	WL-H	DEC 1944	06-07-45	434 SQUAD		08-03-48 DISPOSED	AT VULCAN
KB837	SE-X	DEC 9144	06-07-45	431 SQUAD		24-08-50 DISPOSED	AT CLARESHOLM
KB838	NA-O	DEC 1944	05-07-45	428 SQUAD		15-04-48 DISPOSED	AT CALGARY
KB839	VR-D	JAN 1945	06-07-45	419 & 408 SQUADS	10AR	RETAINED DUNNVILLE	GREENWOOD N.S. ENGINES TO CWH
KB840	WL-N	DEC 1944	06-07-45	434 SQUAD		22-01-47 DISPOSED	AT CLARESHOLM
KB841	VR-A	JAN 1945	06-07-45	419 SQUAD		15-04-48 DISPOSED	AT CALGARY
KB842	WL-L	DEC 1944		*419 & 434 SQUAD		5/6-03-45 CRASHED	LANDED AFTER COLLISION
KB843	WL-Q	DEC 1944	06-07-45	434 & 428 SQUADS FEB	1945	13-05-47 DISPOSED	AT PEARCE
KB844	WL-W	DEC 1944	13-08-45	*419 & 434 SQUAD		08-03-48 DISPOSED	AT CLARESHOLM
KB845	VR-L	DEC 1944		*419 SQUAD		5/6-03-45 CRASHED	DRAYTON PARSLOE
KB846	NA-I	JAN 1945		428 & 434 SQUAD WL-P		15/16-03-45 CRASHED	IN ALLIED LINES
KB847	SE-R	JAN 1945	06-07-45			24-08-50 SOS	AT CLARESHOLM
KB848	NA-G	JAN 1945	06-07-45	428 SQUAD	10DC PX848	03-04-64 SOS	AT GREENWOOD
KB849	WL-T	DEC 1944	06-07-45	434 SQUAD		06-04-50 SOS	AT CLARESHOLM
KB850	WL-O	DEC 1944		*419 & 434 SQUAD		17-01-45	MIA OIL PLANT(ZEITZ)
KB851	VR-W	JAN 1945	06-07-45	419 SQUAD	10DC PX851 DRONE A/C	22-08-61 SCRAPPED	TWO RYAN FIREBEES 23-01-57
KB852	WL-R	DEC 1944	06-07-45	434 SQUAD		08-03-48 DISPOSED	AT VULCAN
KB853	SE-A	NOV 1944		431 SQUAD		11-04-45	MIA
KB854	VR-T	JAN 1945	06-07-45	419 SQUAD	10S No.2 AIR COM	05-10-55 SCRAPPED	No.2 AC 18-03-46
KB855	NA-F	JAN 1945		*419 & 428 SQUAD		20-02-45 CRASHED	LANDED MID.ST.GEO.
KB856	SE-K	MAR 1945	13-08-45	431 SQUAD	No.2 AIR COMMAND	22-01-47 DISPOSED	No.2 AIR COMMAND 1945
KB857	VR-N	FEB 1945	06-07-45	419 SQUAD 405 AG-N	10MR 404,5& 7 SQUADS	02-09-58 SCRAPPED	407 SQUAD 1957,MN857
KB858		FEB 1945		431 SQUAD		05-03-45	MIA
KB859		FEB 1945		431 SQUAD		31-03-45	MIA
KB860	VR-L	NOV 1944	06-07-45	*419 SQUAD		27-01-48 DISPOSED	MEDICINE HAT 1947
KB861	SE-Q	FEB 1945	06-07-45	431 SQUAD	No.2 AIR COMMAND	24-08-54 SOS	2 AIR COMMAND 1945
KB862		FEB 1945	06-07-45	434 SQUAD	No.2 AIR COMMAND	22-01-47 DISPOSED	2 AIR COMMAND 1945
KB863	WL-P	FEB 1945	06-07-45	434 SQUAD	No.2 AIR COMMAND	22-01-47 DISPOSED	2 AIR COMMAND 1945
KB864	NA-S	FEB 1945	06-07-45	428 SQUAD	SPIRIT OF LISTOWEL	16-01-47 DISPOSED	No.2 AIR COMMAND1945
KB865	VR-E	FEB 1945	06-07-45	419 SQUAD	10MR 407 SQUAD 1954	02-06-60 SCRAPPED	
KB866	VR-M	FEB 1945		419 SQUAD		13-04-45	MIA (KIEL)
KB867	NA-L	NOV 1944	06-07-45	428 SQUAD	No.2 AIR COMMAND	15-04-48 SOS	2 AIR COMMAND 1945
KB868	SE-E	MAR 1945	28-06-45	431 SQUAD	10MP 405 SQUAD AG-S	23-06-55 SCRAPPED	STN GREENWOOD 1952
KB869	VR-Q	FEB 1945		419 SQUAD		31-03-45	MIA (HAMBURG)
KB870	VR-K	FEB 1945		419 SQUAD		15/16-03-45 BLEW UP	MIA, AFTER FIGHTER ATTACK
KB871	SE-E	FEB 1945	28-06-45	*419,431,420 SQUADS	10MR 407 SQUAD	06-09-60 SCRAPPED	407 SQUAD 1954 PT-E
KB872	SE-N	FEB 1945	25-09-45	431 & 420 SQUADS	10BR No.2AIR COMMAND	22-01-47 DISPOSED	2 AC 1945
KB873	SE-G	FEB 1945	06-07-45	431 & 434 SQUAD WL-G	No.2 AIR COMMAND	13-05-47 DISPOSED	2 AC 1945
KB874		JAN 1945		DEFFORD, 431 SQUAD		25-03-45	DIA
KB875	VR-Z	JAN 1945	28-06-45	*419 &425 SQUAD KW-U	10MR 407 SQUAD	02-06-60 SCRAPPED	407 SQUAD 1954
KB876	KW-L	JAN 1945	28-06-45	425 SQUAD		22-01-47 SOS	CLARESHOLM 1945
KB877	EQ-S	JAN 1945	28-06-45	408 SQUAD		27-01-48 DISPOSED	MEDICINE HAT 1947
KB878	VR-I	MAR 1945	06-07-45	419 SQUAD	A 538 CI 08-10-46	27-04-54 SOS	2 AC 1945
KB879		MAR 1945		428 SQUAD		30-04-45 CRASHED	FROM 16,000 FT (HIXON)
KB880	WL-L	MAR 1945	06-07-45	434 SQUAD		06-04-50 CRASHED	18-04-45, CLARESHOLM
KB881	VR-C	MAR 1945	06-07-45	419 SQUAD		16-01-47 DISPOSED	PEARCE 1946
KB882	NA-R	MAR 1945	06-07-45	428 SQUAD	10AR 408 SQUAD MN882	26-05-64 SCRAPPED	EDMUNDSTON N.B.
KB883		MAR 1945	06-07-45	434 SQUAD	10MP 407 SQUAD RX883	02-06-60 SCRAPPED	CRASHED MAR 1945
KB884	VR-K	MAR 1945	06-07-45	419 SQUAD	A 526 CI 01-08-46	04-08-49	7 PHOTO WING 1945
KB885	WL-Q	MAR 1945	28-06-45	434 & 420 SQUAD PT-Y	CF-IMF SPARTAN AIR	22-01-47 SOLD	CLARESHOLM 1945
KB886	PT-H	APR 1945	28-06-45	420 SQUAD	No.2 AIR COMMAND	27-01-48 DISPOSED	2 AC 1945
KB887		APR 1945		5 MU		DEC 1946 SCRAPPED	
KB888	SE-O	MAR 1945	06-07-45	*419 & 431 SQUADS	No.2 AIR COMMAND	06-04-50 SOS	No.2 AIR COMMAND 1945
KB889	VR-M	APR 1945	06-07-45	419,428 & 405 SQUADS	10MP 408 SQUAD107 RU	21-05-65 SOLD OSHAWA	D.ARNOLD,U.K. AVM McEWEN 405SQ
KB890		APR 1945	06-07-45	434 SQUAD	10MP 404 SQUAD SP890	25-10-61 SOS	404 SQUAD 1952
KB891	NA-F	MAR 1945	06-07-45	428 SQUAD	No.2 AIR COMMAND	16-01-47 DISPOSED	2 AC 1945
KB892	VR-P	MAR 1945	06-07-45	419 SQUAD	10MP 407 SQUAD AJ892	02-06-60 SOS	407 SQUAD 1954
KB893		FEB 1945	06-07-45	431 & 434 SQUADS	10MP WOODFORD FEB 45	08-05-52 CRASHED	BASED AT TRENTON 1952
KB894	KW-A	MAY 1945	28-06-45	425 SQUAD	10MR 407 SQUAD RX894	10-04-61 SOS	407 SQUAD 1957

KB895	WL-O	MAR 1945	11-09-45	434 SQUAD	No.2 AIR COMMAND 45	22-01-47 SOLD FARMER	C/S USED TO SALVAGE FM213
KB896	VR-V	MAR 1945	28-06-45	419 & 420 SQUAD PT-O	No.2 AIR COMMAND	16-01-47 DISPOSED	No.2 AC 1945
KB897		MAR 1945		218 & 39 MUs		JUN 1947 SCRAPPED	
KB898	PT-W	JAN 1945	28-06-45	420 SQUAD	No.2 AIR COMMAND	22-01-47 DISPOSED	NO.2 AC 1945
KB899	NA-V	APR 1945	28-06-45	428,&425 SQUAD KW-X		27-01-48 DISPOSED	MEDICINE HAT 1947
KB900	SE-C	APR 1945	06-07-45	431 SQUAD		24-08-50 SOS	AT CLARESHOLM 1945
KB901	PT-Q	MAY 1945	28-06-45	420 SQUAD	10MP 404 SQUAD	02-06-60 SCRAPPED	No.2 MOTU
KB902	PT-C	APR 1945	28-06-45	434 & 420 SQUADS	606 C CI 20-07-54	04-04-56 SOS	
KB903	PT-R	MAY 1945	28-06-45	420 & 425 SQUAD KW-R	10MP PROTOTYPE 10MR	02-06-60 SCRAPPED	TORBAY 1955,No.2 MOTU
KB904	EQ-Q	MAY 1945	28-06-45	408 SQUAD	10MP 407 SQUAD	02-06-60 SCRAPPED	407 SQUAD 1954
KB905	EQ-V	APR 1945	28-06-45	408 SQUAD		22-01-47 DISPOSED	AT CLARESHOLM 1945
KB906		APR 1945	22-08-45	20, 32 MUs	10BR No.2AIR COMMAND	13-05-47 DISPOSED	2 AC SQUAD
KB907	EQ-U	MAY 1945	28-06-45	408 SQUAD	10SR C/N 37208	04-04-56SOLD SPARTAN	AIR CF-IMG PHOTO,TRENTON 1951
KB908	PT-P	FEB 1945	28-06-45	420 SQUAD	C/N 37209	15-04-48 DISPOSED	AT NORTH CALGARY 1946
KB909	VR-Y	MAR 1945	28-06-45	419 & 420 SQUAD PT-R	C/N 37210 CF-IMH	04-04-56 SOLD TO	SPARTAN AIR, AT BORDEN 1951
KB910	NA-V	MAR 1945	28-06-45	428 & 420 SQUAD PT-V		16-01-47 DISPOSED	AT PEARCE 1946
KB911		JAN 1945		434 SQUAD		31-03-45	MIA
KB912	KW-Q	JAN 1945	28-06-45	5 MU & 425 SQUAD		27-01-48 DISPOSED	AT MEDICINE HAT 1947
KB913	EQ-X	MAR 1945	28-06-45	5 MU & 408 SQUAD		22-01-47 DISPOSED	AT CLARESHOLM 1945
KB914	WL-A	FEB 1945	28-06-45	434 & 420 SQUAD PT-A	10MR	19-03-53 MISSING	01-02-53 GREENWOOD
KB915	VR-H	MAR 1945	29-06-45	419 & 425 SQUAD KW-H		27-01-48 DISPOSED	AT MEDICINE HAT 1947
KB916	PT-C	APR 1945	28-06-45	420 & 425 SQUAD KW-C		30-01-52 BURNED	AT TRENTON, AT PEARCE 1945
KB917	PT-E	MAR 1945	28-06-45	420 & 425 SQUAD KW-E		02-01-47 SOS	No.9(T) GROUP 1946
KB918	PT-P	JAN 1945	28-06-45	420 & 425 SQUAD KW-P		16-01-47 DISPOSED	AT PEARCE 1946
KB919	EQ-J	APR 1945	28-06-45	408 SQUAD	10MR 1st CONVER.DJ-D	25-08-55 SCRAPPED	No.2 (M)OTU GREENWOOD
KB920	WL-K	MAR 1945	06-07-45	434,428 SQUADS NA-K	10MP 407,405 SQ AF-A	02-06-60 SCRAPPED	407 SQUAD 1957
KB921		APR 1945	06-07-45	419 SQUAD		15-04-48 DISPOSED	AT NORTH CALGARY 1946
KB922		APR 1945	06-07-45	431 SQUAD		22-01-47 DISPOSED	AT CLARESHOLM 1945
KB923	PT-N	APR 1945	28-06-45	420 SQUAD	542C CI 05-11-46	09-12-48 SOS	
KB924	KW-T	MAY 1945	28-06-45	425 SQUAD		15-04-48 DISPOSED	AT NORTH CALGARY 1946
KB925	EQ-E	MAY 1945	28-06-45	408 SQUAD	10MP 407 SQUAD	02-06-60 SCRAPPED	407 SQUAD 1957
KB926	KW-F	MAY 1945	28-06-45	425 SQUAD		27-01-48 DISPOSED	AT MEDICINE HAT 1947
KB927	PT-I	APR 1945	28-06-45	420 SQUAD	10MP 2(M)OTU 404 SQ	25-08-55 SCRAPPED	404 SQUAD 1952
KB928	PT-K	APR 1945	28-06-45	420 SQUAD		22-01-47 DISPOSED	AT CLARESHOLM 1945
KB929	EQ-O	APR 1945	28-06-45	408 SQUAD	10MR No.2OTU 405 AGB	13-09-55 SCRAPPED	2 OTU 1951
KB930	KW-N	MAR 1945	28-06-45	425 SQUAD		16-04-47 SCRAPPED	AT PEARCE 1946
KB931	KW-S	MAR 1945	28-06-45	425 SQUAD		15-04-48 DISPOSED	NORTH CALGARY 1946
KB932	KW-O	MAR 1945	28-06-45	425 SQUAD		16-01-47 DISPOSED	AT PEARCE 1946
KB933	PT-J	MAR 1945	28-06-45	420 SQUAD		16-01-47 DISPOSED	AT PEARCE 1946
KB934	KW-I	MAY 1945	11-07-45	425 SQUAD	10MR	30-01-52 BURNED	AT CLARESHOLM 1945
KN935		MAY 1945		20,32,20 MUs		JAN 1948	SCRAPPED
KB936	KW-G	MAY 1945	11-07-45	425 SQUAD CRASHED	10BR	27-01-48 SCRAPPED	AT MEDICINE HAT 1947
KB937	PT-G	APR 1945	28-06-45	420 SQUAD & 2MOTU	10MP No.2(M)OTU	02-06-60 SOS	AT CLARESHOLM 1945
KB938	PT-D	APR 1945	28-06-45	420 SQUAD	10MP CFS TRENTON1952	13-06-55 CRASHED	25-06-55
KB939	EQ-W	APR 1945	28-06-45	408 SQUAD		27-01-48 DISPOSED	AT MEDICINE HAT 1947
KB940		APR 1945	22-08-45	32 MU	10MR	11-11-52 CRASHED	AT PEARCE 1945
KB941	PT-U	APR 1945	28-06-45	420 SQUAD		22-01-47 DISPOSED	AT PENHOLD 1946
KB942	PT-M	APR 1945	28-06-45	420 SQUAD		22-01-47 DISPOSED	AT CLARESHOLM 1945
KB943		APR 1945	07-09-45	32 MU	10MP 107 RU 943	17-06-65 DISPOSED	AT DUNVILLE
KB944	KW-K	MAR 1945	28-06-45	425 SQUAD	10S STN. GREENWOOD	MUSEUM, OTTAWA,'P'	NAT.AERO. COLLECTION
KB945	LQ-T	MAY 1945	28-06-45	405 SQUAD	10MR 404 SQUAD	19-05-54 CRASHED	404 SQUAD 1952
KB946	PT-Z	MAY 1945	28-06-45	420 SQUAD	10MP No.2OTU 405 AGD	02-06-60 SCRAPPED	No.2 OTU 1955
KB947	EQ-Z	MAY 1945	28-06-45	408 SQUAD		27-01-48 DISPOSED	AT MEDICINE HAT 1947
KB948	EQ-V	MAY 1945	28-06-45	408 SQUAD	10MR No.2(M)OTU	25-08-55 SCRAPPED	No.2 (M)OTU 1951
KB949	LQ-U	MAY 1945	28-06-45	405 SQUAD	10MP 407 SQUAD	10-04-61 SCRAPPED	407 SQUAD 1954
KB950	LQ-O	MAY 1945	28-06-45	405 SQUAD	10MP 2MOTU& 405 AG-L	05-08-55 SCRAPPED	405 SQUAD 1953
KB951	EQ-A	MAY 1945	28-06-45	408 SQUAD		27-01-48 DISPOSED	AT MEDICINE HAT 1947
KB952	LQ-X	MAR 1945	28-06-45	405 SQUAD		27-01-48 DISPOSED	AT MEDICINE HAT 1947
KB953		MAR 1945	04-09-45	32 MU		15-04-48 DISPOSED	NORTH CALGARY 1946
KB954	KW-V	MAU 1945	28-06-45	425 SQUAD	10MR 103 SR&405 SQUA	20-05-55 SOS	103 S&R 1947
KB955	LQ-V	MAY 1945	05-07-45	405 SQUAD	10MR MARITIME AIR CO	28-09-55 SCRAPPED	MAC 1951
KB956	LQ-N	MAY 1945	28-08-45	405 SQUAD	10MR No.2 AIR COM	25-08-55 SCRAPPED	GREENWOOD 1951
KB957	LQ-W	MAR 1945	28-06-45	405 SQUAD	10MP 407 SQUAD	02-06-60 SCRAPPED	407 SQUAD 1954
KB958		MAR 1945	25-07-45	32 MU	10MP 407 SQUAD	02-06-60 SCRAPPED	407 SQUAD 1954
KB959	LQ-Y	MAY 1945	28-06-45	405 SQUAD	10MP 404 SQUAD AF-A	17-05-65 DISPOSED	GREENWOOD
KB960	EQ-F	MAR 1944	28-06-45	408 SQUAD	10MR 2MOTU & 103 S&R	29-09-55 SCRAPPED	103 S&R 1948
KB961	LQ-A	MAY 1945	28-06-45	405 SQUAD	10SR 408 & 404 SQUAD	28-09-55 DISPOSED	404 SQUAD 1952
KB962	KW-D	MAR 1945	28-06-45	425 SQUAD		27-01-48 DISPOSED	MEDICINE HAT 1947
KB963	EQ-H	MAR 1944	28-06-45	408 SQUAD		27-01-48 DISPOSED	MEDICINCE HAT 1947
KB964	LQ-B	MAY 1945	28-06-45	405 SQUAD	10MR 405 SQUAD AG-H	22-01-55 SCRAPPED	405 SQUAD 1951
KB965	LQ-D	MAY 1945	28-06-45	405 SQUAD	10BR 405 SQUAD	16-08-50 CRASHED	405 SQUAD 1949
KB966		MAY 1945	23-07-45	32 MU	10MR 405 SQUAD	04-05-53 CRASHED	405 SQUAD 1952
KB967	LQ-K	MAY 1945	28-06-45	405 SQUAD	10MR 103 RU & No2OTU	23-06-55 SCRAPPED	2 OTU 1951
KB968	LQ-P	MAY 1945	28-06-45	405 SQUAD		15-04-48 DISPOSED	NORTH CALGARY 1946
KB969		APR 1945	22-08-45	5 MU	10BR	16-01-47 SCRAPPED	PEARCE 1946
KB970		MAR 1945	08-08-45	32 MU	WESTERN AIR COMMAND	22-01-47 DISPOSED	WAC 1945
KB971		MAR 1945	14-04-45	20 MU		14-04-45 CRASHED	DURING FLIGHT TESTING
KB972	EQ-C	MAR 1945	28-06-45	408 SQUAD	10MR	30-01-52 BURNED AT	SOS
KB973	LQ-F	MAY 1945	28-06-45	405 SQUAD	10MP AJ973 407 SQUAD	06-09-60 SCRAPPED	407 SQUAD 1954
KB974		MAY 1945	04-09-45	20,5,32 MUs	10MR 404 SQUAD	23-06-55 SCRAPPED	404 SQUAD 1952
KB975		JUN 1945	08-08-45	32 MU		22-01-47 DISPOSED	CLARESHOLM 1945
KB976	MN976	MAY 1945	28-06-45	405 SQUAD	10AR 408 SQUAD 1956	26-05-64WATER BOMBER	STRATHALLAN G-BCOH
KB977	LQ-E	MAY 1945	05-07-45	405 SQUAD	10MR No.2MOTU	28-08-55 SCRAPPED	No.2(M)OTU 1951
KB978		MAR 1945	07-09-45	32 MU		16-01-47 DISPOSED	AT PEARCE 1946
KB979	EQ-L	APR 1945	28-06-45	408 SQUAD		27-01-48 DISPOSED	MEDICINE HAT 1947
KB980		APR 1945		5,32,20 MUs		MAY 1947 SCRAPPED	
KB981		APR 1945	29-08-45	5,32 MUs		27-01-48 DISPOSED	MEDICINE HAT 1947

KB982		APR 1945	22-08-45	32 MU		16-01-47 DISPOSED	AT PEARCE 1946
KB983		APR 1945	30-07-45	32 MU		22-01-47 DISPOSED	CLARESHOLM 1945
KB984		APR 1945	22-08-45	32 MU	10BR	16-01-47 DISPOSED	AT PEARCE 1946
KB985		APR 1945		405 SQUAD MAY 1945		03-06-45 CRASHED	
KB986		JUN 1945	11-08-45	32 MU	10N 561B CI 05-06-47	28-05-57 SOLD	
KB987		APR 1945		5,32,29,22 MUs		JUN 1947 SCRAPPED	
KB988		APR 1945	30-07-45	32 MU		22-01-47 DISPOSED	CLARESHOLM 1945
KB989		APR 1945		20,32,20 MUs		MAY 1947 SCRAPPED	
KB990		APR 1945	08-08-45	32 MU	A 527 CI 24-09-46	10-08-52 DISPOSED	
KB991	LQ-G	MAY 1945	28-06-45	405 SQUAD	10BR	29-07-48 CRASHED	ROCKCLIFFE 22-07-48
KB992		JUN 1945	08-08-45	32 MU	10MR 407 SQUAD 1954	23-06-55 SCRAPPED	
KB993	EQ-U	APR 1945		408 SQUAD		18-05-45 CRASHED	HIT HILL, SHELF MOOR
KB994	EQ-K	JUN 1945	28-06-45	408 SQUAD		22-01-47 DISPOSED	CLARESHOLM 1945
KB995	EQ-B	JUN 1945	28-06-45	408 SQUAD	10MR	16-06-53 CRASHED	STN CONNOX 1952
KB996	EQ-P	MAY 1945	28-06-45	408 SQUAD	10MP 407 SQUAD 1954	02-06-60 SCRAPPED	
KB997	LQ-C	MAY 1945	28-06-45	405 SQUAD	10MR 405 SQUAD AG-M	23-06-55 SCRAPPED	No.2 OTU 1948
KB998	EQ-G	JUN 1945	28-06-45	408 SQUAD		27-06-48 DISPOSED	MEDICINE HAT 1947
KB999	VR-M	JUN 1945	28-06-45	419 & 405 SQUAD LQ.M	10MR 405 SQUAD 1952	22-10-53 CRASH	CHURCH HILL, MALTON MIKE 300TH MK X

INDEX